Milton
and
Catholicism

Milton

and

Catholicism

Edited by

Ronald Corthell
and Thomas N. Corns

University of Notre Dame Press
Notre Dame, Indiana

University of Notre Dame Press
Notre Dame, Indiana 46556
undpress.nd.edu

Published in the United States of America

Library of Congress Cataloging-in-Publication Data

Names: Corthell, Ronald, 1949– editor. | Corns, Thomas N., editor.
Title: Milton and Catholicism / edited by Ronald Corthell and
Thomas N. Corns.
Description: Notre Dame, Indiana : University of Notre Dame Press, 2017. |
Includes bibliographical references and index. |
Identifiers: LCCN 2017024326 (print) | LCCN 2017025753 (ebook) |
ISBN 9780268100834 (pdf) | ISBN 9780268100841 (epub) |
ISBN 9780268100810 (hardback) | ISBN 0268100810 (hardcover)
Subjects: LCSH: Milton, John, 1608–1674—Criticism and interpretation. |
Milton, John, 1608–1674—Religion. | Catholic Church—In literature. |
Christianity and literature—England—History—17th century. |
England—Church history—17th century. | BISAC: LITERARY CRITICISM /
European / English, Irish, Scottish, Welsh. | RELIGION / Christianity /
Literature & the Arts. | LITERARY CRITICISM / Poetry. | HISTORY /
Modern / 17th Century.
Classification: LCC PR3592.R4 (ebook) | LCC PR3592.R4 M53   2017
(print) | DDC 821/.4—dc23
LC record available at https://lccn.loc.gov/2017024326

Contents

List of Abbreviations and Editions   vii

Introduction   1
     RONALD CORTHELL AND THOMAS N. CORNS

1. Milton and the Protestant Pope   17
     ELIZABETH SAUER

2. John Milton and George Eglisham: The English   39
    Revolution and Catholic Disinformation
     ALASTAIR BELLANY AND THOMAS COGSWELL

3. Milton, Sir Henry Vane the Younger, and the   65
    Toleration of Catholics
     MARTIN DZELZAINIS

4. Roman Catholicism, *De Doctrina Christiana*, and   83
    the Paradise of Fools
     THOMAS N. CORNS

5. "How Gird the Sphear"? Catholic Spain in   101
    Milton's Poetry
    ANGELICA DURAN

6. "Coelum non Animum Muto"?: Milton's Neo-Latin   131
    Poetry and Catholic Italy
    ESTELLE HAAN

7. Marian Controversies and Milton's Virgin Mary   169
    JOHN FLOOD

List of Contributors   195

Index   199

Abbreviations and Editions

CPW   *Complete Prose Works of John Milton*, gen. ed. Don M. Wolfe et al. (New Haven, CT: Yale University Press, 1953–82)

CWJM   *The Complete Works of John Milton*, gen. ed. Thomas N. Corns and Gordon Campbell (Oxford: Oxford University Press, 2008–)

ODNB   *Oxford Dictionary of National Biography*, online (Oxford: Oxford University Press)

OED   *Oxford English Dictionary*, online (Oxford: Oxford University Press)

PL   *Paradise Lost*, in *The Riverside Milton*, ed. Roy Flannagan (London: Longman, 1998)

PLat   *Patrologia Latina Cursus Completus*

WJM   *The Works of John Milton*, gen. ed. Frank A. Patterson et al. (New York: Columbia University Press, 1931–38).

Unless otherwise stated, the following editions have been quoted and cited:

For *Paradise Lost*, *The Riverside Milton*, ed. Roy Flannagan (London: Longman, 1998) (abbreviated as *PL*);

For *Samson Agonistes* and *Paradise Regained*, *CWJM*, vol. 2, ed. Laura Lunger Knoppers;

For all other poems by Milton, *CWJM*, vol. 3, ed. Barbara Kiefer Lewalski and Estelle Haan;

For Milton's vernacular regicide and republican tracts, *CWJM*, vol. 6, ed. N. H. Keeble and Nicholas McDowell;

For all other vernacular prose, *CPW*;

For *De Doctrina Christiana*, *CWJM*, vol. 8, ed. John Hale and J. Donald Cullington;

For all other Latin prose, *WJM*.

INTRODUCTION

RONALD CORTHELL AND THOMAS N. CORNS

Milton was a child of a fiercely anti-Catholic society, and manifestations of that tendency permeated his early environment. He was born three years after the Gunpowder Plot, and the fifth of November remained and would remain a persistent reference point in the liturgical calendar of England. "Prayers and thanksgivings to be used by the King's loyal subjects" continued to be printed, presumably to coincide with the anniversary, and sermons each November 5 commemorated the providential deliverance from a Catholic conspiracy of James I and therewith the Protestant faith in England. The event fitted an explicitly articulated pattern of such providential interventions, initiated by the defeat of the Spanish Armada in 1588. As one rather shadowy author, Matthew Haviland, put it in a broadsheet poem of 1635 (reprinted in 1650):

> I, and my house those great things will remember
> And in remembrance sanctifie two days.
> In *August* [commemorating the Armada] one, the other in *November*;
> Both made by GOD for us to give him praise.[1]

On such recurrent and to some extent ritualized anti-Catholic events were mapped profound and sometimes violent peaks of popular response.

1

In May 1618, when Milton was nine, the Defenestration of Prague opened a conflict between the Holy Roman Emperor and his Protestant subjects that reverberated in England. The leader of the Protestant cause, Frederick V, Elector Palatine and son-in-law of James I, found at least moral support among the political nation. The events in continental Europe coincided with and to some extent stimulated the development of English-language news media. As Joseph Frank, in his classic study, puts it, "The English public took a prompt and partisan interest in what was happening in central Europe."[2] Although the government of the day, like the British government in 1938, may have viewed events in the land of which Prague was capital as "a quarrel in a far away country between two people of whom we know nothing," that was not the view of more militant English Protestants.[3] James I excluded national intervention in the interest of his son-in-law, but a volunteer force under Sir Horace Vere attempted to protect his Rhineland territories, though by November 1622 it had capitulated.[4] Vere's exploits were reported in the emergent news media.[5] The crown further stimulated anti-Catholic sentiment through the initially clandestine mission of Charles, Prince of Wales, the future Charles I, to Spain in an abortive attempt to secure marriage to the Infanta. It did not play well with public opinion. However, the prince's return empty-handed proved an inadvertent public relations triumph for the house of Stuart as fireworks, bonfires, peals of bells, and much general roistering greeted him.[6] Milton was fourteen at the time.

Newsbooks and newspapers, both still embryonic, exercised caution through the early Stuart years but nevertheless reflected public concern with events unfolding in continental Europe. In May 1631 the Protestant city of Magdeburg was stormed by the Catholic forces of the Holy Roman Empire, and most of its thirty-six thousand inhabitants were massacred. The court poet Thomas Carew, in a poem not published till the 1640s, congratulated England on its studied neutrality that preserved "Our *Halcyon* dayes" of "Tourneyes, Masques, Theaters," though "the German Drum / Bellow for freedome and revenge"; its noise "Concernes not us."[7] In the nascent public sphere a different perspective emerged, prompted by reports of "the late Deplorable losse of the famous Citty of *Magdenburgh* . . . the like miserable, bloudy and inhumaine Cruelty never committed (since the Seidge of *Ierusalem*) in so short a space."[8] Milton was twenty-two.

A greater horror and greater stimulus to anti-Catholic sentiment, perceived as the worst atrocity ever perpetrated in the British Isles, emerged shortly after Milton returned from his travels in continental Europe. An uprising by indigenous Irish Catholics against English and Scottish Protestant settlers resulted in wide-scale massacres. The events coincided with the collapse of state control of the press, and in the early 1640s hundreds of pamphlets were published, reporting on Irish affairs, many in lurid terms detailing atrocities, floggings, castration, rape, sexual humiliation, genital mutilation, and even cannibalism. The most influential, and apparently the most authoritative, was Thomas Morley's, the title of which explicitly links the catastrophe in Ireland and the political crisis in England: *A Remonstrance of the Barbarous Cruelties and Bloudy Murders Committed By the Irish Rebels Against the Protestants in Ireland . . . Being the examinations of many who were eye-witnesses of the same . . . Presented to the whole kingdome of England, that thereby they may see the Rebels inhumane dealing, prevent their pernicious practises, relieve their poore brethrens necessities, and fight for their Religions, Laws, and Liberties* (London, 1644). A death toll of two hundred thousand was widely accepted.

Milton was sufficiently moved by the plight of Protestants in Ireland to contribute £4 to their relief. Charity was not the only response. Anti-Catholic outrage launched a wave of mob attacks on English Catholics, London embassies of Catholic countries required armed guards, and between 1641 and 1646 twenty-four Catholic priests were killed, often in acts of extreme brutality.[9] That same savage ferocity characterized the worst atrocities perpetrated by the New Model Army, in the ill-treatment of the allegedly Irish camp followers captured after the battle of Naseby, the sack of Basing House, and the better-known massacres of Drogheda and Wexford. Milton lived in bloody times that inevitably shaped his cultural and political consciousness.

His prose and poetry constitute a sustained attack on Catholic ecclesiology and forms of authority. From his Gunpowder Plot juvenilia to *Of True Religion*, published the year before his death, his writing represented Catholicism as inimical to liberty, reformation, and reason. Milton's biography is instructive. His father's career and the wealth it produced were premised on his alienation, on explicitly doctrinal grounds, from his own unbendingly Catholic father, Milton's grandfather. Milton grew up in the parish of a leading and singularly militant anti-Catholic minister, his probable catechist. His earliest known friends included a child of London's community of emigré Italian Protestants and a young poet who wrote to rejoice in a domestic accident, the collapse of a secret chapel, that killed ninety clandestine Catholic worshippers. There is no doubting that, probably from an early age, Milton was, in Arthur Marotti's phrase, an "ideologically impassioned" anti-Catholic.[10] At Cambridge, he followed a familiarly anti-Catholic line in his early neo-Latin poems on the Gunpowder Plot. In the 1640s he showed a particular compassion toward those Protestant settlers attacked and displaced by the rebellion by Irish Catholics. Throughout his prose, he was quick to censure any who could be perceived or represented as compromising with Catholicism. His *Observations* on Irish articles of peace justified Cromwell's implacable Irish campaign that led to Drogheda and Wexford, and his principal arguments against the Restoration included the threat it posed of a restored Catholic queen mother and her entourage. An explicit and partisan anti-Catholicism, in the satirical representation of "eremites and friars" to be exiled to the surface of the moon, jeopardizes the decorum of *Paradise Lost*. His last major prose work attempted to define a broad spectrum of tolerable opinion in terms of its distinction from Catholicism. Recurrently, his concept of the virtuous human life, individual and corporate, was constructed against the Catholic other.

Nonetheless, Milton sufficiently admired from afar the culture of Catholic Italy to master its language, and his Continental travels saw him racing through France to get there. He counted Catholic Italians among his friends and retained correspondence with some after his return home, and he continued to assert, as testimony to his international reputation, that he had been welcomed and celebrated in their academies. He had some social contact with at least two cardinals closely related to the then pope. Anecdotally, back home he helped the petition of an Irish Catholic deprived of his estates. His brother, a lawyer and royalist activist who was knighted and promoted at the Restoration, possibly reverted to the faith of their paternal grandfather, albeit after the poet's death.

Of course, this "some of his best friends were Catholics" qualification of Milton's anti-Catholicism does not mitigate the severity of his public stance against what he and contemporary Protestants habitually termed "popery." And his position and line of attack align with the propensity of both English Protestants and Catholics to define themselves against each other. But that is also just what captures our attention. This is *Milton* we are talking about, after all—in all his rich complexity, hardly a Zeitgeist writer ("Milton! thou shouldst be living at this hour: / England hath need of thee"). Because it is Milton we are dealing with, it is possible to be conflicted about his inflexibility on the Catholic question, at once taken aback by his peculiar intolerance of Catholics as distinct from Protestant sectarians and understanding of his attacks on the church's institutional and intellectual authoritarianism. Milton's mockery of the use and control of imprimaturs in *Areopagitica* brims with his contempt for officious clerics:

> Their last invention was to ordain that no Book, pamphlet, or paper should be Printed (as if S. *Peter* had bequeath'd them the keys of the Presse also out of Paradise) unless it were approv'd and licens't under the hands of 2 or 3 glutton Friers. For example:
>
> > Let the Chancellor *Cini* be pleas'd to see if in this present work
> > be contain'd ought that may withstand the Printing,
> > > *Vincent Rabbatta* Vicar of *Florence.*
> >
> > I have seen this present work, and finde nothing athwart the
> > Catholick faith and good manners: In witnesse whereof
> > I have given, etc.
> > > *Nicolo Cini* Chancellor of *Florence.*
>
> . . . .
>
> Sometimes 5 *Imprimaturs* are seen together dialogue-wise in the Piatza of one Title page, complementing and ducking each to other with their shav'n reverences, whether the Author, who stands by in perplexity at the foot of his Epistle, shall to the Presse or to the spunge. (*CPW*, 2:503–4)

Over the course of his career Milton's ire was directed at the clerical class and controlling hierarchical structures; however, one can be forgiven for feeling uneasy with his seeming insensitivity to the trials of conscience experienced by lay English Catholics struggling as members of a religious minority to maintain their faithfulness and navigate the treacherous waters of "dual loyalty." Why would Milton, champion of conscience, be so unwilling to consider the dilemmas of those caught in the intricate webs woven by religion and politics over the course of a tumultuous century of confessional conflict in his native land? Did the Continental and Irish atrocities summarized at the opening of this introduction entirely override any possibility of identification with English Catholics? A student of early modern English literature might recall John Donne, who struggled with his attachment to the faith. Donne's autobiographical remarks in the preface to *Pseudo-Martyr* (1610), his contribution to the Oath of Allegiance Controversy, famously detail the difficult process of changing religious allegiance:

> They who have descended so lowe, as to take knowledge of me, and to admit me into their consideration, know well that I used no inordinate hast, nor precipitation in binding my conscience to any local Religion. I had a longer work to doe then many other men: for I was first to blot out, certaine impressions of the Romane religion, and to wrestle both against the examples and against the reasons, by which some hold was taken; and some anticipations early layde upon my conscience, both by Persons who by nature had a power and superiority over my will, and others who by their learning and good life, seem'd to me justly to claime an interest for the guiding, and rectifying of mine understanding in these matters.[11]

Of course, Donne's reference to "the Romane religion" is the key to Milton's position—his intolerance of the tyranny of *Rome*. And, as Nigel Smith has put it, "This inability to imagine toleration was very widespread among nearly all religious groups at the time [of the English Revolution]."[12] Alexandra Walsham, in her book *Charitable Hatred: Tolerance and Intolerance in England, 1500–1700*, reminds us that *toleration* was, through most of the early modern period, a word used pejoratively.[13] Still, an element of discomfort, or, perhaps more accurately, disappointment lingers.

Of course, the protracted struggle with the legacy of Roman Catholicism has long been recognized as a key influence on the literary production of early modern England. Our understanding of this relationship has been greatly enriched by the new history of early modern English Catholicism and anti-Catholicism that has been created in the voluminous scholarship of the past twenty years. Following upon the foundational work of John Bossy in the 1960s, historians and literary scholars have since the 1990s been engaged in projects of recovery, revision, and discovery of records of Catholic life and culture during the English Reformation. Beginning with Eamon Duffy's powerful revisionist *Stripping of the Altars*, historians like Alexandra Walsham, Michael Questier, Peter Lake, Christopher Haigh, Anthony Milton, and Thomas McCoog have reshaped and complicated our understanding of Catholicism's place in early modern English religious history, as well as demonstrated the interdependence of Catholicism and Protestantism as ideological mirrors in fashioning religious identities and politics. In concert with this important historical research, literary historians and critics have been reexamining and expanding the early modern English canon by attending to Catholic themes and representations and by recovering Catholic books marginalized or lost over the centuries because of variously motivated forms of omission.[14] Books such as Alison Shell's *Catholicism, Controversy, and the English Literary Imagination, 1558–1660* and *Oral Culture and Catholicism in Early Modern England*; Raymond Tumbleson's *Catholicism in the English Protestant Imagination: Nationalism, Religion, and Literature, 1660–1745*; Peter Lake and Michael Questier's *The Antichrist's Lewd Hat: Protestants, Papists and Players in Post-Reformation England*; and Arthur Marotti's *Religious Ideology and Cultural Fantasy* have complicated and challenged prevailing views of a Protestant framework for English literature of the sixteenth and seventeenth centuries. New scholarship on such important Catholic figures as Edmund Campion, Robert Southwell, and Robert Persons is enriching our understanding of the interplay of complex religio-political texts and contexts in early modern English literary culture.[15]

What recent scholarship has brought to light is the rich diversity of Catholic and anti-Catholic discourses over the period; the multiple subject positions constructed by and for Catholics as they adapted their religious and political allegiances and practices to changing conditions in Tudor and Stuart England; new understandings of martyrdom and martyrology; writing by and about Catholic women in early modern England; and new appreciation for the role of polemic in early modern English literary culture.[16] In this context, we believe a collection focused on Milton's engagement with Catholicism and anti-Catholicism is timely indeed. While new knowledge of Catholic subcultures and anti-Catholic

ideologies has increased significantly, we are only beginning to understand how early modern confessional conflicts between Catholics and
Protestants helped to forge new models and standards of authority, scholarship, and interiority.[17]

Seen in the light of recent scholarship on English Catholics, Milton's
position against toleration of Catholicism stands out even more brightly
than before.[18] Milton could deploy anti-Catholicism as something of a
rhetorical device. As a modern editor points out, his hard line against toleration even of private worship to English Catholics in the late treatise *Of
True Religion* (1673) is harsher than in the earlier *A Treatise of Civil Power*
(1659), which had focused on the "publicke and scandalous use thereof."
In *A Treatise* he writes:

> Nevertheless if they ought not to be tolerated, it is for just reason of
> state more then of religion; which they who force, though professing
> to be protestants, deserve as little to be tolerated themselves, being
> no less guiltie of poperie in the most popish point. Lastly, for idola-
> trie, who knows it not to be evidently against all scripture both of the
> Old and New Testament, and therfore a true heresie, or rather an im-
> pietie; wherin a right conscience can have naught to do; and the
> works therof so manifest, that a magistrate can hardly err in pro-
> hibiting and quite removing at least the publick and scandalous use
> therof. (*CPW*, 7 [rev. ed.]: 254)

Here Milton comes as close as he ever did to allowing there might be a
private, inner space where English Catholics could feel free from inter-
ference from the English state; his equation of the "forcing" of religion,
even for Catholics, as in fact a form of "poperie" is consistent with the
thinking of some his radical friends. In the later work Milton wishes to
distinguish between toleration of Protestant sects, which he supports, and
toleration of Roman Catholicism, which had been extended in limited
form under the Declaration of Indulgence.[19] To express his support of
Parliament's withdrawal of the Declaration of Indulgence and thereby to
align himself and Protestant nonconformists with Parliament against the
common enemy, Milton deploys *popery* as a kind of scare-word in *Of True
Religion*. Here are the opening phrases of the final three paragraphs of the
pamphlet:

> The next means to hinder the growth of Popery will be. . . .
> Another means to abate Popery arises from. . . .
> The last means to avoid Popery, is. . . .

Milton concludes: "Let us therefore using this last means, last here spoken of, but first to be done, amend our lives with all speed; least through impenitency we run into that stupidly, which now we seek all means so warily to avoid, the worst of superstitions, and the heaviest of all Gods Judgements, Popery" (*CPW*, 8:433–40).

But more than a rhetorical device, anti-Catholicism does seem to have played the role for Milton that Lake and other scholars have described as a type of Protestant self-fashioning, "a means of labelling and expelling tendencies that seemed to jeopardise their integrity."[20] What is particularly interesting about Milton's anti-Catholicism is the way it aligns with his understanding of inwardness and conscience and illuminates one of the central conflicts between Catholics and Protestants in the period. Through most of the later sixteenth and seventeenth centuries, from Burghley's *Execution of Justice in England* (1583) and William Allen's response in *A True, Sincere, and Modest Defense of English Catholics* (1584), through the Oath of Allegiance controversy (1606), the Royal Declaration of Indulgence in 1672, and its withdrawal in 1673, to the fictitious conspiracy known as the Popish Plot (1678–81), English Protestants and Catholics wrangled over the entanglement of religious belief and political loyalty. In his famous *Humble Supplication to her Majestie* (1600), Robert Southwell sought, problematically, to separate his religious commitment from loyalty to Elizabeth.[21] In *A Brief Discourse containing certayne Reasons why Catholiques refuse to go to Church* (1580), the prolific Jesuit polemicist Robert Persons had made the case for recusancy to both English Catholics and Protestants "on the grounds that a person who acted in defiance of his inner beliefs committed a grevious sin."[22] The particular complications of conscience for English Catholics became especially evident in arguments over the Oath of Allegiance (1606). The key passage in the Oath, one that precipitated debates between Catholics and between Catholics and Protestants in England, and that continues to be debated among historians, can help us gain entry into Milton's thinking on Catholics and conscience: "I do further swear that I do from my heart abhor, detest and abjure, as impious and heretical, this damnable doctrine and position, that princes which be excommunicated or deprived by the Pope may be deposed or murdered by their subjects or any other whatsoever."[23] The chief debating point, in the early seventeenth century and continuing into the present day among historians, is whether the oath was focused on the doctrine of the papal deposing power and therefore functioned as a loyalty test, or whether, as Michael C. Questier argues, it was centered on "the novel 'impious and heretical' clause rejecting the 'damnable doctrine' that excommunicated or deprived princes 'may be deposed or murdered by their subjects'" and therefore functioned as a means of branding papal doctrine as heresy and indirectly conceding the king's supremacy over the church.[24] In her recent book *Law and Conscience* Stefania Tutino highlights the change Catholics perceived in the oath:

> In other words, in an oath designed to test, according to its author's [James I] intention, the "civill Obedience" of subjects, there appears the statement that the doctrine of the legitimate deposing of a king excommunicated by the pope is "impious and heretical. . . . If one starts off from an assumption that only political loyalty, and not religious beliefs, was the object of discussion, stating that a founding point in Catholic doctrine regarding the Church of England was to be deemed "impious and heretical" led dangerously into the very forum of conscience that the sovereign himself claimed he wanted to respect.[25]

Milton shows little concern in his antipapal writings with issues of Catholic loyalty, but a doctrine, *held in conscience*, of papal supremacy in spiritual matters goes to the heart of his inability to tolerate Catholicism. To put it simply: What is the pope doing in someone's conscience?

Milton's intolerance of Catholicism is grounded in this concept of "implicit faith." An explanation of the term from the Catholic side can be found in another Persons tract, *The Warn-word to Sir Francis Hastinges Wast-word* (1602). Following the church father Athanasius of Alexandria, Persons argues that salvation depends on holding to the Catholic faith, which Persons interprets to mean every article of doctrine: "Thus saith that creed [traditionally, if erroneously attributed to Athanasius] shewing us the dreadful daunger of him that erreth, or doubteth of any one article of the Catholic faith, which infinite people of England must needs do at this day, who have no other guide, direction, or certainty to bring them to resolve in matters of controversy, but eyther their owne reading, or to believe some other as uncertayne as their owne judgment in this behalf."[26] Persons explains the two kinds of faith, "fide explicita" and "fide implicita": explicit faith is "a cleare, distinct and particular faith or belief of any article, point or parcel of Christian Religion"; implicit faith, on the other hand, comprises "a more darcke, secret or hidden faith, implied as it were or wrapped . . . in the belief of an other more general point" (*Warn-word*, Z6r). The key idea, which Milton, following Calvin, cannot countenance, is that for Persons Catholics unversed in theology "believe the Catholike Churche, and all that shee beleeveth, which *implyeth* so much as is necessary to any mannes salvation" (*Warn-word*, L14v–L15r; our emphasis). As Milton writes in *Of True Religion*, "If they say that by removing their Idols we violate their Consciences, we have no warrant to regard Conscience which is not grounded on Scripture" (*CPW*, 8:432). Or, as he phrased it in *A Treatise of Civil Power* in a passage preceding and canceling his caution regarding "forcing" of religion, "Besides, of an implicit faith, which they profess, the conscience also becoms implicit; and so by voluntarie servitude to mans law, forfets her Christian libertie. Who then can plead for such a conscience, as being implicitly enthrald to man instead of God, almost becoms no conscience, as the will not free, becoms no will" (*CPW*, 7 [rev. ed.]: 254). Here is the conundrum from Milton's point of view: Catholic inwardness is a contradiction, since it includes submission to the pope on spiritual matters; the notion of Catholic "conscience" is unconscionable.

That said, Milton's intolerance of Catholicism is not joined to any program of persecution of Catholics. Even in the *True Religion*, punishment is reserved only for those who threaten "the security of the State" (*CPW*, 8:431). He does recommend the destruction of images and prohibition of Masses. However, the pamphlet concludes with positive prescriptions that apply to both Catholics and Protestants: "The next means to hinder the growth of Popery will be to read duly and diligently the Holy Scriptures, which as St. *Paul* saith to *Timothy*, who had known them from a child, *are able to make wise unto salvation*" (*CPW*, 8:433). Milton tellingly does not limit this exhortation to Catholics: "most men in the course and practice of their lives" place earthly before heavenly things "and through unwillingness to take pains of understanding their Religion by their own diligent study, would fain be sav'd by a Deputy. Hence comes implicit faith. . . . till want of Fundamental knowledge easily turns to superstition or Popery" (*CPW*, 8:434–35). Thus are Catholics and Protestants both brought under Milton's censure, as he closes: "The last means to avoid Popery, is to amend our lives" (*CPW*, 8:438). Milton's intolerance of Catholicism was an active, lifelong campaign against "the popery within."

❋   ❋   ❋

This collection of essays investigates a rich variety of approaches to Milton's career-long engagement with Catholicism and its relationship to reformed religion, picking open latent tensions and contradictions, exploring the nuances of his relationship to the easy commonplaces of Protestant compatriots, and disclosing the polemical strategies and tactics that often shape that engagement. Milton writes so often in dialogue—or debate—with the thought and work of others, and this volume seeks, among other objectives, to make more audible the other parts of those conversations and controversies. This is not, however, a casebook or companion. Broadly speaking, the collection moves from the fine-grained engagement with events and texts to a larger consideration with a wider view, sometimes, indeed, an overview. But it would be misleading to overschematize the structure of a project, the primary aim of which was to give a platform for a diverse and multifaceted investigation into a complex and little-explored field in Milton studies.

NOTES

1. Matthew Haviland, *A Monument of Gods most gracious preservation of England from Spanish Invasion, Aug. 2 1588. and Popish Treason, Novem. 5. 1605* ([London, 1635]).

2. Joseph Frank, *The Beginnings of the English Newspaper, 1620–1660* (Cambridge, MA: Harvard University Press, 1961), 4.

3. Neville Chamberlain, radio broadcast on Germany's annexation of the Sudetenland, September 27, 1938.

4. J. V. Polisensky, *The Thirty Years War*, trans. Robert Evans (London: New English Library, 1971), 167.

5. Frank, *Beginnings*, 9.

6. Thomas Cogswell, *The Blessed Revolution: English Politics and the Coming of War, 1621–1624* (Cambridge: Cambridge University Press, 1989), 6–9.

7. Thomas Carew, "In answer of an Elegiacall Letter upon the death of the King of Sweden," lines 95–98, in *The Poems of Thomas Carew with His Masque "Coelum Britannicum,"* ed. Rhodes Dunlap (1949; repr., Oxford: Clarendon Press, 1964), 74–77.

8. *The Continuation of our weekely Avisoes, since the 16. of May to the 4. of June* (London, 1631), title page.

9. Gordon Campbell and Thomas N. Corns, *John Milton: Life, Work, and Thought* (Oxford: Oxford University Press, 2008), 172. The following biographical account draws on this study passim.

10. Arthur F. Marotti, *Religious Ideology and Cultural Fantasy: Catholic and Anti-Catholic Discourses in Early Modern England* (Notre Dame, IN: University of Notre Dame Press, 2005), 5.

11. John Donne, *Pseudo-Martyr, Wherein Out of Certaine Propositions and Gradations, This Conclusion Is Evicted, That Those Which Are of the Romane Religion in This Kingdome, May and Ought to Take the Oath of Allegiance*, ed. Anthony Raspa (Montreal: McGill-Queen's University Press, 1993), 13.

12. Nigel Smith, *Literature and Revolution in England, 1640–1660* (New Haven, CT: Yale University Press, 1994), 121.

13. Alexandra Walsham, *Charitable Hatred: Tolerance and Intolerance in England, 1500–1700* (Manchester: Manchester University Press, 2006), 4.

14. John Bossy's influential works include "The Character of Elizabethan Catholicism," *Past and Present* 21 (1962): 39–59, and *The English Catholic Community, 1570–1850* (London: Darton, Longman and Todd, 1975). See also Christopher Haigh, *English Reformations: Religion, Politics, and Society under the Tudors* (Oxford: Clarendon Press, 1993), "The Continuity of Catholicism in the English Reformation," *Past and Present* 93 (1981): 37–69, and "From Monopoly to Minority: Catholicism in Early Modern England," *Transactions of the Royal Historical Society*, 5th ser., 31 (1981): 129–47; J. J. Scarisbrick, *The Reformation and the English People* (Oxford: Blackwell, 1984); Eamon Duffy, *The Stripping of the Altars: Traditional Religion in England, 1400–1580* (New Haven, CT: Yale University Press, 1992); Peter Lake, "Anti-Popery: The Structure of a Prejudice," in *Conflict in Early Stuart England: Studies in Religion and Politics, 1603–1642*, ed. Richard Crust and Ann Hughes (London: Longman, 1989), 72–106; Anthony Milton, *Catholic and Reformed: The Roman and Protestant Churches in English Protestant Thought, 1600–1640* (Cambridge:

Cambridge University Press, 1995); Alexandra Walsham, *Church Papists: Catholicism, Conformity and Confessional Polemic in Early Modern England* (Woodbridge: Royal Historical Society and Boydell Press, 1993) and *Charitable Hatred*; Thomas McCoog, ed., *The Reckoned Expense: Edmund Campion and the Early English Jesuits* (Woodbridge: Boydell, 1996).

15. Alison Shell, *Catholicism, Controversy, and the English Literary Imagination, 1558–1660* (Cambridge: Cambridge University Press, 1999) and *Oral Culture and Catholicism in Early Modern England* (Cambridge: Cambridge University Press, 2007); Raymond Tumbleson, *Catholicism in the English Protestant Imagination: Nationalism, Religion, and Literature, 1660–1745* (Cambridge: Cambridge University Press, 1998); Peter Lake and Michael C. Questier, *The Anti-Christ's Lewd Hat: Protestants, Papists and Players in Post-Reformation England* (New Haven, CT: Yale University Press, 2002); Arthur F. Marotti, ed., *Catholicism and Anti-Catholicism in Early Modern English Texts* (London: Macmillan, 1999), and *Religious Ideology*. Other recent literary and cultural studies include Frances E. Dolan, *Whores of Babylon: Catholicism, Gender, and Seventeenth-Century Print Culture* (1999; repr., Notre Dame, IN: Notre Dame University Press, 2005); Ronald Corthell, Frances E. Dolan, Christopher Highley, and Arthur F. Marotti, eds., *Catholic Culture in Early Modern England* (Notre Dame, IN: University of Notre Dame Press, 2007); Scott R. Pilarz, *Robert Southwell and the Mission of Literature, 1561–1595: Writing Reconciliation* (Burlington, VT: Ashgate, 2004); Anne Sweeney, *Robert Southwell: Snow in Arcadia, Redrawing the English Lyric Landscape, 1586–95* (Manchester: Manchester University Press, 2006); Victor Houliston, *Catholic Resistance in Elizabethan England: Robert Persons's Jesuit Polemic, 1580–1610* (Burlington, VT: Ashgate, 2007); Raymond Tumbleson, *Catholicism*; Dennis Flynn, *John Donne and the Ancient Catholic Nobility* (Bloomington: Indiana University Press, 1995); Ceri Sullivan, *Dismembered Rhetoric: English Recusant Writing, 1580–1603* (Madison, NJ: Fairleigh Dickinson University Press, 1995).

16. On the diversity of Catholic and anti-Catholic discourses, see especially Shell, *Catholicism, Controversy* and *Oral Culture*; Sullivan, *Dismembered Rhetoric*; Tumbleson, *Catholicism*; and Marotti, *Religious Ideology*. On Catholic subject positions, see Bossy, "Character of English Catholicism" and *English Catholic Community*; Haigh, *English Reformations*, "Continuity of Catholicism," and "From Monopoly to Minority"; Duffy, *Stripping of the Altars*; and Walsham, *Church Papists*. On martyrdom, see Anne Dillon, *The Construction of Martyrdom in the English Catholic Community, 1535–1603* (Aldershot: Ashgate, 2002); Susannah Monta, *Martyrdom and Literature in Early Modern England* (Cambridge: Cambridge University Press, 2005); Brad S. Gregory, *Salvation at Stake: Christian Martyrdom in Early Modern Europe* (Cambridge, MA: Harvard University Press, 1999); John R. Knott, *Discourses of Martyrdom in English Literature, 1563–1694* (Cambridge: Cambridge University Press, 1993); Eliza-

beth Hanson, *Discovering the Subject in Renaissance England* (Cambridge: Cambridge University Press, 1998). On writing by and about Catholic women, see Dolan, *Whores of Babylon*; Heather Wolfe, *The Literary Career and Legacy of Elizabeth Cary, 1613–1680* (New York: Palgrave Macmillan, 2007). On the role of polemic, see Tumbleson, *Catholicism*; Sullivan, *Dismembered Rhetoric*; Lake, "Anti-Popery"; Houliston, *Catholic Resistance*; and Marotti, *Religious Ideology*.

17. On models of authority, see, for example, Robert Weimann, *Authority and Representation in Early Modern Discourse*, ed. David Hillman (Baltimore: Johns Hopkins University Press, 1996); on models of scholarship, see Anthony Grafton, *The Footnote: A Curious History* (1997; rev. ed., Cambridge, MA: Harvard University Press, 1999); on models of interiority, see Katherine Eisaman Maus, *Inwardness and Theater in the English Renaissance* (Chicago: University of Chicago Press, 1995).

18. For a concise overview of the features of Catholicism that underlay Milton's intolerance, see Andrew Hadfield, "Milton and Catholicism," in *Milton and Toleration*, ed. Sharon Achinstein and Elizabeth Sauer (Oxford: Oxford University Press, 2007), 186–99.

19. Keith Stavely in *CPW*, 8:431–32. Milton wishes to express his support of Parliament's withdrawal of the Declaration in order to persuade Parliament to see him and nonconformists as allies against popery and, therefore, worthy of toleration. Stavely also claims that Milton's convictions about Catholicism were consistent throughout his career, somewhat undermining his rhetorical argument in *Of True Religion*.

20. Walsham, *Charitable Hatred*, 27; Lake, "Anti-Popery"; Anthony Milton, "A Qualified Intolerance: the Limits and Ambiguities of Early Stuart Anti-Catholicism," in Marotti, *Catholicism and Anti-Catholicism*, 85–115.

21. See Ronald Corthell, "'The Secrecy of Man': Recusant Discourse and the Elizabethan Subject," *English Literary Renaissance* 19 (Autumn 1989): 272–90.

22. Walsham, *Charitable Hatred*, 242.

23. Quoted in Stefania Tutino, *Law and Conscience: Catholicism in Early Modern England, 1570–1625* (Burlington, VT: Ashgate, 2007), 133.

24. Michael C. Questier, "Loyalty, Religion and State Power in Early Modern England: English Romanism and the Jacobean Oath of Allegiance," *Historical Journal* 40 (1997): 318–19. The debate is summarized by Johann P. Sommerville, who argues for the oath as a loyalty test in "Papalist Political Thought and the Controversy over the Jacobean Oath of Allegiance," in *Catholics and the "Protestant Nation": Religious Politics and Identity in Early Modern England*, ed. Ethan Shagan (Manchester: Manchester University Press, 2005), esp. 172–78.

25. Tutino, *Law and Conscience*, 133. Tutino argues that the inclusion in the oath of a renunciation of the doctrine of papal primacy "offered a new

formulation of the separation between inner beliefs and outer conduct, shifting in a fundamental way . . . the 'boundary between the internal and external forum'" (321–22).

26. Robert Persons, *The Warn-word to Sir Francis Hastinges Wast-word; conteyning the issue of the three former Treatises, the Watch-word, the Ward-word and the Wast-word (1602)*, in *English Recusant Literature, 1558–1640*, ed. D. M. Rogers, vol. 302 (Ilkley: Scolar Press, 1976), L14v. Subsequent citations are to this edition and are given parenthetically in the text.

CHAPTER 1

MILTON AND
THE PROTESTANT POPE

ELIZABETH SAUER

[The bishops] brought in many *Popish Innovations*, and in their
Surplices, Copes, and Hoods, had well nigh ushered the Pope
into *England*.
—Mercurius Britanicus, *Communicating the affaires of great
Britaine: For the better Information of the People* (1644)

In early modern England, Catholics disputed the nature and terms of
their relationship to the international church, their allegiances to the
state, and their subjection to Catholic bishops appointed by Rome. English Catholic clerics themselves protested against the Jesuits and their
missionizing in England and abroad, and thereby contributed to the anti-
Jesuit rhetoric of the day, at the same time that they added their voices to
the prevailing anti-Puritan sentiment. That the discontents and divided

loyalties of Catholics, who conformed to varying degrees to the Church of England, continued in later decades is evidenced in the distinction between lay English Catholics and what the anonymous author of the seventeenth-century *Letter from a Gentleman of the Romish Religion* calls "Missionary Priests in this Kingdom." By virtue of their ordination and oath of obedience to the pope, the foreign priests subscribe to "the mad Doctrine of Popes having power to depose Princes," the letter's author complains. Resistance to kingship was a known principle of the Jesuit tradition. The professor of the "Romish Religion" explicitly distances himself from this Jesuitical position and assures his brother, the ostensible addressee, that no renunciation of one's allegiance to the king is demanded on the part of Catholic laity, who are subject to and will be protected by England's laws.[1]

Neither English Protestant conformists nor Puritans were prepared to entertain the possibility of a loyal Catholic citizen. As "an ideal polemical tool" and "a free-floating term of opprobrium . . . defined by its place in a longstanding ideological code," antipopery was a rallying cry for a Protestant nation that defined itself in opposition to Catholic Rome—the origin of all ills.[2] A term of derision, *popery* was a universal charge, and *papist* "a magic epithet" that offered an effective means of immediately vilifying those designated as undesirable or different.[3] In Stuart England, popery would have had to be invented if it didn't exist, points out Peter Lake in his study of anti-Catholic prejudice.[4] Antipapist sentiment was prevalent in many circles in England, but largely as an invention of the historical and literary imagination at a time when the emerging nation had a strong religious orientation. The identification of "an other" or a common adversary and the rhetorical, ideological, and cultural existence of antipopery were necessary for the coalescence of disparate Protestant groups and consolidation of an English identity. Milton buys into prejudices of the time and deploys and supplements the popular anti-Catholic rhetoric in establishing his role as architect and champion of Protestant nationhood. He does so in relation first to Laudianism, on which this chapter concentrates, and later in relation to monarchism, which he reviles as popish. When he justifies the regicide at the end of the decade, Milton also seizes the opportunity to assault the English pope, the archbishop of Canterbury, and his "late Breviary" (a Catholic prayer book for clerics) (*CWJM*, 6:291). Laud remains a target long after his sentencing and the demise of the episcopacy because he represents for Milton an English counterpart of an ever-threatening papal power and a malignant popish influence on a justly executed king, who, like his father, "shiver[ed] between Protestant and Papist all his life" (*CWJM*, 6:357).

I

Throughout his writing career Milton rehearses a series of errant practices and erroneous beliefs that he associates with popery. He condemns the doctrine of purgatory (*CPW*, 1:702). In *The Doctrine and Discipline of Divorce* (1643) he derides the papists' designation of marriage as sacramental rather than as an arrangement intended for "human Society" (*CPW*, 2:275). In *The Judgement of Martin Bucer Concerning Divorce* (1644), Milton contrasts literal (usually Catholic) approaches to scriptures with "the direct analogy of sense, reason, law, and Gospel" (*CPW*, 2:431) in order to refute the English church's papistical interpretation of Matthew 5 and its subscription to canon laws on marriage. Also, like his Puritan contemporaries, Milton rejects the designation of sacredness with specific institutions or individuals. He expresses contempt for the idolatrous accouterments of ceremonial and sacramental worship, represented by the Mass, clerical vestments, religious art and images, and "easy Confession, easy Absolution, Pardons, Indulgences" (*CPW*, 8:439). But there were also menacing aspects to Catholicism: in a 1641 speech addressed to Parliament, John Pym, who brought the Grand Remonstrance before the House of Commons, warned, "The Religion of the Papists is a Religion incomputable to any other Religion, destructive to all others, and doth not endure any thing that doth oppose it; and whosoever doth withstand their Religion, (if it lie in their power) they bring them to ruine."[5] When it is cited in religious nationalist discourses and when it is politicized, Catholicism becomes especially detestable and dangerous. Romish intolerance and tyranny in turn justify Protestant intolerance of Catholicism, if not outright persecution of Catholics. When political and religious interests meet, as they regularly do in Milton's imaginative and polemical works, "political intolerance will not allow condoning the religious component."[6] Collapsing the differences between a politicized popery and the doctrine and discipline of the Roman Catholic Church became central to

Milton's polemical strategy. "Their religion the more considerd, the less can be acknowledgd a religion; but a Roman principalitie rather," as he writes in *A Treatise of Civil Power in Ecclesiastical Causes: Shewing that it is not lawful for any power on earth to compel in matters of Religion* (1659), which warns the new parliament of the injustices and dangers of politico-ecclesiastical institutions and doctrines that repress liberty of conscience (*CPW*, 7:254). Popery is a twofold menace, "Ecclesiastical, and Political, both usurpt, and the one supporting the other," Milton declares in *Of True Religion*, in which he takes parting shots at popery (*CPW*, 8:429).

From the outset of his career, Milton maps binary oppositions between good and evil onto his literary representations of Protestantism and Catholicism. In "In quintum Novembris"—likely designed to observe the anniversary of Guy Fawkes Day and deliverance from the popish plot to overthrow the king—Milton hails James as a restorer of peace and order, while describing the punishment of the conspirators.[7] Though he initially eulogized James, Milton later faults the king for his indulgence of Roman Catholics.[8] This chapter reviews some of Milton's early writings on church government and his 1644 anticensorship tract, in which he elides differences between Laudianism and Catholicism and politicizes both as popery. In a recent study of *Areopagitica: A Speech of Mr. John Milton For the Liberty of Unlicenc'd Printing*, Stephen Dobranski points out that the censure of Catholicism in the tract is also a denunciation of the Laudian church.[9] Earlier attacks on pseudo-Catholic Laudianism appear in "Lycidas," which captures the collusion of political and ecclesiastical affairs in the line about papistical prelates "Creep[ing] and intrud[ing], and climb[ing] into the fold" (115). Whether detecting radical elements in Milton's early works or aligning the young Milton with Laudian conservatism, Miltonists have generally interpreted "Lycidas" as the poet-polemicist's first decisive antiepiscopal statement.[10] The poem exerts pressure on the conventions of the pastoral mode through its incursion and digression into church polity and its detection and excoriation of an internal foe.

Indeed, beginning in the 1630s, Milton's antipopery rhetoric, while designed to expose the threat of an anti-Christian outsider, was also deployed to designate as foreign and corrosive the internal "*tyranny* [that] invaded the *Church*" (*CPW*, 1:822–23). Laud and Charles viewed the divinely ordained office of the prelacy as a corollary of *jure divino* monarchism. Milton in contrast focused on discrediting the former, in part by implicating the archbishop and popish prelates in a plot to destabilize just kingship. What Protestants saw as the Catholic Church's claims over conscience were interpreted as a compromise of national allegiances and sovereignty, including disobedience to kings. Milton thus deploys the rhetoric of popery to designate as alien and subversive the contagion that exists *within*—"the Pope, with his appertinences the Prelats" (*Areopagitica, CPW,* 2:549). By relying on the language of the other— the stranger, the intruder, the malefactor—antipopery allowed for the labeling and externalizing of internal conflicts.

II

In the early modern era, English Protestants accused the papacy of spreading superstition and sedition and dictating the observance of false rituals, which transformed an active and engaged congregation into blind followers. Catholicism was perceived as contaminating court politics and church government, in part through the conspiracy of the king's counselors and an Episcopalian Church subject to non-English influences. Through its association with foreign allegiances and menacing foreign powers, popery was judged to be "a solvent of the ties of political loyalty" as well as of Protestant unity.[11] Alleged associations with Roman Catholicism shook the Caroline government and accounted in part for its downfall. In the late 1620s, John Cosin prepared, presumably at the behest of Charles I, the *Collection of Private Devotions,* an Anglican manual for use by court ladies and specifically for Susan Fielding (née Villiers), Countess of Denbigh, who was leaning toward Rome.[12] Cosin's prayer anthology, modeled on books of hours, was intended to counter the Counter-Reformation liturgy that encouraged conversions to popery. At the same time, Cosin was heavily involved in the defense of high church practices that resembled Catholicism, and in that regard he was engaged in the same exercise as his friend and correspondent William Laud, the archbishop of Canterbury and chief ecclesiastical administrator. In 1628 Cosin participated in the prosecution of Peter Smart, who vilified popery from the pulpit of the Cathedral of Durham, where the subject was frequently broadcast. Smart was held in custody for over a decade by the Court of High Commission for what William Prynne described as the "popish *Innovations* [he and his confederates] brought into that Church . . . , as Images, Copes, Tapers, Crucifixes, bowing to the Altar, praying towards the East, turning the Cōmunion Table of wood . . . into an Altar of stone."[13] Like Laud, Cosin would be accused of undermining the king's authority over the church and of attempting to divert the king's subjects from the true religion by "seducing" them to popery.[14]

Not only did Prynne and Henry Burton vehemently attack Cosin's book, they implicated it in a plot to subject England to Roman authority. Prynne designates the book as "*Popish*, both in the forme, and matter of it," and declares its intent to "Vsher *Poperie* into our Church." Establishing parallels between Cosin's prescriptions and popish discipline, Prynne judges that the book is leading the English Church back to the Romish origins it renounced when the Reformation took hold.[15] Burton likewise maintains that the one unified church, which Cosins defends, enslaves England to Rome once again. Since this "Popish booke," declares Burton, renders the English church "no otherwise distinct from the Church of Rome," the pope will usurp kingly power and "with his foote strike[] off his crowne."[16]

The threat posed by a foreign adversary was thus overshadowed by internal court and church affairs. According to the Venetian ambassador in England, Anzolo Correr, Roman Catholics after 1636 were tolerated to a greater degree than before, and Mass attendance in the queen's chapel increased.[17] "Catholics are no longer hated or persecuted with the old severity," he reports. Worse yet, they are permitted, if not welcomed, at the court: "The public services in the queen's chapel are most freely frequented by very great numbers, while those of the ambassadors are crowded," Correr continues. Queen Henrietta Maria would be linked to popish plots in the late 1630s. As for Laud, he is now lording over the national church "*so that they commonly call him the pope of England.*" Those who feared the infestation of Catholicism in their country also drew upon examples of proselytization at court. In October 1637, the conversion (known as the perversion) of Lady Newport, one of the queen's ladies and wife of Mountjoy (Earl of Newport)—confirmed suspicions about the influence of Catholicism on those close to the monarchy.[18] George Con, who served at the queen's court until 1639, was accused of attempting to bring England in line with Rome. As Ambassador Correr informed the Doge and Senate, the king of England, had he not doted so much on the queen, would surely have enacted "some resentful measure" against the papal agent, whose removal from the court was urged, lest England "be brought to obedience to the Roman pontiff."[19] The joining of England with Rome was a regular refrain at the time, and the king's failure to resist the sway of Rome and its agents was increasingly troubling and ultimately treacherous.

Laud's actions and his theology supported the authoritarianism of the king and privileged royal prerogative over the liberties of the subject. Laudian reforms were seen as supporting a counter-reformation and as imposing a contrived and repressive conformity on the national church. Among the more popular works of the day that identified Laudianism as a vanguard for popery was John Bastwick's *Letany of John Bastwick . . . Also a full Demonstration, that the Bishops are . . . Enemies of Christ . . .* (1637). The book, which John Lilburne helped bring out at his own peril, exposes the collusion of prelacy and popery. In 1637, the *Letany* would bring Bastwick to the Court of the Star Chamber and then to pillory, where he would be joined by Prynne and Burton for their paper-contestations against the prelates.[20] Lilburne would be punished in the following year. The dangers inherent in Laudianism and Catholicism were powerfully conflated in the popular imagination and enabled the antiepisopalian and antipopish movement to gain momentum.

Laud and his clerics, who supported his ecclesiastical policies, gradually became disinclined to condemn popery or popish innovations, a strategy that had in fact proven futile in encouraging recusants to join the English church.[21] In an effort to lure conformists inclined toward Catholicism back to the Church of England, pro-Laudian clergy sought to depict Rome as a true, if flawed, church and to downplay the differences between the doctrine and discipline of the English Protestant and Catholic churches. Bringing recusants into the fold was "infinitely more urgent" than attempting to reconcile with Puritans whom they despised.[22] When Correr reported that Laud had assumed the title of the "pope of England," he explained that Laud condoned Catholicism in the court and at the same time set his sights on destroying "the party of the Puritans, which has grown so much as to cause apprehension to the government."[23] Laudians ascribed the rise of dissent and discontent with the English government to unauthorized preaching, which in his mind had upset the balance between church and state and had poisoned vulnerable minds. Reckoning Laud receptive to their religion, Catholics decided that Catholicism could be tolerated within a monarchically governed English church.[24] There was a danger in the refusal to denounce the Church of Rome, which the Reformers generally detested and feared: the Laudians themselves became implicated in popery. Charges of crypto-Catholicism were directed particularly at Laud himself. Laud ardently sought to demonstrate his opposition to Catholicism, though hardly with the same intensity or commitment that he exhibited in the fight against Puritanism.[25]

The "fear of popery" connects the religious controversies of the Laudian era with the wars of religion that raged during and following the archbishop's demise.[26] Again, popery continued to serve an imaginative, ideological, and polemical function more than it posed an actual threat. Until the early 1640s, there was a reluctance to see the king as complicit in popery, though he was seen as surrounding himself with counselors and ecclesiasts with papist leanings and aspirations.[27] The December 11, 1640, "Root and Branch" Petition challenged the legislation introduced by Laud's 1640 *Constitutions and Canons Ecclesiasticall*, which reinforced the relationship between monarchical and episcopal authority.[28] Milton would shortly thereafter refute the notion that "no forme of Church government is agreeable to monarchy, but that of Bishops" (*CPW*, 1:573). "The First and Large Petition . . . For a Reformation in Church-government"—the formal title of the Root and Branch Petition—demanded the abolition of the prelacy, given its approximation to and support of Catholic polity and authority. Listed here are grievances occasioned by the practices of the prelates that include "the publishing and venting of Popish, Arminian, and other dangerous Bookes and Tenets, as namely, that the Church of Rome is a true Church" (Art. 10); "the Liturgie for the most parts framed out of the *Romish Breviarie Ritualium* Masse-book, also the Book of Ordination, for Archbishops and Ministers, framed out of the roman Pontificall" (Art. 18); and the "expectation of the *Romish* part, *that their superstitious Religion will ere long be fully planted in this Kingdom again*" (Art. 28.1). The tenets of the petition are invoked in Milton's antiprelatical works, including *Animadversions upon the Remonstrants Defence*, which presents a defense of what was known as the "City Petition." *Animadversions* mentions its favorable reception by Parliament, which not only judged it worthy of support but secured the MPs' commitment to its principles. Opposition to the petition represents an affront to parliamentary authority, Milton points out (*CPW*, 1:677). The petitioners had campaigned against future incursions of the episcopacy in state affairs, and Milton takes up the same cause in his polemical writings. In doing so, he, like his Puritan contemporaries, availed himself of anti-Laudian, antiprelatical, and anti-Romanist propaganda in the war of religion that preceded and accompanied the civil wars.

III

It is noteworthy that Milton's humanism and his participation in a republic of letters could trump his anti-Catholicism or, perhaps more accurately, modulate his staunch English Protestant nationalism. One might turn to Milton's early remarks on his sojourn to Italy for confirmation of this. "I knew beforehand that Italy was not, as you think, a refuge or asylum for criminals, but rather the lodging-place of *humanitas* and of all the arts of civilization, and so I found it" (*CPW*, 4:609).[29] While still at Naples he learned from merchants "of plots laid against me by the English Jesuits, should I return to Rome, because of the freedom with which I had spoken about religion" (*CPW*, 4:619). But Rome beckoned again. Later, when he recalled his trip to Rome, Milton portrayed himself as an embattled but resolute protector of the faith, that is, as a "Protestant soldier,"[30] who championed national interests (and thereby his own), though encompassed round with dangers: "What I was, if any man inquired, I concealed from no one. For almost two more months [January–February 1639], in the very stronghold of the Pope, if anyone attacked the orthodox religion, I openly, as before, defended it" (*CPW*, 4:619). Nicolaas Heinsius, Dutch scholar, philologist, and poet, whose correspondence sheds light on the reception of Milton's Latin writings on the international stage, mentions that the antipopish Englishman had incensed his hosts during his tour of their country, which Heinsius regularly visited:[31] "Imo invisus est Italis Anglus iste [Miltonus] inter quos multo vixit tempore, ob mores nimis severos, cum & de religion libenter disputaret, ac multa in Pontificem Romanum acerbe effutiret quavis occasione" (In fact, that Englishman was hated by the Italians, among whom he lived a long time, on account of his over-strict morals, because he both disputed freely about religion, and on any occasion whatever prated very bitterly against the Roman Pontiff).[32]

Milton's Puritan sympathies and disillusionment with the prospect of a church career resulted in a dedication to the Presbyterian cause probably not long after his return to England in the late summer of 1639. By the time of the issuing of the aforementioned Laudian *Canons* in 1640, Milton had decided against a formal religious vocation.[33] He committed himself instead to taking up arms for Protestant cause in an alternative arena: while the conflict between Charles and Parliament was heating up, Milton set out to defend the interests of religion and liberty of conscience against the incursions of the episcopate. In doing so, he does not rebel against civil authority. In fact in the antiprelatical tracts of 1641–42 he registers his continued support of monarchical government, answerable to the law and the interests of the people as represented by Parliament. Monarchy, he insists, is defined in terms of "the Liberty of the subject, and the supremacie of the King" (*CPW*, 1:592).

Church tyranny is Milton's enemy, which he brands as papistical. Popery is for him an external invader but also, as repeatedly observed in the present chapter, an internal adversary, manifested in the ungodly prelates and the archbishop of Canterbury, who conspire to usurp the authority of the English subjects and monarch. In a discussion of Milton's antiepiscopal prose, Thomas N. Corns refers to the polemicist's strategy of "cheerfully lump[ing] the errors of Protestant bishops with those of their Catholic predecessors" in an "exuberant disregard for church history."[34] The compressed history of the Postscript to the Smectymnuan *An Answer to a Booke* offers an illustration of this.[35] "A Postscript" traces England's church government since the establishment of the See of Canterbury, with its founder "Austin the Monk" (*CPW*, 1:966). Thereafter, Dunstan (the Anglo-Saxon archbishop of Canterbury), Edward the Confessor, William the Conqueror, and Archbishop Anselm, followed by a long line of English prelates through to the Elizabethan era, are indiscriminately accused of imposing Roman ceremonies on the church and subjecting kings and the state to the papal authority.

Roughly concurrent with his Postscript, *Of Reformation* traces the history of a church whose reforms are constantly intercepted and overturned by Romish intruders and imitators. At the outset of the tract, John

Wycliffe is credited with sparking reform through his opposition to papal authority and doctrine, but, explains Milton, his blaze was quenched by the pope and popish English dynasties, extending from Henry VIII (*CPW*, 1:525, 526). Designed to expose the connections between England and Rome, the pamphlet *The English Pope* declares that "*Roman* Prelates" seeking to erect an "Ecclesiasticall Empire" were discovered in England over a century ago and that Henry VIII made no attempt to deliver his "subjects liberty from popish thraldome."[36] England, as Milton laments, was reduced to a schism and a scandal to the Reformation when the prelates restricted the ordination of ministers and introduced ceremonies into the liturgy, thus supporting "the *pompe* of *Prelatisme*" and sending the country "sliding back to *Rome*" (*CPW*, 1:527). The "*See* of *Canterbury*," the seat of the archbishop's authority, became a satellite for the papacy (*CPW*, 1:529). The elevation of the prelate will prove to be his tragic downfall, Milton predicts, as he divests the position and Laud himself of authority: "When hee steps up into the Chayre of *Pontificall* Pride, and changes a moderate and exemplary House, for a mis-govern'd and haughty *Palace, spirituall Dignity* for carnall *Precedence*, . . . then he *degrades*, then hee *un-Bishops* himselfe; hee that makes him *Bishop* makes him no *Bishop*" (*CPW*, 1:537–38).

Milton recounts that in the course of church history, and especially beginning with the rule of Constantine, the office of the ecclesiast became increasingly undemocratic in contrast to the communal arrangement of the primitive church. The "Canon-wise Prelate" was exalted at the expense of the people of God, the laity, whose status was diminished to that of "impure ethnicks, and lay dogs" (*CPW*, 1:547). Further, the prelates themselves, far from demonstrating their allegiance to king and country, became guilty of undermining both: "What good upholders of Royalty were the Bishops, when by their rebellious opposition against King John, Normandy was lost, he himself depos'd, and this Kingdom made over to the Pope" (*CPW*, 1:581). Since then, the episcopate had assumed the same tyrannical powers in England as the papists had on the Continent. Thus "wise and famous men" would support Milton's verdict that "the Protestant *Episcopacie* in *England*" was as much to be feared as the papacy (*CPW*, 1:581). Had not English ecclesiasts disputed the supremacy of the monarchy? Certainly the chief ecclesiast was guilty of exactly that and thereby incriminated himself. Laud, Milton testifies, shortly after the archbishop was impeached for treason, is "accus'd out of his owne Booke, and his *late Canons* to affect a certaine unquestionable *Patriarchat*, independent and unsubordinate to the Crowne" (*CPW*, 1:594). The aforementioned Laudian Canons rendered the church immune to Parliament's authority. Underscoring the dangers posed by the bishops, Milton develops parallels between the episcopacy and the papacy: "If *Episcopacie* be taken for *Prelacie*, all the Ages they can deduce it through, will make it no more venerable then *Papacie*." Juxtaposed in order to convey identification, "Episcopacie," "Prelacie," and "Papacie," which converge in the "See of Canterbury," constitute a "dolefull succession of illiterate and blind guides" (*CPW*, 1:602–3). As the See of Canterbury, Laud is a whole institution, which Milton seeks to dismantle. As he draws near to a conclusion in *Of Reformation*, Milton, still endorsing kingship, imagines the prospect of Charles governing without Laud: "The King shall sit without an old disturber, a dayly incroacher, and intruder" (*CPW*, 1:599).

The theme of the danger that popish English bishops pose to monarchs runs through Milton's antiprelatical tracts, including not only *Of Reformation* and *Of Prelatical Episcopacy*, produced about a month later (June or July 1641), but also *Animadversions* (July 1641), a response to the April 12, 1641, *Defence of the Humble Remonstrance*, by Bishop Joseph Hall. Hall had been asked by Archbishop Laud to produce a defense of episcopacy, which was titled "Episcopacie by Divine Right Asserted" (February 10, 1640). The *Defence* sparked a print war over the subject of church government, about which Hall combated with the Smectymnuus authors. Milton entered the arena with his first two antiepiscopal tracts, while reserving his direct assaults on Hall for *Animadversions*, in which the Remonstrant is cast as a backer of Romish doctrines and practices. *Animadversions* aligns the Remonstrant or protester's position on *jure divino* episcopacy with the pope's own defiance about "his ungainsaid authority" (*CPW*, 1:674), the opponents of which are condemned as heretics. Milton hails the liberation of the nation by virtue of the distinctly Protestant protest against Romish superstition: "*Brittains* God hath reform'd his Church after many hundred yeers of *Popish* corruption," releasing the people from the "intolerable yoke of *Prelats*, and *Papall* Discipline"—once again deemed as interchangeable (*CPW*, 1:704). "Every true protested *Brittaine*" must now render thanks that the night of popish thralldom is giving way to "the morning beam of Reformation" (*CPW*, 1:704, 705).

The fourth antiprelatical pamphlet, *The Reason of Church-government Urg'd Against Prelaty*, again utilizes the genre of animadversion tract and countertract, as Milton opposes church tyranny, partly represented by bishops' return to the House of Commons on December 29, 1641. He excises them from history by cross-examining their defenders and by exposing their popish roots. Written in response to *Certain Briefe Treatises . . . Concerning the Ancient and Moderne Government of the Church* (1641), *Church-government* (*CPW*, 1:783) exposes the historical connection between the bishopric and the papacy.[37] Under the pretense of securing order, the office of the bishopric gave rise to the pope and papacy (*CPW*, 1:783). If all churches joined together under the prelacy in the name of quelling dissent, an "Arch-primat, or Protestant Pope" would emerge and issue a "finall pronounce or canon" (*CPW*, 1:783). The consequence thereof, Milton warns, would be the subjection of the people to servility, a betrayal of the liberation or deliverance promised by the Gospel. He also describes the corresponding social, material, and legal violations committed by the prelates who deprive citizens of their civic rights and estates: when "they have stufft their Idolish temples with the wastefull pillage of your estates," they will, like the merchants of Babylon—identified with Rome—sell your souls, "your bodies, your wives, your children, your liberties, your Parlaments," and, "by their corrupt and servile doctrines," permanently enslave you (*CPW*, 1:851).

IV

In the same year as *Church-government* was produced, the aforementioned John Pym, the unofficial head of Parliament, appealed for the indulgence of supplicants, especially those pleading for free speech. "This great Councell . . . is the soul of the Common-wealth, wherein one may hear and see, all the grievances of the Subjects . . . amongst whom, the greatest priviledge is liberty of Speech."[38] The "company of Seminary Priests" that exists as long as papal agents continue to infest England, explains Pym, endangers the church from without, but as great a danger lies within, from those who serve the church for the sake of worldly prefer-ments.[39] Milton's speech "For the Liberty of Unlicenc'd Printing," begins as Pym's did by flattering Parliament for its willingness to hear its citizens' appeals: after rehearsing the epigraph from Euripides appearing on the title page to *Areopagitica*, in which he states, "This is true Liberty when free born men / Having to advise the public may speak free," Milton in his exordium declares, "When complaints are freely heard, deeply con-sider'd, and speedily reform'd, then is the utmost bound of civill liberty attain'd, that wise men looke for" (*CPW*, 2:487). Liberation from Rome is hailed thereafter as an act of God and secondarily as the work of the Lords and Commons of England. As noted above, the assault on Catholi-cism prevalent throughout *Areopagitica* is partly a recrimination against the Laudian church, but it is also aimed at the very Parliament whose "laudable deeds" and "indefatigable vertues" Milton otherwise celebrates (*CPW*, 2:487). *Areopagitica* was in preparation during Laud's trial (which ended August 31), and the Areopagus serves for Milton as the site of the inquisition of the Laudian institution and the corresponding policies of the Roman Church. At the same time Milton urges Parliament, which adopted those policies by reintroducing licensing, to repeal its own op-pressive quasi-popish practices.

In July 1641, Star Chamber and the High Commission were abol-ished, and with that the jurisdiction that the bishops held over licensing ended. But in 1643, the Stationers Company was invested with the power to regulate the printing trade by searching printing houses, seizing presses, and apprehending authors, printers, bookbinders, and distributors of "scandalous or unlicensed" materials.[40] Milton's defense of critical reading involves a rebuke of governmental authorities who, in imitation of the church prelates, enforce censorship, prohibit book publication, and dis-courage active interpretation, thus thwarting the progress of the Refor-mation. Laud may be on trial and "the Prelats" may have "expir'd" (*CPW*, 2:491) on February 13, 1642 (insofar as they were removed from the House of Lords and deprived of their authority over licensing),[41] but various vestiges of Laudianism remained intact. "The ghost of a linen decency yet haunts us" (*CPW*, 2:564), Milton complains. The ghost lingered after the scaffold took care of the rest.

In *Areopagitica*, Milton's most optimistic statement on England's Reformation, the nation is figured as chosen and privileged by virtue of the "great measure of truth which [it] enjoy[s], especially in those main points between us and the pope, with his appertinences the Prelats" (*CPW*, 2:549). The political institution of the papacy stands in the way of true liberty, the cherished value and defining feature of the Reformation. "The Popes of *Rome*" were the first censors, Milton, reminds his audience; "Engrossing what they pleas'd of Politicall rule into their owne hands, [the papists] extended their dominion over mens eyes, as they had before over their judgements, burning and prohibiting to be read, what they fansied not" (*CPW*, 2:501–2). Having historicized the connection between Rome and licensing in his oration, Milton challenges Parliament to reaffirm the difference between the liberty-embracing English nation and intolerant foreign papists. In *Areopagitica*, censorship is represented as Romish, as well as Spanish, but this originally popish practice threatens England from within: the English press is "gag[ed]" by its own ecclesiasts (*CPW*, 2:519). The situation is thus all the more complicated when the tyranny Milton exposes and rails against prevails even after the "Bishops [were] abrogated and voided out of the Church" (*CPW*, 2:541). Maintained by a system in which "Episcopall arts begin to bud again" (*CPW*, 2:541), the restraint of press freedoms is upheld by parliamentary issued licensing policies whose associations with Romish censorial and Inquisitorial operations Milton was determined to publish and censure.

Areopagitica outlines strategies for combating popish influences and effects on various fronts, including at the level of the individual, whose spiritual inertia, Milton warns, leads to errancy: "There is not any burden that som would gladlier post off to another, then the charge and care of their Religion. There be, who knows not that there be of Protestants and professors who live and dye in as arrant an implicit faith, as any lay Papist of Loretto" (*CPW*, 2:543–44). Errant faith is untried and untested and, in its stagnation, breeds superstition even among Protestants, Milton is keen to emphasize. *Areopagitica* thus sets up comparisons between "the dignity of labour, manual and intellectual, and . . . the lazy, loitering easy life readily imaged in the beneficed clergy or Roman church," as Michael Wilding observes.[42] When Milton translates the obligations and rights of the people as God's chosen into civil rights and individual liberties, he further distances Protestant expressions of faith from an "implicit faith" and from the blunting and numbing doctrine and discipline of the

Roman Catholic Church. To resist popery is to promote "reason, scripture, and conscience," which is Milton's rallying cry throughout his antiepiscopal tracts.[43] The exercise of the faculty of reason and the active engagement with scripture ward off superstition and its custodians.

Does the antipopery of *Areopagitica* compromise the defense of liberty of speech? Not at all, Milton protests. An intolerant religion invalidates itself: while toleration should be broadly extended to embrace as many Christians as possible, "Popery," that is, "open superstition," is intolerable: "As it extirpats all religions and civill supremacies, so it self should be extirpat" (*CPW*, 2:565). Though a papist practice, censorship can justly be used to rein in papists, and thus what may appear to qualify or even subvert his argument for freedom of the press is turned into a principle assured of achieving consensus and broad support. Resistance to Catholic and Episcopalian authoritarianism brings Protestants into agreement with each other. By establishing common ground through the opposition to popish conformity, Milton takes the first step toward confronting Parliament about a licensing act that he codes as Romish.

The scene of the Court of the Areopagus gives way only a short while later to a site of judgment on Tower Hill: "This is a very uncomfortable place to preach in," confessed Laud in his final performance—on the scaffold. At the same time that he defends his work as archbishop in his last dying speech, Laud laments the rise of dissenters who destabilize the true Protestant religion and nation: "The Pope never had such an harvest since the Reformation as he hath now by these sects that are among us."[44] In his last breath, Laud again identifies as his primary target the sectaries who impede the progress of the Reformation and thereby inadvertently aid the pope's cause. When Laud was executed, Samuel Pecke printed a transcript of the archbishop's speech in his *Perfect Diurnall*. Although clearly a Puritan partisan, Pecke gave his adversaries space to air their views, but not without his own animadversions, which he describes as "observations." All the interpolations in the transcription of Laud's speech implicate the archbishop in popery.[45] "If the Pope heard you," states Pecke, in response to Laud's declaration that the pope is reaping the benefits of internal divisions in England, "*heed* [he would] *scarce believe you in this; what? a better Harvest than when Jesuites, Priests and Fryers, and a world of Popish trumperie were tollerated.*"[46] Pecke is determined to pen the last words for Laud, whose reputation as an apologist for Rome would follow him to the grave and beyond. When William Prynne in 1646, for example, retried his late persecutor, he again highlighted the archbishop's indulgence of the pope and Romish priests and decried his hostility to the Reformed churches and the Reformation movement.[47]

This chapter has sought to unsettle the binary between English Protestantism and Roman Catholicism in a review of Milton's early condemnation of Laud. The antiepiscopal tracts in particular exhibit Milton's elision of differences between Laudianism and popery and his politicization of both. For Milton, for whom a key polemical strategy in the works on church government is the repeated reinforcement of the prelacy-papacy connection, the Reformation remains a protestation; and given that the shadow of Rome still hangs over the state and church, the English religion is defined in terms of opposition or negation as Protestantism (after the Lutheran *protestatio*). *Areopagitica* builds on the antiprelatical writings by identifying licensing with a Romish Laudian era (*CPW*, 2:555). But Milton has another objective in mind in *Areopagitica*: the anti-Catholic directive and imperative designed to unite Protestants gives way to affirmations of liberty and prepares the way for the accommodation of those "cry'd out against for schismaticks and sectaries," whom Laud especially despised (*CPW*, 2:555). "Many moderat varieties and brotherly dissimilitudes" make up the new "Temple of the Lord" Milton envisions, soon to be reconceived as an invisible church (*CPW*, 2:555). The erection of the heterodox Reformed church in the place of Laud's "mis-govern'd and haughty *Palace*" (*CPW*, 1:537) would represent the ultimate victory in the disciplinary controversy, the debate over church government, and the "wars of Truth" (*CPW*, 2:562) that constituted Milton's civil war.

NOTES

1. Caroline Hibbard, *Charles I and the Popish Plot* (Chapel Hill: University of North Carolina Press, 1983), 64; *A Letter from a Gentleman of the Romish Religion, To his Brother a Person of Quality of the same Religion* (London, 1674), 27, 26. William Castell notes the Jesuits' argument that princes should be subordinate to the pope, who has the power to depose kings (*The Jesuits undermining of parliaments and Protestants with their foolish phancy of a toleration, discovered, and censured* [London, 1642], 2).

2. Peter Lake, "Anti-popery: The Structure of a Prejudice," in *Conflict in Early Stuart England*, ed. Richard Cust and Ann Hughes (London: Longman, 1989), 91, 96. On early modern anti-Catholic rhetoric, see Martin J. Havran, *The Catholics in Caroline England* (Stanford, CA: Stanford University Press, 1962); Arthur Marotti, ed., *Catholicism and Anti-Catholicism in Early Modern English Texts* (Basingstoke: Palgrave, 1999); Alison Shell, *Catholicism, Controversy and the English Literary Imagination, 1558–1660* (Cambridge: Cambridge University Press, 1999); Ethan H. Shagan, ed., *Catholics and the "Protestant Nation": Religious Politics and Identity in Early Modern England* (Manchester: Manchester University Press, 2005); Raymond Tumbleson, *Catholicism in the English Protestant Imagination: Nationalism, Religion, and Literature, 1660–1745* (Cambridge: Cambridge University Press, 1998).

3. Don M. Wolfe, introduction to *CPW*, 1:70–72.

4. Lake, "Anti-popery," 83.

5. John Pym, *March 17. Master Pyms Speech in Parliament* (London, 1641/2), 6.

6. John T. Shawcross, "'Connivers and the Worst of Superstitions': Milton on Popery and Toleration," *Literature and History*, 3rd ser., 7, no. 2 (1998): 57.

7. John Milton, "In Quintum Novembris," in *The Shorter Poems*, ed. Barbara K. Lewalski and Estelle Hann, *CWJM*, 3:166. Quotations of Milton's shorter poems are taken from this edition.

8. Thomas N. Corns, "James I," in *The Milton Encyclopedia*, ed. Thomas N. Corns (New Haven, CT: Yale University Press, 2012), 190. See, for example, *CWJM*, 6:357–58.

9. Stephen B. Dobranski, "Principle and Politics in *Areopagitica*," in *The Oxford Handbook of Literature and the English Revolution*, ed. Laura Lunger Knoppers (Oxford: Oxford University Press, 2012), 195.

10. Elizabeth Sauer, "Milton and Caroline Church Government," *Yearbook of English Studies* 44 (2014): 199–200; John Spencer Hill, *John Milton: Poet, Priest and Prophet: A Study of Divine Vocation in Milton's Poetry and Prose* (London: Macmillan, 1979), 39–40; Thomas N. Corns, "Milton before 'Lycidas,'" in *Milton and the Terms of Liberty*, ed. Graham Parry and Joad Raymond (Cambridge: Brewer, 2002), 23–36; Edward Jones, "Milton's Life, 1608–1640," in *Oxford Handbook of Milton*, ed. Nicholas McDowell and Nigel Smith (Oxford: Oxford University Press, 2009), 13; Edward Jones, ed. *Young Milton: The Emerging Author, 1620–1642* (Oxford: Oxford University Press, 2013); Nicholas McDowell, "The Caroline Court," in *Milton in Context*, ed. Stephen B. Dobranski (Cambridge: Cambridge University Press, 2010), 237–47; Neil Forsyth, "The English Church," in Dobranski, *Milton in Context*, 296,

298. On Milton's "disengagement" from Laudianism, see also Gordon Campbell and Thomas N. Corns, *John Milton: Life, Work, and Thought* (Oxford: Oxford University Press, 2008), 95.

11. Lake, "Anti-popery," 79.

12. John Cosin, *Collection of Private Devotions: In the Practise of the Ancient Church, Called the Houres of Prayer* (London, 1627).

13. William Prynne, *Canterburies Doome. or The First Part of a Compleat History of The Commitment, Charge, Tryall, Condemnation, Execution of WILLIAM LAUD Late Arch-Bishop of Canterbury* (London 1646), 93 (misnumbered in original source).

14. *Diurnall Occurrences* (1641), quoted in *The Journal of Sir Simonds D'Ewes: From the Beginning of the Long Parliament to the Opening of the Trial of the Earl of Strafford*, ed. Wallace Notestein (New Haven, CT: Yale University Press, 1923), 57n20.

15. William Prynne, *A Briefe Suruay and Censure of Mr Cozens his Couzening Deuotions Prouing both the Forme and Matter of Mr Cozens his Booke . . . to be Meerely Popish* (London 1628), 3, 82.

16. H. B. (Henry Burton), *A Tryall of Private Devotions: or, a Diall for the Houres of Prayer* (London 1628), A4r, Hr.

17. Venice: May 16–31, 1637, in *Calendar of State Papers Relating to English Affairs in the Archives of Venice*, vol. 24, *1636–1639*, ed. Allen B. Hinds (London: HMSO, 1923), 210–18. See also Anthony Milton, *Catholic and Reformed: The Roman and Protestant Churches in English Protestant Thought, 1600–1640* (Cambridge: Cambridge University Press, 1995), 61–62.

18. William Prynne, *A Breviate of the Life of William Laud . . . Collected and Published . . . as a Necessary Prologue to the History of His Tryall* (London, 1644), 21.

19. Venice: November 13, 1637, in Hinds, *Calendar*, 24: 312–28.

20. Bastwick identifies Laud as pope in his account of the Puritans' pillorying in *A Breife Relation of Certain Speciall and Most Materiall Passages . . . June the 14th. 1637. At the censure of those three worthy Gentlemen, Dr. Bastwicke, Mr. Burton and Mr. Prynne* (Amsterdam, 1638), 16.

21. A. Milton, *Catholic and Reformed*, 64, 77. As Laud declared at his trial, no "understanding Papist" could be persuaded and converted by the denunciation of the Pope as Anti-Christ (William Laud, *The History of the Troubles and Tryal of . . . Laud, The Works of . . . William Laud*, ed. W. Scott and J. Bliss, 7 vols. [Oxford: John Henry Parker, 1847–60], 4:309).

22. Alexandra Walsham, "The Parochial Roots of Laudianism Revisited: Catholics, Anti-Calvinists and 'Parish Anglicans' in Early Stuart England," *Journal of Ecclesiastical History* 49, no. 4 (1998): 639.

23. Venice: May 16–31, 1637, in Hinds, *Calendar*, 24:217.

24. Michael C. Questier, ed., *Newsletters from the Caroline Court, 1621–1638: Catholicism and the Politics of the Personal Rule* (Cambridge: Cambridge University Press, 2005), 19.

25. Ibid., 21n62. That Laud rejected Catholicism as he rejected Puritanism is discussed in Samuel Rawson Gardiner, *History of England from the Accession of James I to the Outbreak of the Civil War, 1603–1642*, 10 vols. (1884; repr., New York: AMS Press, 1965), 7:301–2.

26. Kevin Sharpe, *The Personal Rule of Charles I* (New Haven, CT: Yale University Press, 1992), 938–39.

27. See, for example, *Sir Francis Seymor his honourable, and worthy speech, spoken in the high court of Parliament . . . And how the splendor of His Majestyes glory is eclipsed with toleration of Iesuits, seminary priests, and bad ministers* (London 1641).

28. *The First and Large Petition of the City of London and of Other Inhabitants Thereabouts: For a Reformation in Church-government, as also for the Abolishment of Episcopacy* (London, 1641), in *CPW*, 1:976–84; *Constitutions and Canons Ecclesiasticall* (London, May 17, 1640), E203 (2), sig. B6.

29. See Catherine Gimelli Martin, "Italy," in Dobranski, *Milton in Context*, 319–22.

30. Diana Trevino Benet, "The Escape from Rome," in *Milton in Italy: Contexts, Images, Contradictions*, ed. Mario A. Di Cesare (Binghamton, NY: Center for Medieval and Early Renaissance Studies, 1991), 47.

31. Barbara K. Lewalski, *Life of John Milton: A Critical Biography* (Oxford: Blackwell, 2000), 98–99.

32. Nicolaas Heinsius, "Letter to Isaac Vossius" (1653), quoted in *The Life Records of John Milton*, ed. J. Milton French, 5 vols. (1949–58; repr., New York: Gordian Press, 1966), 3:321; trans. David Masson, *The Life of John Milton*, 6 vols. (1877; repr., Gloucester, MA: Peter Smith, 1965), 4:475.

33. Hill, *John Milton*, 49. This was in part an expression of his opposition to the prelatical system (John T. Shawcross, *The Arms of the Family: The Significance of John Milton's Relatives and Associates* [Lexington: University Press of Kentucky, 2004], 179).

34. Thomas N. Corns, "Milton's Antiprelatical Tracts and the Marginality of Doctrine," in *Milton and Heresy*, ed. Stephen B. Dobranski and John P. Rumrich (Cambridge: Cambridge University Press, 1998), 43.

35. See Don Wolfe, preface and notes to "A Postscript," in *CPW*, 1:961–65.

36. *The English Pope, or a Discourse Wherein the Late Mysticall Intelligence betwixt the Court of England, and the Court of Rome is in Part Discovered* (1643), 3–4.

37. *Certain Briefe Treatises, Written by Diverse Learned Men, Concerning the Ancient and Moderne Government of the Church. Wherein . . . the Primitive Institution of EPISCOPACIE is Maintained* (Oxford, 1641).

38. Pym, "March 17. Master Pyms Speech," 3.

39. Ibid., 4.

40. "The Licensing Order of 1643," ed. Ernest Sirluck (1959), in *CPW*, 2:798.

41. Episcopacy itself, however, was not abolished until October 9, 1646.

42. Michael Wilding, "Milton's *Areopagitica*: Liberty for the Sects," in *The Literature of Controversy: Polemical Strategies from Milton to Junius*, ed. Thomas N. Corns (London: Routledge, 1987), 17.

43. Corns, "Milton's Antiprelatical Tracts," 47.

44. *A Perfect Diurnall of Some Passages in Parliament*, no. 76 (January 6–13, 1645), 603, 604; see also William Laud, "The Speech of the Lord Archbishop of Canterbury, spoken at his Death, upon the Scaffold on the Tower-hill, Jan. 10, 1644," in Laud, *History of the Troubles*, 4:430–40.

45. *Perfect Diurnall*, January 10, 1645, 603.

46. Ibid., 604.

47. Prynne, *Canterburies Doome*, e.g., 391.

CHAPTER 2

JOHN MILTON AND
GEORGE EGLISHAM

The English Revolution and Catholic Disinformation

ALASTAIR BELLANY AND THOMAS COGSWELL

John Milton's celebrated defenses of the regicide and the new English republic, *Eikonoklastes* (1649) and *Pro Populo Anglicano Defensio* (1651),
contain a rather odd recurring allusion. In his response to *Eikon Basilike*,
Milton began his indictment of the recently executed king by noting that
Charles I had dissolved the 1626 Parliament "for no other cause then to
protect the Duke of Buckingham against them who had accus'd him, besides other hainous crimes, of no less then poysoning, the deceased King
his Father." This shocking charge, Milton argued, needed no elaborate
rehearsal, since "The Declaration of No more addresses, hath sufficiently
inform'd us." Later in *Eikonoklastes*, he again referred to "the suspected
Poysoning of [Charles's] Father, not inquir'd into, but smother'd up, and
him [Buckingham] protected and advanc'd," even though the duke "was
accus'd in Parlament to be Author of the Fact."[1] In 1651, Milton refuted
Salmasius's attack on the regicide by charging "Charles with his father's

39

death." At first Milton was cautious: "I do not use the word murder, although all the signs of poison were in evidence upon his father's body." Buckingham was the culprit; but "Charles did not only absolve that slayer of the king and of his father from all blame in the highest council of state, but also dissolved Parliament to keep the whole affair from any Parliamentary investigation." He then maintained that Charles "who snatched from the arms of the law the Duke who was guilty of the poisoning was himself guilty too." More emphatically he proclaimed that "Charles used poison to kill his father and his king!"[2]

The editors of Milton's works duly noted Milton's debt to the February 1648 *Declaration* justifying the Vote of No Addresses. Yet they did not investigate the history of the allegation that James had been murdered and that his son had somehow been involved in the conspiracy. If they had, they would have discovered that the first systematic allegation of James's murder dated back to 1626 and to a short tract, published in Latin, English, and German versions by George Eglisham and titled, in English, *The Forerunner of Revenge upon the Duke of Buckingham*.[3] Eglisham's pamphlet probably encouraged the 1626 Parliament to open hearings into James's death, and its allegations stalked Buckingham to his grave; indeed, the book may have encouraged John Felton to assassinate the duke in 1628. Eglisham's book continued to influence English politics into the civil wars and revolution. It was reprinted at least five times in 1642 and generated at least one creative adaptation that same year.[4] It was translated into Dutch in 1644 and was republished in a severely abridged form in 1648.[5] Yet the continuing popularity of Eglisham's 1626 tract was more than a little surprising.

The 1640s and '50s were a highly uncomfortable period for English Catholics. At the beginning of the Civil War, John Pym and his associates constantly conjured up the specters of innumerable popish plots in which foreign Catholic powers and English priests and laity purportedly sought to subvert Parliament and the Protestant Reformation. This storm surge of anti-Catholicism never abated among the supporters of Parliament, who were all too willing to act on this rhetoric. Its soldiers were often reluctant to accept the surrender of Catholic troops, especially if they were Irish. Meanwhile the public executioners were kept busy through the Civil War, eviscerating priests at a pace not seen since the late sixteenth century. Six of them were drawn and quartered in 1642 alone, and at least sixteen in all between 1641 and 1646. These Catholics were so despised that in London the crowds reportedly played football with Father Green's head.[6] Amid this extraordinary outburst of religious hatred, Eglisham's continuing fame and influence was, to put it mildly, rather ironic. The origins of his tract have long been shrouded in mystery. According to their title pages, the English edition and one of the Latin ones were purportedly published in Frankfurt. But we have been able for the first time to trace the book to its actual origins in a print shop in Brussels with close ties to the Spanish regime, ties that, it turns out, George Eglisham shared. In short, Eglisham was a Catholic, and his tract laying out the case for James's murder, and thus the origins of Milton's 1649 and 1651 allusions, was a remarkably successful piece of Catholic "disinformation" designed to sow confusion among English Protestants during the opening phase of England's ill-fated interventions in the Thirty Years' War. We offer here a genealogy of one strain in Milton's republican polemic, tracking how a charge framed by a Catholic libel became a shibboleth of radical Protestant republicanism.

I

A Scotsman with close ties to the Marquis of Hamilton's family, George Eglisham was a doctor, poet, and polemicist. His Catholicism was long-standing. He was educated at Louvain in the Spanish Netherlands, where he spent some time in a Jesuit college. He was identified as a recusant while working as a tutor for a Yorkshire gentry family and would later surface in Rouen and Paris, where he taught philosophy and practiced medicine.[7] He was married in secrecy in a Catholic ceremony at London's Clink Prison in 1617. By the time of his marriage, Eglisham had been settled in London for about three years. Thanks to a pair of Latin tracts he had written against the Arminian Conrad Vortsius in 1612, he attracted the favor of James I, who made him an extraordinary royal doctor and granted him a royal patent to establish a new London livery company of Goldbeaters.[8] Unfortunately his prosperous new world in London was short-lived. The 1621 Parliament attacked his new company as one of the dangerous monopolies plaguing the commonwealth, and James was forced to withdraw its patent. Then, during the negotiations for the Spanish Match when Catholics seemed destined for favor, Eglisham abandoned his attempt to keep his religion from public notice and engaged in disputations over transubstantiation with Archbishop Abbot's chaplain Daniel Featley. Early in March 1625, with an anti-Catholic mood now back on the ascendant, Eglisham became involved in a rash attempt to convert the dying Marquis of Hamilton to Rome. Though Catholic writers insisted Hamilton had converted, Protestants maintained he had not, and they blamed Eglisham for the entire scandalous affair.[9] With Archbishop Abbott and James himself furious at Eglisham's behavior, Eglisham first went into hiding and then fled to Brussels in June 1625.

Jean Baptiste Van Male, the Archduchess Isabella's longtime diplomatic representative in London, wrote directly to her in Brussels, requesting support for Eglisham, who had been "persecuted by the Archbishop of Canterbury and others for having caused the conversion of the Marquis of Hamilton." The doctor was, Van Male added, "a person of great parts and letters" capable of performing "useful services." William Trumbull, James's Brussels agent, reported Eglisham's arrival and his welcome from Cardinal Cueva, one of Isabella's councillors. Meanwhile a Scottish priest who came to Brussels with details of a possible Catholic rising late in 1626 connected Eglisham with another key figure, the Conde de Gondomar, the veteran Spanish ambassador to London who was then in Brussels organizing Spanish intelligence gathering in England.[10] One or several of these figures at the heart of the Brussels regime—Van Male, Gondomar, and/or Cueva—was likely involved in arranging for the publication of Dr. Eglisham's most celebrated tract, the *Forerunner of Revenge*.

The English edition, and one of the two Latin ones, carried Frankfurt imprints, and because these editions scrupulously avoided any overt Catholic sentiments, readers may have been deceived by the imprint connecting the book to the German Lutheran city and printing center. This masking was quite deliberate. Working with the Plantin-Moretus bookshop registers in Antwerp and using close comparison of typography, we have been able to link the English and Latin "Frankfurt" editions of *The Forerunner* to the print shop of Jan Van Meerbeeck in Brussels. Meerbeeck, a young printer who had already worked with prominent figures in the Brussels political and intellectual elite, was entrusted by the regime with several high-profile works of propaganda and disinformation in 1626. Eglisham's *Forerunner* thus belonged both to a long tradition of masked Flemish libels aimed at English readers—works such as the Elizabethan *Leicester's Commonwealth* (1584) and the Jacobean *Corona Regia* (1615)—and to the more tightly focused propaganda campaign launched by the Habsburgs in 1625–26 to unsettle their English, French, and Dutch enemies.[11]

An anonymous Spanish intelligencer noted that on his arrival in Brussels Eglisham was eager to broadcast the news that "they gave poison to the Marquis of Hamilton," and Hamilton's murder takes up the bulk of *The Forerunner's* narrative. Hamilton had quarreled with Buckingham over a marriage alliance, and the favorite had cruelly poisoned him. The marquis's corpse had spectacularly revealed the murder, swelling "in such sort that his thighes were as big as the belly of an oxe, his armes as big as the natural quantitie of his thighs, his necke so broad as his shoulders, his cheekes over the tope of his nose, that his nose could not be seene or distinguished, the skinne of forehead over his eyes . . . two finger high swelled." His hair came out "as easily as if one had pulled hay out of an heape of hay," and his body was covered with blisters, "some white, some blacke, some red, some yeallow, some greene, some blew." As an addendum to his detailed account of Hamilton's death, Eglisham added two and a third pages describing how Buckingham had poisoned King James. Without the royal doctors' knowledge, the favorite had applied a plaster to the old king's chest and given him a potion to which he had added some white powders. James "immediatly became worse and worse, falling into many soundings and paynes, and violent fluxes of the belly so tormented, that his Maiestie cryed out aloud, o this white powder! this white powder! wold to God I had never taken it, it will cost me my liffe." His corpse also exhibited the same telltale symptoms as Hamilton's: "The Kings body and head swelled above measure, his haire with the skin of his head stucke to the pillow, his nayles became loose upon his fingers and toes." Eglisham appealed to King Charles to see justice done on his father's murderer, but he had little hope, since "your Maiestie suffereth your selfe so farre to be led" by Buckingham. Indeed, Eglisham told Charles that "your best subiects ar in doubt, whether he is your king or you his."[12]

Eglisham had witnessed Hamilton's death but had been in hiding when James died and had to rely on rumors circulating at court about Buckingham's unadvised medical interventions during the king's final illness. He called on Charles and Parliament to collect "the examinations upon oath of all those that were about the King and the Marquis of Hamilton in there sicknes, or at there death." Charles declined to follow his advice, but the Parliament-men, eager to destroy Buckingham and stalled in their attempts to impeach him, spent three days in late April 1626 hearing the testimony of the doctors and attendants. Their last-minute decision to launch this inquiry was almost certainly catalyzed by the arrival of the first copies of Eglisham's tract in London. Though none of the royal physicians suggested that James had been poisoned, they confirmed that Buckingham had meddled in James's treatment, possibly to damaging effect, confirming enough of Eglisham's details for the Commons to add Buckingham's actions to the impeachment charges as "an act of transcendent presumption of dangerous consequence." Neither Eglisham nor the impeachment charge made any claims about Charles's involvement in James's death. The guilt was Buckingham's. But from the start, it was clear that the accusations were highly volatile. Charles had both Sir John Eliot and Sir Dudley Digges imprisoned after their presentations of the impeachment charges to the Lords, convinced that the two Parliament-men had insinuated his involvement in Buckingham's actions. Eventually convinced that the two men had meant no such thing, Charles released them. Four weeks later, frustrated with the Commons's refusal to pass the all-important subsidy bill, Charles dissolved Parliament before the Lords had rendered a verdict on Buckingham's impeachment.[13]

Buckingham ended the session a widely hated figure, and allegations about his poisonings became standard fare in the underground verse libels that dogged his reputation for the rest of his days. There is evidence of considerable frustration at Charles's dissolution of Parliament, and anger at his refusal to surrender the duke to justice. But few contemporaries were willing to think through what the dissolution might suggest about the young king's role in James's death. The private musings of the godly Thomas Scott of Canterbury, however, reveal what was thinkable. Scott had little doubt that Buckingham was guilty of James's death. Though he could not decide if Charles was also involved in the murder, Scott thought that the young king's decision to dissolve Parliament implicated him as an accessory after the fact. This left the awkward question of what was to be done: Scott found the answer in the pages of his Bible and in his copy of the notorious Calvinist resistance tract *Vindicae contra Tyrannos*. With Eglisham's pamphlet running through his head, Scott sketched out the moral and political logic for a revolt led by the lesser magistrates to execute Buckingham and to try Charles.[14] Scott was an outlier in 1626; but this kind of reasoning would come to dominate public discourse about the murder of James I during the 1640s.

II

Eglisham's accusations did not die with Buckingham in 1628; indeed, by late 1642 the guilt of his father's death was starting to become more firmly attached to Charles I. Charles's dissolution of the 1626 Parliament became the key incriminating evidence against him. In the early fall of 1642, a radical tract *King Iames His Iudgement* presented an indictment of Charles that began with the covering up of James's murder: "When our geud King Iames his death was by one of his Phisitians tendered to the King and Parliament to be examined," the tract wondered, why was "the Parliament . . . eft soone dissolved?" Though it provided no clear answer to its own question, the pamphlet had ventured onto dangerous terrain, and Parliament ordered the printers imprisoned. Nevertheless, questions about James's death and the 1626 dissolution would not go away.[15] Within weeks of the publication of *King Iames His Iudgement*, there began a massive, and seemingly coordinated, campaign to republish and revive Eglisham's *Forerunner*, which now became freely available for sale in London bookshops for the first time. Details of Buckingham's murder of the old king quickly became a recurrent motif in parliamentarian propaganda, but few writers pursued the awkward questions raised by *King Iames His Iudgement*. Since Parliament was then ostensibly fighting to separate the king from his evil councillors, the Commons could support attacks on the wicked deeds of royal favorites but not a direct criminal accusation against the monarch they were fighting to redeem. And it was primarily as a critique of favorites that Eglisham's reprinted *Forerunner* was marketed in late 1642. Given the centrality of antipopish rhetoric in parliamentarian propaganda, it was not surprising that Eglisham's old accusations also acquired an explicitly anti-Catholic twist during the First Civil War. William Prynne, for instance, identified an ongoing Jesuit-popish plot that was controlling Charles by threatening to poison him as they had previously poisoned his father. Prynne's repeated references to this popish plot treated James's murder as an uncontroversial fact and cited Eglisham's pamphlet as his proof. The violently anti-Catholic Prynne apparently had no idea he was using a Catholic work to substantiate his antipopish polemic. Eglisham's life story was little discussed during this period, and indeed one late 1642 adaptation of *The Forerunner* explicitly Protestantized the Scotsman by claiming he had fled England not for Catholic Brussels but for Calvinist Holland.[16]

During the First Civil War, polemic on the murder of James I remained primarily focused on the problems of popery and favorites. Early in 1648, however, Eglisham's old allegations were stunningly reinvented into a protoregicidal charge against Charles I. In January 1648, frustrated by its inability to reach a settlement with an apparently perfidious king and fearful that Charles was secretly negotiating with the Scottish Presbyterians, the Commons voted 141 to 92 to break off talks with the king and to prohibit any future ones. To justify its actions, Parliament issued a powerful printed declaration. Parliamentary litanies of Charles's offenses had become commonplace after the 1641 Grand Remonstrance—the early Caroline past was one of the major polemical battlegrounds of the war. But the 1648 *Declaration*'s list of particulars began with the question that Thomas Scott had pondered in private two decades earlier and that *King Iames His Iudgement* had briefly and controversially aired in print in 1642. The *Declaration* stated that in 1626 Charles had sabotaged the Commons's attempt to prosecute his favorite for "an act of transcendent presumption, and of dangerous consequence" by sending constant "messages and interruptions . . . while they had the said charge in agitation." He had imprisoned Digges and Eliot, who had "specially managed" the impeachment charge on James's death. Finally, as the Commons prepared to secure "judgement against the said Duke," Charles had "a suddain purpose to dissolve the Parliament" before "Justice could be done." Subsequently no other "legal inquiry" had been made "concerning the death of the said King." The *Declaration* concluded ominously: "We leave the world now to judge where the guilt of this remains." Very quickly, this question became almost impossible to avoid—the Commons printed no fewer than five thousand copies of their *Declaration* for distribution around the country, and the publication triggered a massive and multi-dimensional print response.[17]

The *Declaration* was supported by other radical tracts. A new and much-abbreviated version of *The Forerunner* appeared in concert with the *Declaration* and urged readers to take note of Eglisham's discussion of "King James His Protestation concerning our Soveraign Lord the King that now is." King James had "often publikly protested even in the presence of his apparent Heire, *That if His owne sonne should commit Murther, or any such execrable act of injury, he would not spare him, but would have him dye for it, and would have him more severely punished then any other*." By highlighting James's speech, this new edition insinuated, like the *Declaration*, that Charles was his father's murderer and deserved no mercy.[18] These carefully phrased insinuations overlapped with an emerging discourse around Charles's "blood-guilt," and for a few months in 1648 they drove much of the increasingly radical debate about what to do with Charles Stuart. Lest anyone was uncertain about the possible consequences of such charges, Matthew Simmons, a printer with ties to the army and the Independents, printed the first English edition of the *Vindiciae contra Tyrannos*, the famous 1579 Huguenot justification for the deposition of a monarch who violated divine law. Brisk sales quickly prompted Simmons to issue a second edition. The Eglisham revival in 1648, some radicals clearly hoped, would help ignite what Royalists feared would be a "bonfire for monarchy."[19]

The royalists could not ignore such a formidable polemical challenge. Years later, Edward Hyde recalled that the *Declaration* signaled that for the first time a majority in the Commons, casting aside the "duty and respect" hitherto used when talking of "the King's person," had made a "direct insinuation as if he had conspired with the Duke of Buckingham against the life of his father."[20] Other Royalists agreed with this interpretation: "They accuse him of his Fathers Murther," wrote one pamphleteer, and another opined that "these desperate and bloody usurpers" had used the Commons's "grand manifesto" to accuse Charles "of parricide."[21] In 1626, the regime had made no public response to *The Forerunner*, lest it draw increased attention to the libel. Now desperate to counter the *Declaration*, Royalist authors spent much of 1648 pounding away at the old allegations. Newsbooks like *Mercurius Pragmaticus* insisted that the *Declaration* attempted to "render his Majesty odious in the eyes of his people" by charging him with "Treason . . . against his Father King Iames, as if hee had been accessary to his Death."[22] Short tracts like *Treasons Anatomie* offered to vindicate "His Gracious Soveraigne, against those horrid Aspersions . . . conserning His Fathers Death."[23] Books like Sir Edward Nicholas's *Royall Apologie* maintained that "the sole end and scope of inserting this particular in their Declaration is evident to be, to make the King odious, as judging that nothing could more incense the world against Him . . . than to have it insinuated unto the people that amongst many Articles against Him, one is concerning the death of his father."[24] The Royalist tracts worked over in great detail the circumstances of James's death, all in an effort to discredit *The Forerunner*'s allegations. And in the process, they attempted to unmask George Eglisham for what he really was: a popish malcontent.

The 1626 tract had been, as we have seen, carefully produced to conceal its Brussels origins and Eglisham's Catholicism, and by the mid-1640s Eglisham had been explicitly Protestantized and his charges subsumed into an antipopish worldview. Some contemporaries in 1626 had noted Eglisham's Catholicism, but it seems few English readers at the time were aware that the attack on Buckingham had come from a popish pen. Indeed, it was all too easy to link claims that Buckingham was a poisoner to claims that he was a Catholic—to English eyes, poison was, after all, a quintessentially popish crime. At least two Royalist responses to the 1648 *Declaration*, however, tried to deflate the Parliament's case against Charles I by exposing George Eglisham's religion. George Bate, one of Charles's doctors, presented a devastating medical critique of Eglisham's charge but also undid Eglisham's posthumous Protestantization by proclaiming that he was "a Papist, or rather of no Religion."[25] Likewise Sir Edward Hyde, the former chancellor of the Exchequer then in exile in Jersey, denounced the *Declaration*'s "odious and groundlesse discourse of the death of King James, which though they have alwaies whisper'd, they never thought to own till now." After rebutting Eglisham's allegations, Hyde seconded Bate, describing Eglisham as "an infamous Scotch-man, and a Papist" who was motivated by "an ambition to be taken notice of as an Enemy to the Duke" and broadcast that the tract had been printed in Flanders.[26]

By this point, however, the allegations about James's death had taken on a life of their own. For radicals convinced that a settlement with Charles was impossible, Charles's complicity in his own father's murder had become a virtual shibboleth. Their version of James's murder either Protestantized Eglisham or elided him. Indeed, with the *Declaration* as their lead, the radicals now tended to attribute the accusation that James had been murdered not to Eglisham's *Forerunner* but to the 1626 Parliament. The Royalists insisted (correctly) that Parliament had not accused Buckingham of murder, only of recklessness, and a number of key Royalist works linked the original murder accusation to a popish malcontent. But political opinion was so polarized that these factual revelations carried little weight. Stories and perceptions were becoming fixed. The situation was captured neatly in *A Satyrical Catechisme*, which had a "Newter" ask whether the king did ever "conspire against his owne Father King James." A Roundhead assured him, "Believe it and credit it, for it is as sure as I am a saint." At which point, the Royalist author interjected that "'tis as false as God is true thou son of Belial."[27]

III

The Vote of No Addresses, the *Declaration*, and the repeated references to James's poisoning also helped set the stage for the king's trial and execution. Those determined to bring Charles to justice in the summer and autumn of 1648 repeatedly harked back to the *Declaration*'s case against the king. In September 1648, the *Moderate*, a radical newsbook, attacked Parliament's reopened negotiations with the king by emphasizing that only a few months earlier Parliament had charged Charles "with all the blood that had been shed by this War in the three Kingdoms, the death of his father King James, etc, and therefore no further addresses to be made to him." A petition from Leicestershire similarly insisted that Parliament had "declared him to be guilty of the death of King Iames."[28] In October, *Mercurius Militaris* mocked the notion that Charles was the Lord's anointed and asked, "When was it done? after the poysoning of his brother Harry or his Father?"[29] In November, a *Humble Petition* from Rutland asked, "How durst our Parliament think of Treating with such a man" given the accusation against him concerning "the death of his father."[30] And in December a tract argued that in James's final months Charles and Buckingham had "agreed to divide the Empire upon condition of poysoning the old man."[31] Following Pride's Purge, as radicals and soldiers began deliberating a formal charge against the king, some contemporaries assumed that it would include the poisoning allegation. The Royalist tract *The Charge of the Army*, for example, imagined a nine-point indictment, highlighting the accusation that Buckingham "by his [Charles's] consent, laid a Plaster to King Iames, and gave him a Drinke, . . . although the sworne Physitians had forbidden any to presume to give the King any thing without their Direction." This much recycled the duke's 1626 impeachment, but now Charles as well as Buckingham was guilty, not of "an Act of a transcendent presumption," but "of the highest Treason, and cannot be judged by us any other then Murder and Patricide."[32]

In the end, nothing about the poisoning allegation, or indeed any act before 1640, appeared in the formal charge. The commissioners of the High Court had discussed draft charges detailing Charles's misrule in the 1620s and '30s, and official newsbooks described a draft circulating on January 15 as "very large." But John Cook, the solicitor general appointed to prosecute the king, later claimed that, although "some would have had a very voluminous and long Charge," he had been "utterly against it," thinking it "not fit and requisite, that any thing should be put in." Contemporary newsbooks indicated that the majority of his fellow commissioners came to agree that the charge should "be abbreviated." On January 17, the commissioners still thought an edited version "too large" and ordered that it "be yet made more brief," although Col. Thomas Harrison reportedly argued for a longer, more inclusive charge, since "it will be good for us to blacken him, what we can."[33] None of these drafts survive, but it was likely that the much-discussed case against Charles set out in the 1648 *Declaration* was under active consideration as grist for the king's prosecution just days before his trial began.

The king famously refused to enter a plea at his trial, a decision that prevented John Cook from presenting the full case against him. But within ten days of the king's execution, Cook made his planned speech public in *King Charls his Case*.[34] The "most part" consisted of "that which was intended to have been delivered at the Bar" if Charles had entered a plea; but Cook also added what he called "additional Opinion," focusing on "the Death of King James, The loss of Rochel, and, the Blood of Ireland."[35] Although it is not always easy to pick apart the intended speech from the "additional Opinion," it is clear that Cook had planned to use James's murder to aggravate the case against Charles in open court. He had intended, for instance, to bring up the 1626 arrest of Sir John Eliot as an example of Charles's tyrannical impulses. The allusion to the arrest would have allowed Cook to make a brief aside before the court on the question of Charles's blood guilt: "For sure there is no Turk or Heathen but will say that if he [Charles] were any way guilty of his Fathers death, let him die for it."[36] Turning from his planned speech to his additional opinion, Cook noted that there was no need to rehearse this accusation at any length, adding, "I would not willingly be so injurious to the honest Reader as to make him buy that again which he hath formerly met with in the Parliaments *Declaration*." Instead, he thought, "A marginal reference may be sufficient." In 1626, "When the Earl of Bristol had exhibited a Charge against the said Duke, the 13. Article whereof concerned the death of King James, [Charles] instantly dissolved that Parliament, that so he might protect the Duke from the justice thereof, and would never suffer any legal inquiry to be made for his Fathers death." While the *Declaration* had stopped here, asking the readers to judge for themselves where the guilt lay, Cook's additional opinion spelled out what the *Declaration* had left unsaid. What, he asked, could have restrained a son from discovering the truth about his father's death, especially when the son "hath all power in his hands to do justice"? He then sketched out the conundrum: "There is one accused upon strong presumptions at the least, for poisoning that Kings Father," and yet "the King protects him from justice." The next question was obvious: "Do you believe that [Charles] himself had any hand in his Father's death?" After all, "Had the Duke been accused for the death of a begger, he ought not to have protected him from a Judicial Trial." At the very least, Cook argued, Charles helped conceal his father's murder, and "To conceal a Murder, strongly implies a guilt thereof, and makes him a kind of Accessary to the fact."[37] James's murder, Cook suggested, revealed Charles's deformed nature. Good kings sought justice; but Charles had "no nature to do justice," even "to his own Father." Good kings were paternal; but Charles lacked all "natural affection," even "to his own Father." Good kings followed scriptural precepts, but Charles had forgotten the apt biblical precedent of Amaziah, the new king of Judah, who "did justice upon those servants which had killed his father Joash: he did not by any pretended prerogative excuse or protect them." Instead, rather than make "the Law of God his delight," Charles had studied Ben Jonson and William Shakespeare.[38]

Cook's version of the story was typical of the regicidal retellings of James I's murder—Eglisham was elided; the 1626 Parliament was assumed to have accused Buckingham of murder; and important details were blurred or fudged (Cook conflated Bristol's treason allegations against Buckingham in the Lords with the Commons's impeachment and implied that the dissolution had followed immediately upon the poisoning allegations). The continued use of the charges unsurprisingly drew further Royalist responses. In July 1649, James Howell's anonymously published *An Inquisition after Blood* bitterly asserted that "this businesse about the playster was sifted & winnow'd as narrowly as possibly a thing could be in former Parlements," so that it was "strange that these new accusers shold make that a parricide in the King, which was found but a presumption in the Duke."[39] Likewise *The Royall Legacies of Charles the First*, published in May 1649, charged that Parliament had "falsly loaded Him with horrible Reproaches, viz. the Death of His Father, and the Blood of His People." The tract also was weary of the poison allegation: "(Without going to a Witch) every man knowes that King James dyed in the Cold Fit of a Tertian Ague, a Disease most incongruous to the operation of Poyson."[40]

The most important and influential Royalist response to the regicide, *Eikon Basilike*, offered no explicit engagement with the poison accusations, though it made much of Charles's love for parliaments and concluded with an affecting portrait of the king's sorrows in the wake of the Vote of No Addresses. But the story of James's murder offered ammunition to those men who set out on the difficult task of breaking the remarkable hold of the king's book over the popular political imagination. In August 1649, *Eikon Alethine*'s robust assault on the king's book asked whether any could "beleeve" that "the late King would professe that . . . he never wilfully opposed or denied any thing that was in a faire way, after full and free debates propounded to him by the two Houses." The incredulous author "could not but remember the dissolving the Parliament, for questioning the D. of Buckingham for poysoning his Father, when he was bound by all ties of justice and Nature, to have heard them, and the least shadow of reason could not appeare to preswade the contrary." Confronted with Charles's alleged boast about "a 17 yeares reigne in such a measure of Justice, Peace, Plenty and Religion, as all Nations about either admired, or envied," the author listed examples of "the base neglect of his subjects blood so perfidiously slain," which began with "the breaking up the Parliament for questioning the poysoners of his Father."[41] *Eikon Alethine* prompted its own rebuttal, and in September, *Eikon e Piste* defended Charles against the allegation that he had dissolved the 1626 session when the Commons began "questioning the Duke of Buckingham for poysoning his Father." First of all, "There were other reasons . . . why that Parliament was dissolv'd, therefore that cannot be held to be the reason." Furthermore, "There is a difference between dissolving the Parliament *that* questioned the Duke of Buckingham, and dissolving Parliament *for* questioning the Duke of Buckingham." Finally, *Eikon e Piste* observed, "It is very likely the King did not believe any such thing," and "It may be he had reasons for his beliefe." Consequently, to suggest that Charles had been "a conniver at his Fathers murder" was preposterous.[42]

This tart Royalist response was followed by Milton's official assault on *Eikon Basilike* in *Eikonoklastes*, an intellectually complex work dismantling the seductive edifice of the martyr-king, which appeared in October 1649. In *Eikon Basilike*, Charles argued that, out of his "own choice and inclination," he had summoned Parliament in 1640, believing that "the right way of Parliaments" was "most safe for my Crown, and best pleasing to my People." Milton responded by cataloguing Charles's longstanding hostility to Parliament, which he "never call'd . . . but to supply his necessities; and having supply'd those, as suddenly and ignominiously dissolv'd it, without redressing any one greevance of the people." Following the script established by the 1648 *Declaration*, and conflating the parliaments of 1625 and 1626, Milton made clear the reasons for the first of these ignominious dissolutions: "The first he broke off at his comming to the Crown; for no other cause then to protect the Duke of Buckingham against them who had accus'd him, besides other hainous crimes, of no less then poysoning the deceased King his Father."[43] Given the extensive discussion of the case in the 1642 and 1648 Eglisham reprints as well as in the 1648 *Declaration* and in Cook's presentation, Milton knew he only had to allude to the charge to score his point. Like Cook, Milton deployed the narrative developed by the *Declaration*, focusing on the 1626 Parliament, asserting that the Parliament-men had charged Buckingham with murder, and drawing attention to the suspicious nature of the dissolution. Milton had no doubt read George Eglisham; but he had almost certainly also read the Royalist attacks exposing Eglisham's Catholicism. Like other radical variations on *The Forerunner*'s original accusations, Milton's attack chose to elide the Scottish doctor from the case against Charles.

IV

When Milton returned to Eglisham's accusations in February 1651, he did so in a new polemical context. In June 1650 Prince Charles landed in Scotland, and the entire country, Royalists as well as Covenanters, rallied around him, raising a large army of seasoned Scottish veterans. The resulting Third Civil War pitted the new republic against fellow reformed Protestants and former allies. These were not godless malignants in need of righteous chastisement; rather, they were brethren who had strayed and had to be made to see the error of their ways. Given this formidable challenge, the regime supported Cromwell's military efforts with a concerted press campaign to stiffen English resistance and to make their former Scots allies think long and hard about their new king. This propaganda centered to a great extent on scandalous stories about the Stuart past, including allegations about the murder of James I.[44]

Shortly after his arrival in Scotland, the young prince had issued an extraordinary declaration. As "a dutifull son," he honored "the memory of his Royall Father" and "the person of his Mother," but he was "afflicted in spirit before God, because of his Fathers hearkening to, and following evil Counsels, and his opposition to the work of Reformation." Anxious to avoid "visiting the sins of the Fathers upon the Children," Charles publicly acknowledged "all his own sins, and all the sins of his Fathers house."[45] Marchamont Nedham, then editing the official newsbook *Mercurius Politicus*, scoffed at Charles's attempt to neutralize the past and offered a devastating counterhistory of the House of Stuart, in which the murder of James I played a prominent polemical role. The Scots Presbyterian ministers, he noted, "were the Beagles wherewith they hunted his great Grandam [Mary Queen of Scots], grand-sire [James VI and I], and Daddy [Charles I], out of Scotland into England." He then added in passing that none of these three "dyed a naturall death" and that "Jamy's was more unnaturall than any, except Prince Henry." Nedham then urged the Scots to abandon their quixotic effort to rehabilitate that "Scottish Fatall Family," since disaster and defeat had "followed the whole Family for many Generations." James's father—"if we may say the Lord Darnly was his Father," Nedham snidely added—"was hanged in Scotland, and by the consent (or rather conspiracy) of his own Wife." Mary Queen of Scots and her grandson Charles I were both beheaded, while "K. James himselfe, and his eldest Son Henry" were "more then suspected to be both poysoned." Since the young prince's French ancestors were equally cursed, this clearly providential pattern of events made it clear that no cause could thrive "that admits of a Combination with that wretched Family."[46]

Other defenders of the republic quickly seconded Nedham's polemics. The veteran parliamentarian polemicist Henry Parker edited, and may even have written, a detailed critique of the young pretender's claim to the throne.[47] *The True Portraiture of the Kings of England* used the long history of monarchical tyranny to celebrate the regicide. "We have conquered the Conqueror, and got the possession of the true English title, by justice, and gallantry," the pamphlet concluded; "Let us not lose it again, by any pretence of a particular, and debauched person."[48] In this account, Charles I had established "the most absolute monument of Monarchy, and example of tyranny and injustice that was ever known in England." But before Charles could act, James had to die: "He now grows old and was judged only fit to lay the Plot, but not to execute it; the design being now ripe, and his person and life the only obstacle and *Remora* [hindrance] to the next Instrument, he is conveyed away suddenly into another world, as his son Henry was, because thought unsuteable to the Plot, it being too long to waite, untill Nature and Distemper had done the deed." James's killer was not Buckingham; it was Charles. And the young pretender was his father's son, "bred up under the wings of Popery and Episcopacy, and doubtless suckt both brests," and stained with all the blood needlessly shed during his father's wars.[49]

More sensational was Sir Anthony Weldon's much-reprinted *Court and Character of King James*, first "Published by Authority" in 1650 though drafted in the 1640s.[50] The publishers' preface encouraged readers to "give glory to God, in acknowledging his Justice, in the ruining of that Family," and its providentialist message could not have been plainer: "Take heed how they side with this bloody House, lest they be found opposers of Gods purpose, which doubtlesse is, to lay aside that Family, and to make it an example to posterity." The book identified five "remarkable passages" that revealed this providential lesson. One was "the fearfull imprecation made by King James against himselfe and his Posterity, in the presence of many of his Servants, and the Judges, even upon his knees, if he should spare any that were found guilty in the poysoning businesse of Sir Thomas Overbury" in 1615. James's failure to fulfill this oath, the preface argued, had incurred God's wrath, and the first blow fell on the king himself. "How the Justice of God hath been, and is upon himselfe and Posterity, his owne death, by poyson, and the sufferings of his Posterity, doe sufficiently manifest."[51] Weldon's narrative later described the details of James's death. He noted that James and Buckingham had begun quarreling and that while James had not dared to disgrace his favorite, Buckingham had had "more courage": "Although the King lost his opportunity on Buckingham, yet the black plaister and powder did shew Buckingham lost not his on the King." Weldon's account focused on Buckingham but implicated Charles: "Nor could any but Buckingham answer it with lesse then his life at that present, as he had the next Parliament, had it not been dissolved upon the very questioning him for the Kings death, and all those that prosecuted him, utterly disgraced and banished the Court."[52]

In February 1651, a few days before Milton's next intervention in the debate on the republic, Weldon's printer-publisher issued a large broadside, "Published by Authority," narrating "The True Manner of the Crowning of Charles the Second King of Scotland." It ridiculed the "swarthy" young man crowned at Scone, a "Scottish vapour, exhaled by French distillation," the puppet of "his mothers [French and Catholic] counsels" and subject to the Scottish kirk's command. God, the broad-

side was certain, stood squarely behind the Commonwealth that had executed Charles's father and abolished the monarchy. Indeed, the writer
marveled that anyone would support the new Scottish king given "such
evident manifestations of the Lords so visibly owning" the anti-Stuart
cause. "He that sitteth in the heavens shal laugh," the text predicted, and
"the Lord shal have them in derision." Charles could read his providen-
tially prescribed doom in the black legend of his own family: "His unhap-
pinesse in his fatall Progenitors, he may read in Capitalls, engraven even
on the Throne he sits in, where is legible to his eyes, the ecodemical [*sic*]
disasters of the Family out of which he sprang, His Father was beheaded,
His Grand-Father (as some Phisitians have declared) poysoned, His great
Grand-Father, and so on to several assents before, successively cut off, by
disastrous deaths."[53]

It was in this polemical context that Milton published his major
defense of the republic in late February 1651. Thirteen months earlier,
the Council of State had asked him to reply to Salmasius's attack on the
regicide, but the pressure of business and his "precarious health" had delayed him. Milton knew many of the polemicists who had raked over
the murderous Stuart past to attack the pretensions of the new king of
Scotland. He was well acquainted with Nedham, whom Anthony Wood
called the poet's "great crony," and Milton's position as the government
censor for Nedham's newsbook brought the two men into regular weekly
contact, furthering their political and intellectual collaboration.[54] For all
its learning, Milton's *Pro Populo Anglicano Defensio* shared something
of the content and scabrous tone of the more demotic polemic of the
1650–51 Scottish crisis. Under real pressure to destroy Salmasius's case,
Milton marshaled a formidable mixture of scriptural exegesis and ancient
and modern history; but he relied too on polemical invective, returning
once more to Eglisham's old allegations and playing with the newly current polemical trope of the cursed Stuart dynasty.

Milton made much, for instance, of Charles's close relationship with
his favorite. He wondered how Salmasius could praise "the purity and
continence of one who is known to have joined the Duke of Buckingham
in every act of infamy," someone who "kisses women wantonly, enfolds
their waists, and to mention no more openly, plays with the breasts of
maids and mothers." Milton delved into the same scandalous Scottish

histories that Nedham had exploited. Pondering Salmasius's comparison between Charles and Solomon, Milton suggested that James was a better parallel, because Solomon had been "the son of David, who was originally Saul's musician," just as James had been the child of another musician named David—David Riccio, the Italian lover of Mary, Queen of Scots. Milton repeated George Buchanan's story that Darnley had caught Riccio "on a nocturnal visit to his queen's bedroom" and killed him. "For such a reason," Milton wryly noted, "was the ancestry of King James more illustrious, and he was called a second Solomon." In 1650, it was David Riccio's great-grandson who was "confessing and lamenting before the people of Scotland on that stool for public repentance." Milton then turned to Charles I, retorting to Salmasius, "If you like parallels so well, let us compare Charles with Solomon." The Israelite king began by justly punishing his brother, while the Briton's reign began "with his father's death." With a show of care, Milton claimed he would not "use the word murder, although all the signs of poison were in evidence upon his father's body." But when Buckingham came under suspicion, Charles "did not only absolve that slayer of the king and of his father from all blame in the highest council of state, but also dissolved Parliament to keep the whole affair from any Parliamentary investigation." For Milton, James's death clearly stood at the head of all Charles's crimes. Dismissing Salmasius's claims that the English Parliament itself had behaved more like "Nero than the Roman senate," Milton mocked "this insatiable passion of yours for gluing together the most foolish comparisons." The parallel, he told Salmasius, had to be adjusted, for it was the English king who most obviously resembled the quintessential Roman tyrant: "How like Nero Charles was. 'Nero,' you say, 'killed his own mother' with a sword; Charles used poison to kill his father and his king! To pass over other proofs, it must be that the one who snatched from the arms of the laws the Duke who was guilty of the poisoning, was himself guilty too."[55] Here Milton turned James's murder into a classical republican argument connecting poison to tyranny. John Eliot had made a similar move in 1626—comparing Buckingham's "venefices" to those of Sejanus, favorite of the tyrant Tiberius. Accusations that had taken their first clear form in a work of Catholic disinformation and propaganda had now been reworked as part of a learned republican case in defense of a Free State.

V

Milton was simply repeating, and developing, what had become, since early 1648, an article of faith among English radicals. A charge originating in a Brussels print shop, published by the Spanish Habsburgs to sow confusion among their Protestant English enemies, had been thoroughly absorbed into English Protestant political culture—utilized by the Parliament-men of 1626, mobilized by libelous poets, pondered by radical Puritans, and then reinvented and revived during the civil wars before being used to justify a radical break with Charles I and the execution of a king. His religion, though not his name, masked in 1626, George Eglisham remained an authoritative source on the murder of James I through the 1640s. By the time the Royalists had exposed his Catholicism and his Flemish connections, Eglisham's secret history of James I's murder had escaped its old confessional identity; it had been fused with a distorted memory of the 1626 Parliament, allowing Eglisham himself to fade from the narrative while his claims of poison at court lived on. In an irony that neither George Eglisham nor John Milton would likely have appreciated, a Catholic "libel" from the 1620s provided polemical grist for a radical Protestant revolution.

NOTES

1. John Milton, *Eikonoklastes* (London, 1649), in *Vernacular Regicide and Republican Writings*, ed. N. H. Keeble and Nicholas McDowell, *CWJM*, 6, 286, 332–33. For more on these charges and about their author and reception, see Alastair Bellany and Thomas Cogswell, *The Murder of King James I* (New Haven, CT: Yale University Press, 2015).

2. John Milton, *A Defence of the People of England* (London, 1651), in *CPW*, 4:371–72, 408, 451.

3. George Eglisham, *The Forerunner of Revenge Upon the Duke of Buckingham for the poysoning of the most potent King Iames of happy memory King of great Britan, and the Lord Marquis of Hamilton, and others of the nobilitie* (Frankfurt, 1626); *Prodromus Vindictæ in Ducem Buckinghamiæ, pro Virulenta Cæde Potentissimi Magnæ Britanniæ Regis Jacobi; nec-non Marchionis Hamiltonij, ac Aliorum Virorum Principum* (two editions: Frankfurt, 1626, and n.p., 1626);

and *Prodromus Vindictae, Das ist: Vorlauffer oder Vorbott der billichen Raach, vber den gifftmörderischen Fürsten von Buckingham, vmb wegen der grewlichen hinrichtung deß Grossmächtigen Monarchen Iacobi Königs in Groß-Britanien, &c* (Augsburg, 1626).

4. For the 1642 editions, see George Eglisham, *The Fore-runner of Revenge* (London, 1642; ESTC R9597, R18976, R176655, R206483, R206484, and R206486).

5. *Strange Apparitions, or The Ghost of King Iames, With a late conference between the ghost of that good King, the Marquesse Hameltons, and George Eglishams, Doctor of Physick, unto which appeared the Ghost of the late Duke of Buckingham concerning the death and poysoning of King Iames* (London, 1642); George Eglisham, *A Declaration to the Kingdome of England. Concerning the poysoning of King James of happy memory, King of Great Brittain* (London, 1648; TT E.427/5); and George Eglisham, *Een moordadich, schrickelijck, ende heel wonderbaer Secreet, in Engelandt ontdeckt* ([Amsterdam?], 1644).

6. Caroline Hibbard, *Charles I and the Popish Plot* (Chapel Hill: University of North Carolina Press, 1983); and Michael Braddick, *God's Fury, England's Fire* (London: Penguin Books, 2008), 200.

7. Thomas Dempster, *Historia Ecclesiastica Gentis Scotorum* (Edinburgh, 1829), 271; Edward Peacock, ed., *A List of the Roman Catholics in the County of York in 1604* (London, 1872), 6; and A. G. Dickens, "The Extent and Character of Recusancy in Yorkshire, 1604" (1948), and (with John Newton), "Further Light on the Scope of Yorkshire Recusancy, 1604" (1955), both reprinted in *Reformation Studies*, by A. G. Dickens (London: Hambledon Press, 1982).

8. George Eglisham, *Crisis Vorstiani Responsi* (Delft, 1612), *Hypocrisis Apologeticae Orationis Vorstianae* (Delft, 1612), *Duellum Poeticum* (London, 1618 and 1619), and James F. Larkin and Paul L. Hughes, eds., *Stuart Royal Proclamations: James I* (Oxford: Clarendon Press, 1973), 1:441–46.

9. Larkin and Hughes, *Stuart Royal Proclamations*, 1:513; letter from George Eglisham, January 18, 1630, in National Archives (NA) State Papers Domestic 16/158/60; T. H. B. M. Harmsen, *John Gee's Foot Out of the Snare* (Nijmegen: Cicero Press, 1992), 297; John Chamberlain, *The Letters of John Chamberlain*, ed. Norman Egbert McClure (American Philosophical Society: Philadelphia, 1939), 2:605; *Supplementary Report on the Manuscripts of the Earl of Mar and Kellie*, ed. H. Paton (Historical Manuscripts Commission: London, 1930), 2:222–25; and *Calendar of State Papers Relating to English Affairs in the Archives of Venice*, vol. 18, *1623–1625*, ed. Allen B. Hinds (His Majesty's Stationery Office: London, 1912), 621. See also Bellany and Cogswell, *Murder of King James I*, chaps. 4 and 5.

10. Van Male to Infanta Isabella and Charles della Faille, March and May, 1625, Belgien Fasz. 62, fols. 160, 243, 247, Haus-, Hof- und Staatsarhiv,

Vienna; Trumbull to Conway, NA State Papers Flanders 77/18/149–50; and anonymous report, July? 1626, NA State Papers Domestic 16/32/117. We are grateful to Patrick O'Neill for help translating the Van Male material.

11. "Libraires étrangers et anversois, 1613–1633," MS 744, fol. 347, Plantin-Moretus Archive, Antwerp. See also Bellany and Cogswell, *Murder of King James I*, chap. 6.

12. Anonymous report from Brussels, Estado 2516, fol. 115, Archivo de General Simancas, Flanders; and Eglisham, *Forerunner*, 4, 15, 21–22. Thanks again to Patrick O'Neill for translating the Spanish report.

13. Thomas Cogswell, "The Return of the 'Deade Alive': The Earl of Bristol and Dr. Eglisham in the Parliament of 1626 and in Caroline Political Culture," *English Historical Review* 128 (2013): 535–70; Bellany and Cogswell, *Murder of King James I*, chaps. 8–12.

14. On Scott's "meditations," 1626, see Knatchbull MSS, U951, Z17, Kent History and Library Centre. See also Bellany and Cogswell, *Murder of King James I*, chap. 16.

15. *King Iames His Iudgement of a King and of a Tyrant* (London, 1642), sig. A3v.

16. William Prynne, *Romes Master-Peece. Or, The Grand Conspiracy of the Pope and his Iesuited Instruments, to extirpate the Protestant Religion* (London, 1643; TT E.249/32), 34; *Strange Apparitions*, 7. For a sampling of other variants, see John Vicars, *Prodigies & Apparitions or Englands Warning Pieces* (London, 1643), 3, 12–20; *The Second Part of the Spectacles* (London, 1644; TT E.53/21), 3, 6, 7; John Booker, *No Mercurius Aquaticus, But A Cable-Rope, Double twisted for Iohn Tayler, The Water-Poet* (London, 1644; TT E.2/22), 7–8; *Parliaments Kalender of Black Saints* (London, 1644; TT E.7/9), 3–4; and *A Dog's Elegy, or Rupert's Tears, For the late Defeat given him at Marston-moore* (London, 1644; TT E.3/17), esp. 6–8. See Bellany and Cogswell, *Murder of King James I*, chaps. 18 and 19.

17. Parliament, *A Declaration of the Commons of England In Parliament assembled; Expressing Their Reasons and Grounds of passing the late Resolutions touching No farther Address or Application to be made to the King* (London, 1648; TT E.427/9), 17–18. See also Bellany and Cogswell, *Murder of King James I*, chap. 20.

18. Eglisham, *Declaration to the kingdome*, title page, 1–2, adapting *Forerunner*, 9.

19. *Kingdoms Weekly Account*, no. 7 (February 23, 1648), 53; *Perfect Occurrences*, nos. 60–61 (February 25 and March 3, 1648), 422, 500–501; *Vindiciae contra Tyrannos: A Defence of Liberty against Tyrants . . . Being a Treatise written in Latin and French by Junius Brutus* (London, 1648; TT E.430/2); *Mercurius Pragmaticus*, no. 22 (February 15, 1648), sigs. Y1v–2r.

20. Edward, Earl of Clarendon, *The History of the Rebellion and Civil Wars in England*, ed. W. Dunn Murray, 6 vols. (Oxford: Clarendon Press, 1888), 4:281–85.

21. *Great Britans Vote: Or, God save King Charles* (London, 1648; TT E.431/26), 8; and *The Hamilton Papers: Being Selections from Original Letters in the Possession of His Grace the Duke of Hamilton and Brandon, Relating to the Years, 1638–1650*, ed. Samuel Rawson Gardiner, Camden Society, n.s., 27 (London, 1880), 162.

22. *Mercurius Pragmaticus*, no. 22 (February 15, 1648), sigs. Y1v–2r, and no. 23 (February 22, 1648), sig. Z3r. For similar efforts, see *Mercurius Aulicus*, no. 3 (February 17, 1648), sigs. C2r–v; *Mercurius Bellicus*, no. 4 (February 20, 1648), 2; *Mercurius Elencticus*, no. 9 (January 26, 1648), 65–66, and no. 11 (February 9, 1648), 81; and *Mercurius Melancholicus* no. 25 (February 19, 1648), 145.

23. *Treasons Anatomie* (London, 1648), 4–7. See also *The Kingdomes Briefe Answer, to the Late Declaration* (London, 1648; TT E.431/9), 1, 18; *White-hall Fayre* (London, 1648; TT E.434/16); *The Declaration Declared Or an Examination of the Declaration in the name of the house of Commons the 11. of February 1647* (n.p., 1648), 6–8, 14; and [Edward Hyde], *An Answer To a Pamphlet, Entitled, A Declaration of the Commons of England* ([London], 1648; TT E.438/3), 9. Our thanks to the James Ford Bell Library, University of Minnesota, for digital images of *The Declaration Declared*.

24. [Edward Nicholas], *The Royall Apologie; or An Answer to the Declaration* (London, 1648), 11–13.

25. [George Bate], *The Regall Apology: Or, The Declaration of the Commons, Feb. 11. 1647 Canvassed* (London, 1648; TT E.436/5), 24.

26. Edward Hyde, *A Full Answer to An Infamous and Trayterous Pamphlet* (London, 1648), 13–14.

27. *A Satyrical Catechisme* (London, 1648; TT E.449/1), sig. A2. See also *Troy-Novant Must Not Be Burnt* (London, 1648; TT 669.f.12/21).

28. *The Moderate*, no. 8 (September 5, 1648), sig. H1v; no. 10 (September 19, 1648), sig. K1r; and no. 11 (September 26, 1648), sig. L1v; and the Leicestershire Petition, late September 1648, in *The Moderate*, no. 12 (October 3, 1648), sig. M3r. See also Bellany and Cogswell, *Murder of King James I*, chap. 21.

29. *Mercurius Militaris*, no. 2 (October 17, 1648), 13–14.

30. *The Humble Petition, or Remonstrance . . . of Rutland* (London, November 24, 1648; TT 669.f.13/47).

31. *The People Informed of their Oppressors and Oppressions* (London, 1648; TT E. 536/17), esp. 3–6.

32. *The Charge of the Army, and Counsel of War Against the King. With a brief Answer thereunto by some of the Loyall Party* (n.p., 1648; TT E.536/20), 3.

33. *Perfect Occurrences*, no. 107 (January 19, 1649), 801, 803; *Kingdomes Weekly Intelligencer*, no. 295 (January 23, 1649), 1226–27; *An Exact and most Impartial Accompt Of the Indictment, Arraignment, Trial, and Judgment (according to Law) of nine and twenty Regicides* (London, 1660), 44, 54v, 119.

34. On Cook, see Geoffrey Robertson, *The Tyrannicide Brief: The Story of the Man Who Sent Charles I to the Scaffold* (New York: Vintage, 2005).

35. John Cook, *King Charls his Case: Or, An Appeal To all Rational Men, Concerning His Tryal At the High Court of Justice* (London, 1649; TT E.542/3), title page.

36. Ibid., 10–11.

37. Ibid., 11–12.

38. Ibid., 12–13.

39. [James Howell], *An Inquisition After Blood* (n.p., [July 17], 1649; TT E.531/23), 11–12, also reprinted in *Some of Mr Howel's Minor Works, Reflecting upon the Times Upon Emergent Occasions* (n.p., 1654). On Howell, see Daniel Woolf, "Conscience, Constancy, and Ambition in the Career and Writings of James Howell," in *Public Duty and Private Conscience in Seventeenth-Century England: Essays Presented to G. E. Aylmer*, ed. John Morrill, Paul Slack, and Daniel Woolf (Oxford: Oxford University Press, 1993). From 1643 to 1651, Howell was imprisoned in the Fleet.

40. *The Royall Legacies of Charles the First* (London, 1649; TT E.557/1), 43.

41. *Eikon Alethine* (London, 1649; TT E.569/16), 37, 47.

42. *Eikon e Piste* (London, 1649; TT E.573/11), 32, 40.

43. Milton, *Eikonoklastes*, in *CWJM*, 6:286; Philip A. Knachel, ed., *Eikon Basilike* (Ithaca, NY: Cornell University Press, 1966), 3.

44. On war with Scotland and Charles II in 1650–51, see Austin Woolrych, *Britain in Revolution, 1625–1660* (Oxford: Oxford University Press, 2002), 480 ff. See also Bellany and Cogswell, *Murder of King James I*, chap. 22.

45. Charles II, *A Declaration by the Kings Majesty* (n.p., 1650; TT 1030/8), 1–2; and *The Answer of the Parliament* (London, 1650; TT E.613/2), 12.

46. *Mercurius Politicus*, no. 14 (September 12, 1650): 209–11.

47. [Henry Parker], *The True Portraiture of the Kings of England* (London, 1650; TT E 609/2). See also Michael Mendle, *Henry Parker and the English Civil War: The Political Thought of the Public's "Privado"* (Cambridge: Cambridge University Press, 1995), 166–68.

48. [Parker], *True Portraiture*, pp. 4–5, 39, 42.

49. Ibid., sigs. A2r–v and pp. 12, 15–16, 37–42.

50. Sir Anthony Weldon, *The Court and Character of King James* (London, 1650). For the Wright-Ibbitson 1650 editions, see ESTC R209127, R204065, and R186354. For the Ibbitson-Collins 1651 editions, see T301136, R229346, and R34738. See also Alastair Bellany, *The Politics of Court Scandal in Early*

Modern England: News Culture and the Overbury Affair, 1603–1660 (Cambridge: Cambridge University Press, 2002), 266.

51. Weldon, *Court and Character* (1650 ed.), sigs. A2r–3r.

52. Weldon, *Court and Character* (1651 ed.), 138–41, 144–49.

53. *The True Manner of the Crowning of Charles the Second King of Scotland, on the First day of January, 1650* (London, 1651). Thanks to Jane Rickard for bringing this broadside to our attention.

54. Blair Worden, *Literature and Politics in Cromwellian England: John Milton, Andrew Marvell, Marchamont Nedham* (Oxford: Oxford University Press, 2007), 54–81; and Joad Raymond, "Hall, John (bap. 1627 – d. 1656)," in *ODNB*.

55. John Milton, *Pro Populo Anglicano Defensio, CPW*, 4:372, 408, 451. For the English editions, see ESTC R31234, R32430, R382, R39745, and R31233; for the Dutch ones, R226367, R234384, R228714, R21409, R40028, R31896, and R12770.

CHAPTER 3

MILTON, SIR HENRY VANE THE YOUNGER, AND THE TOLERATION OF CATHOLICS

MARTIN DZELZAINIS

In the peroration to the first edition of *The Readie & Easie Way to Establish a Free Commonwealth*—in print by March 3, 1660—Milton defiantly summed up the tenor of his pamphlet by declaring that "what I have spoken, is the language of the good old cause" (*CWJM*, 6:520).[1] Within weeks, circumstances had changed so much that the second edition had to be radically revised and expanded. Amid the political turmoil, Milton found time to fine-tune the sentence: "What I have spoken, is the language of that which is not call'd amiss *the good old Cause*" (*CWJM*, 6:521). The effect of the insertion ("that which is not call'd amiss") and the italics is to reify, and underscore his commitment to, a cause that was increasingly being vilified in print and on the streets (*CWJM*, 6:509). What Milton meant by the slogan is summed up just before the peroration when he announces that the "whole freedom of man consists either in spiritual or civil freedom." And "liberty of conscience," he adds, can have "no government more inclinable not to favor only but to protect, then a free Commonwealth" (*CWJM*, 6:515).[2] He then turns to the "other part of our freedom," which "consists in the civil rights and advancements of every person according to his merit: the enjoyment of these never more certain, and the access to these never more open, then in a free Common-wealth" (*CWJM*, 6:515).[3] In short, the good old cause amounted to the enjoyment of one's civil and religious rights in a free commonwealth.

As Austin Woolrych showed in his classic survey of the literature of the good old cause, this "catena of ideas" was first formulated by Sir Henry Vane the Younger (1612–62) in *The Healing Question propounded and resolved*, one of several works published in 1656 in opposition to the regime of the Lord Protector.[4] The reason why "the whole party of Honest men adhering to this Cause" had gone to war in the first place, Vane pointed out, had been to "subdue the common Enemy, and restore to this whole body their just naturall Rights in civil things, and true freedome in matters of conscience."[5] But these could not be secured so long as the Protector's army continued to dominate the civil power. Vane's tract was judged seditious and led to his imprisonment.[6] But following Cromwell's death and the overthrow of the Protectorate he was again at the center of the political stage, trying to put his stamp on the shape of a republican settlement by insisting that it include a standing council or senate—as Milton was also to do.[7]

Given that Milton had already known Vane for at least a decade when he nailed his colors to the mast of the good old cause, it is hard to explain why so little scholarly attention has been paid to their relation-ship.[8] One reason may simply be a reluctance to engage with Vane's no-toriously difficult prose. Richard Baxter remarked that his "Doctrines were so clowdily formed and expressed that few could understand them," though this was possibly by *"design*, because he could speak plainly when he listed."[9] Clarendon similarly drew a distinction between Vane's spoken and written style; the "usual clearness and ratiocination in his discourse, in which he used much to excel the best of the company he kept," was absent from his writings, where "in a crowd of very easie words the sence was too hard to find out."[10] Modern commentators have been less chari-table. Vane's *The Retired Mans Meditations* (1655), says Michael Fixler, can have "influenced few who demanded sustained intelligibility in what they read."[11] Christopher Hill, in *The Experience of Defeat*, compared Milton at length not with Vane but with Vane's protégé, Henry Stubbe, because he "shrank from the impenetrable thickets of [Vane's] prose," while, more recently, Blair Worden has averred that "Vane's opaque political ideas and religious beliefs are now barely intelligible."[12] Yet the difficulties seem overstated.[13] Vane's family sermons, for example, were perspicuous, and his prose is capable of great subtlety. It is no surprise that he was in demand for his skills as a legislative and diplomatic draftsman; whenever a tricky proviso, clause, letter, narrative, or declaration needed to be drawn up, Vane was often the first to be nominated.[14]

There are, however, genuine obstacles. One is that Milton did not withdraw from politics like Vane and other republicans when Cromwell dissolved the Rump in 1653 or come out in opposition to the Protectorate in 1656. More important still is the deep fault line apparently separating the two on the question of toleration, especially in relation to Roman Catholics. The most influential recent statement of this case is by John Coffey, who argues that Milton's refusal of toleration for Catholics "is profoundly puzzling, since his close friends Vane and [Roger] Williams had both argued at length for the toleration of idolaters. In most respects Milton went along with his fellow Puritan tolerationists, but with regard to the Catholic issue he was unwilling to follow the radical view through to its logical and startling conclusion." For Coffey, the key distinction is between those like Oliver Cromwell and John Owen for whom liberty of conscience meant "liberty for conscientious protestants" only and those "within the puritan community who argued passionately for the toleration of *false* religion."[15] On this view of the matter, Milton belonged to the former and Vane to the latter group. The main aim of this chapter is to challenge this contention, and to do so as much in relation to Vane as to Milton.

My starting point is the remarkable sonnet that Milton sent to Vane on July 3, 1652, but that remained unpublished until 1662, the year of Vane's trial and execution.

VANE, young in years, but in sage counsel old,
Then whom a better senator ner'e held

The helme of *Rome*, when Gowns not Arms repell'd
The fierce *Epeirot* and the *African* bold.
Whether to settle peace or to unfold
The drift of hollow states, hard to be spell'd,
Then to advise how war may best, upheld,
Move by her two main Nerves, Iron and Gold
In all her Equipage: besides to know
Both spiritual power and civil, what each meanes,
What severs each, thou hast learn't, which few have done.
The bounds of either Sword to thee we owe;
Therefore on thy firm hand Religion leans
In peace, and reckons thee her eldest Son.

                              (*CWJM*, 3:291)[16]

If the outbreak of war with the Dutch furnishes the context for the first part of the poem, that for the second comprises the sequence of events that began on February 10, 1652, when the leading Independent divine, John Owen, together with fourteen others, complained to Parliament about the recent London edition of the *Catechesis Ecclesiarum Quae in Regno Poloniae* (the Latin translation of the notorious Racovian Catechism), a complaint that led to the setting up of one committee that eventually examined Milton for having licensed publication of the *Catachesis* on August 10, 1650, and another to receive proposals for establishing a state church.[17] Owen's proposals, submitted to the committee on February 18, were later supplemented by fifteen "fundamentals" designed to test ministers' orthodoxy—particularly on the Trinity—and hence their eligibility for state maintenance. The response from those opposed to a state church was a campaign organized by Roger Williams, to which he recruited Milton and Vane among others.[18] Williams himself published pamphlets in favor of unlimited toleration and the separation of church and state.[19] Vane, who had defended the Socinian John Biddle in 1647, the anti-Trinitarian MP John Fry in 1651, and the Massachusetts Socinian William Pynchon in 1652, supplied a treatise on idolatry, *Zeal Examined: Or, A Discourse for Liberty of Conscience in Matters of Religion.*[20] For his part, Milton, as we have seen, addressed one sonnet to Vane and another, as the partially crossed-out title in the Trinity Manuscript has it, "To the Lord Generall Cromwell May 1652 On the proposalls of certaine ministers at yᵉ Commtee for Propagation of the Gospell," possibly in the hope of detaching Cromwell from his protégé Owen.[21]

The draft of the sonnet to Vane in the Trinity Manuscript shows Milton had difficulty stabilizing the meaning of lines 5 to 11—a block of verse that forms the core of the poem and precludes a conventional division of it into octave and sestet. Two lines were especially troublesome; before being canceled, line 10 read, "What powre the Church & what the civill meanes," which is plainly ungrammatical, while line 11 successively read, "Thou teachest best, which few have ever done" and "Thou hast learnt well, a praise which few have won" before, in the margin, Milton came up with the final version: "What severs each thou hast learnt, wᶜʰ few have don."[22] The most significant change is in the choice of verb to secure what R. F. Hall calls "syntactic closure"; that is to say, are "to settle," "to unfold," "to advise," and "to know" all things that Vane *teaches* or are they all things that he *has learned*?[23] Is Vane to be seen as one who instructs others how to know the difference between religious and civil power or as one who has understood for himself the difference between the two? And what is the significance of the change in roles from teacher to learner?

While Milton greatly admired Vane, he would not have wanted to appear at all indebted to him intellectually. A similar (over-)sensitivity informs the preface to Milton's translation of *The Judgement of Martin Bucer, Concerning Divorce* (August 1644), where he wishes, on the one hand, to stress the coincidence between his views and those of the sixteenth-century reformer and, on the other, to insist that it was "*not as a lerner, but as a collateral teacher*" that he had first encountered Bucer's work "*wel-nigh three month*" after the second edition of *The Doctrine and Discipline of Divorce* appeared early in February 1644 (*CPW*, 2:435–36).[24] It is hardly surprising therefore that Milton opted for the suggestion that Vane, in learning these things, had joined a select "few" of whom Milton was already one.

However, this still leaves the question of what kind of teaching Milton had in mind when he wrote of Vane in the first instance that

> to know
> What powre the Church & what the civill meanes
> Thou teachest best, which few have ever don.

One possible answer can be retrospectively inferred from the preface to Milton's *A Treatise of Civil power in Ecclesiastical causes: Shewing That it is not lawful for any power on earth to compell in matters of Religion*, which he addressed to Richard Cromwell's first parliament in 1659 and which he had "*prepar'd . . . against the much expected time of your sitting*" (*CPW*, 7 [rev. ed.]: 239). Anticipating that the Parliament would address the issue of a national confession of faith that had dogged the Commonwealth and the Protectorate, he harked back to an earlier and more constructive phase of religious debates in the Council of State:

> *One advantage I make no doubt of, that I shall write to many eminent persons of your number, alreadie perfet and resolvd in this important article of Christianitie. Some of whom I remember to have heard often for several years, at a councel next in autoritie to your own, so well joining religion with civil prudence, and yet so well distinguishing the different power of either, and this not only voting, but frequently reasoning why it should be so, that if any there present had bin before of an opinion contrary, he might doubtless have departed thence a convert in that point, and have confessd, that then both commonwealth and religion will at length, if ever, flourish in Christendom, when either they who govern discern between civil and religious, or they only who so discern shall be admitted to govern.* (*CPW*, 7 [rev. ed.]: 240)

We have already seen what Baxter and Clarendon thought of Vane's powers of speech. Was Milton here expressing a comparable regard for the contributions of Vane to religious debates in the Council of State between 1649 and 1653? And, in that event, was he also simultaneously recalling the terms of his sonnet to him?[25] After all, the preface is effectively paraphrasing its argument when it praises members for "*so well joining religion with civil prudence, and yet so well distinguishing the different power of either*" and "*reasoning*" with such force as to "*convert*" those who thought otherwise. On this view, one reason why Milton could assure Vane in 1652 that "thou teachest best" was precisely because he had heard him doing just that in council.

Another explanation of why Milton would have thought of Vane as a teacher first and foremost in 1652 is that he had just read and been impressed by his arguments in *Zeal Examined* (the bookseller George Thomason received his copy of the tract on June 15, less than three weeks before Milton dispatched the sonnet). If so, this would make it especially appropriate for Milton in his tribute to speak of Vane as a teacher in the present tense.

The treatise itself is in two parts. Vane says that the first (pages 1–27) was written and sent to an unnamed friend *"about a twelvemonth since, without a thought of making it more* publique." It consists of an answer in twenty-six sections to the question of "Whether the *Magistrate* professing *Christianitie*, ought to punish *Idolaters*, according to the Law of *Moses*, or otherwise";[26] it was prompted by an *"occasionall* Dispute" in which Vane says he dealt *"too sharply"* with his friend (1)—a disagreement that may have been occasioned by the Blasphemy Act, the terms of which Vane apparently tried to moderate when it was passed in August 1650. The second part (pages 29–47) consists of *An additionall Discourse, more particularly directed against the inmost Spirit of persecution, and against some fleshly and legall Principles relating thereunto, with a Word to the Magistrate,* arranged in fourteen sections. The discourse appears to have been written directly in response to the Humble Proposals of 1652, as its hostile reference to the "Rulers of the people" being prompted by the "Whore of fleshly wisedome" to erect "some one publique profession of Religion" would suggest (45).

Blasphemy itself was one area where there seems to have been a measure of agreement between Milton and Vane. The former thoroughly approved of the Blasphemy Act, referring to it in *A Treatise of Civil Power* as "that prudent and well deliberated act *August 9.* 1650; where the Parlament defines blasphemie against God, as far as it is a crime belonging to civil judicature," and has done so "more warily, more judiciously, more orthodoxally then twice thir number of divines have don in many a prolix volume" (*CPW*, 7 [rev. ed.]: 246–47).[27] This was because the emphasis in the act was on the social and political rather than the doctrinal dimension of blasphemy. For his part, Vane expressed a wish, in *Zeal Examined*, "that all of us, who pretend to the advancement of true Christianity in the world, would desist from any endeavours to separate ourselves from Heretickes, by any publique forme of doctrine or discipline established by a fleshly power." In short, he was opposed to any attempt whatsoever to impose doctrinal orthodoxy. But he was also aware "that the provocations by those grosse opinions, and filthy fleshly practices in some that are full of high notions, have been very great," even if he could not quite bring himself to rule out the possibility that "this false fleshly liberty might possibly be a fore-runner of some true spiritual liberty, to break forth in an extraordinary manner." But when it had eventually become apparent to Vane that some of these "poor creatures" had "cast themselves down into abominable practices," he found he could not "exempt . . . their outward and fleshly defilements from all jurisdiction of the Magistrate, though I wish he might be sparing of life to men, as men, in all such like cases" (33–34). It is hard to see the scope for any essential disagreement between Vane and Milton on this issue.

At first sight, idolatry was a different matter. In the preface to *Zeal Examined*, Vane sets the threshold for the success of his argument as high as possible: "*For if it be evinced that* Idolaters *ought not to bee punished by the* Magistrate *as such; it will follow that damnable* Hereticks *must be also spared by him, and if those* Tares *be left alone, then will the* Wheat *escape also*" (sig. A2v). Vane's ultimate aim was to secure toleration for conscientious Christians, but rather than proceed by first defining that group and then arguing exclusively on its behalf, he sought to secure a maximal degree of toleration that would necessarily include them; to make the case for idolaters would be to make it for everyone else. The first part of *Zeal Examined* is thus taken up with a string of arguments for why it is wrong or counterproductive or even self-destructive for the magistrate to punish instances of idolatry.

As we shall see, there *is* evidence to suggest that Milton found some of these arguments persuasive. But the consensus is that his sense of how far toleration extended was much narrower than Vane's. This is held to be especially evident in what Milton has to say about Roman Catholics.[28] The *locus classicus* for this view is in *Areopagitica* (1644), written before he met Vane, so far as we know. The passage in question nevertheless begins in maximal style by declaring that, since "it is not possible for man to sever the wheat from the tares," doing so "must be the Angels Ministery at the end of things." The general principle of toleration follows directly from this, but it is affirmed only to be withdrawn in the next breath: "If all cannot be of one mind, as who looks they should be? this doubtles is more wholsome, more prudent, and more Christian that many be tolerated, rather then all compell'd. I mean not tolerated Popery, and open superstition, which as it extirpats all religions and civill supremacies, so it self should be extirpat, provided first that all charitable and compassionat means be us'd to win and regain the weak and the misled" (*CPW*, 2:565). This notorious crux has become the central feature of most commentaries upon the tract.[29] In principle, however, Willmoore Kendall was quite right when he said that we will have "learned to read the *Areopagitica* only when we can read this passage [about popery] and *not* find in it any inconsistency" (though the consistency Kendall himself found in the work is of a deeply antilibertarian kind).[30] It can be pointed out in mitigation that in using such violent language Milton was merely echoing public documents with which his readers—and especially the Presbyterians among them—would have been familiar. Thus article 191 of the Grand Remonstrance (1641) alleged that "the religion of the Papists hath such principles as do certainly tend to the destruction and extirpation of all Protestants," while the wording of Article 2 of the Solemn League and Covenant (1643) committed Parliament to "endeavour the extirpation of Popery."[31] And it would be true to say that Milton's position is substantively no different from that of John Locke, whose "liberalism," as Mark Goldie usefully reminds us, is simply "not . . . the same as modern secular liberalism."[32] But even if, by the standards of the time, Milton was not saying anything untoward or somehow contradicting himself when he denied toleration to popery, the question remains of why he was prepared to do so at all when some of his closest friends and colleagues were not.

Milton returned to the topic of popery in 1659. He begins *A Treatise of Civil Power* by congratulating "the governors of this commonwealth" who "since the rooting out of prelats have made least use of force in religion, and most have favord Christian liberty of any in this Iland before them since the first preaching of the gospel." (Having just finished drafting much of *The History of Britain*, Milton could assert this with some confidence.) But he now wanted "to incite them also to enlarge" this liberty. His main contention was thus "that for beleefe or practise in religion according to . . . conscientious perswasion no man ought be punishd or molested by an outward force on earth whatsoever" (*CPW*, 7 [rev. ed.]: 241–42). Once again, however, this claim did not encompass Catholics and idolaters.

But as for poperie and idolatrie, why they also may not hence plead to be tolerated, I have much less to say. Their religion the more considerd, the less can be acknowledgd a religion; but a Roman principalitie rather, endevouring to keep up her old universal dominion under a new name and meer shaddow of a catholic religion; being indeed more rightly nam'd a catholic heresie against the scripture; supported mainly by a civil, and, except in *Rome*, by a forein power: justly therfore to be suspected, not tolerated by the magistrate of another countrey. Besides, of an implicit faith, which they profess, the conscience also becoms implicit; and so by voluntarie servitude to mans law, forfets her Christian libertie. Who then can plead for such a conscience, as being implicitly enthrald to man instead of God, almost becoms no conscience, as the will not free, becoms no will. Nevertheless if they ought not to be tolerated, it is for just reason of state more then of religion; which they who force, though professing to be protestants, deserve as little to be tolerated themselves, being no less guiltie of poperie in the most popish point. Lastly, for idolatrie, who knows it not to be evidently against all scripture both of the Old and New Testament, and therfore a true heresie, or rather an impietie; wherin a right conscience can have naught to do; and the works therof so manifest, that a magistrate can hardly err in prohibiting and quite removing at least the publick and scandalous use therof. (*CPW*, 7 [rev. ed.]: 254–55)

The first thing to note is that Milton is at least now prepared to argue rather than simply state his case, suggesting he may have become more sensitized to the issues at stake in consequence of the weight of pro-tolerationist work—especially Vane's—that had been published since 1644. Nevertheless, he does little more than expand upon his earlier views: Catholicism is not so much a religion as an alien political entity, and since Catholics have an implicit faith (believe what they are told to believe rather than conscientiously arriving at their beliefs for themselves), they have no conscience as such on behalf of which liberty might be claimed. The refusal to extend toleration to popery is thus a political decision ("for just reason of state") rather than a religious one, and any attempt by Protestants to use force to change the beliefs of papists would in effect be to behave in a popish fashion themselves and hence lose their own claim to toleration.[33] As for idolatry, any public display of it was straightforwardly liable to be prohibited by the magistrate.

How did Milton's stance compare to that of Vane? As we have seen, Vane's general position was to maintain that not even idolatry could be punished by the magistrate. However, Vane too drew the line at popery in *Zeal Examined*:

> *But by excusing of* Idolaters, *I doe not intend a necessary* Toleration *of* Papists, *much lesse of* Priests *and* Jesuites, *for though they may not come within the* Magistrates Cognizance, *by their worshipping of* Images *or the* host *in the* Sacrament, *yet they may as they maintain the* Jurisdiction *of a forreign power over their* Consciences, *if that forreign power doe maintain* Principles *that are inconsistent with all* Magistrates *and* People *that are not of his* Religion. *Now that the* Pope *doth so is most apparent, for he doth not onely declare us all to be* Hereticks, *but likewise that such* Hereticks *ought to be put to death when ever his* Disciples *have the power over them.* (sig. [A3]v)

So although Vane personally had no wish to see lay Catholics suffer ("*in regard there is not many of them in this Nation, and those that are, have already suffered much: I could wish there might bee more tenderness used towards the seduced people, what ever become of the* Priests *and* Jesuites"), he was in complete agreement with Milton about denying toleration to Catholics on political grounds alone (sig. [A3]v). Both men were in fact in the mainstream of seventeenth-century opinion on the issue of popery and toleration. So when Richard Baxter accused Vane of being a closet Catholic, his disciple Henry Stubbe indignantly sprang to his defense, protesting that "there is not a man in this Nation who hath more layed his Ax to the roote of Popery, then Sr. *Henry Vane*."[34]

Perhaps the point that both Vane and Milton should have been required to address was the one posited by Stubbe in *An Essay in Defence of the Good Old Cause, Or A Discourse concerning the Rise and Extent of the power of the Civil Magistrate in reference to Spiritual Affairs* (1659). Toward the end of the *Essay*, he proposed a way round the stumbling block of the Catholics' political unreliability by drawing attention to the existence of what he called "the *Widdringtonian Catholicks* now in *England*."[35] He was referring to followers of the teachings of the Benedictine monk Roland

Preston (1567–1647), who had sided with James I against Cardinal Bellarmine in the controversy over the Oath of Allegiance, writing under the pseudonym Roger Widdrington.[36] His aim in doing so was to make clear that it was possible for Catholics to be loyal subjects of the British crown in precisely the way that those like Vane and Milton thought impossible. As an example of this, Widdrington had reproduced a declaration of loyalty to Elizabeth I signed by thirteen Catholic priests, and Stubbe seized on this to suggest that "our State might obtain the like declaration" from the "the multitudes of the *Romish* Church; who might thereupon enjoy a *Toleration* moderated according to the conveniency of the Republique."[37] Impractical as Stubbe's scheme may have been, he was at least prepared to think about what it might take to make Catholicism *politically* acceptable.

However, Vane and Milton did share some rather less orthodox positions. This stemmed from the fact that for both of them the categories of papist and Protestant were ultimately irrelevant. The fundamental distinction in matters of faith was between beliefs that were conscientiously arrived at by the individual believer and those held in consequence of an implicit faith. There was therefore a sense in which even a Protestant could be a papist. This was a position Milton had already arrived at by the time he wrote *Areopagitica*, announcing that "there be, who knows not that there be of Protestants and professors who live and dye in as arrant an implicit faith, as any lay Papist of Loretto" (*CPW*, 2:543–44). For Vane, too, the dangers of implicit faith cut across confessional boundaries: he writes in *Zeal Examined* that "those, who can leap into a publick *Catechism* as soon as they see it, because that they are told it is *Orthodox*, doe plainly declare, that they are but *Papists* in *principles*, though they call themselves *Protestants*" (3). The crucial thing for Vane, exactly as for Milton, was always how the believer had come to hold the beliefs that he or she held, regardless of whether they were theologically correct or not.

Vane was further prepared to concede that the Catholic Church's reliance on implicit faith meant that it made only limited, predictable, and achievable demands of its faithful, unlike the open-ended demands made by its Protestant counterparts: "Was it not much fairer in the *Papist* to keep the *worship* in an *unknown tongue*, and to shut up the *Bible* from all that had not speciall *licence*, that so they might not be tempted to any *Inquirie*, and consequently to their own *punishment*, then for us to in-courage people to read the *Scriptures*, and not to be lead by an *implicite faith*, and yet when they are instructed according to the *measure* of their *growth* from thence, then to destroy them because they are not of our Pitch?" (2–3). It is this willingness to see the internal logic of the Catholic position and to contrast it with Protestant incoherence that Milton seems to have acquired from Vane.[38] Certainly it informs his extended contrast between the papist and the Protestant in *A Treatise of Civil Power*.

> For the papist, judging by his principles, punishes them who beleeve not as the church beleevs though against the scripture: but the protestant, teaching every one to beleeve the scripture though against the church, counts heretical and persecutes, against his own principles, them who in any particular so beleeve as he in general teaches them; them who most honor and beleeve divine scripture, but not against it any humane interpretation though universal; them who interpret scripture only to themselves, which by his own position none but they to themselves can interpret; them who use the scripture no otherwise by his own doctrine to thir edification, then he himself uses it to thir punishing: and so whom his doctrine acknowledges a true beleever, his discipline persecutes as a heretic. The papist exacts our beleef as to the church due above scripture; and by the church, which is the whole people of God, understands the pope, the general councels prelatical only and the surnam'd fathers: but the forcing protestant though he deny such beleef to any church whatsoever, yet takes it to himself and his teachers, of far less autoritie then to be calld the church and above scripture beleevd: which renders his practise both contrarie to his beleef, and far worse then that beleef which he condemns in the papist. (*CPW*, 7 [rev. ed.]: 253–54)

Whereas Catholics who do not do what their church requires of them are quite reasonably deemed to have failed, Protestants who do exactly what is required by the fundamental principles of their faith may nevertheless still be found wanting—and be punished for it. Milton's apprehension of the sheer perversity of some aspects of Protestant practice again seems to owe something to Vane's probings in *Zeal Examined*.

Another aspect of Vane's assault on implicit faith is the role he assigns to inward illumination. In *Zeal Examined*, he asserts that practicing one's

religion according to one's inner light, even if one is an idolater, is prefer-
able to being in the right on someone else's say-so: "Whether a man be a
Christian or an *Idolater*, he is more excusable in practising according to
the darkest *measure* which is according to the best light which is in his
own *heart*, then he that takes up an higher and better way of *worship*, by
an *implicite Faith* in any other mens authoritie: And therefore seeing the
Magistrate cannot tell when a Man acts by the *light* in him, and when not,
he is not fit to determine which are fit Members to be cut off" (20).
Milton did not go all the way with this argument, endorsing the doctrine
of inner light only in the case of a Christian engaging with the scriptures:

> It cannot be deni'd, being the main foundation of our protestant re-
> ligion, that we of these ages, having no other divine rule or autoritie
> from without us warrantable to one another as a common ground
> but the holy scripture, and no other within us but the illumination
> of the Holy Spirit so interpreting that scripture as warrantable only
> to our selves and to such whose consciences we can so perswade, can
> have no other ground in matters of religion but only from the scrip-
> tures. And these being not possible to be understood without this
> divine illumination, which no man can know at all times to be in
> himself, much less to be at any time for certain in any other, it fol-
> lows cleerly, that no man or body of men in these times can be the
> infallible judges or determiners in matters of religion to any other
> mens consciences but thir own. (*CPW*, 7 [rev. ed.]: 242–43)

But, as can be seen, he did wholeheartedly adopt the second point made
by Vane to the effect that the unverifiability of inward illumination was
sufficient in and of itself to inhibit the magistrate from intervening.

It is when rooting out types of religious hypocrisy that Vane adopts
his most challenging positions. For example, while we (Protestants) might
wish to punish the "poor outward Idolater," the very sense of our own
rectitude in such a case might mean that we were actually in a worse state
"and that the poor Papist who stands far from *Christ*, and dares not approach him, but by a Saint or an *Image*, having a deep sence of his own
unworthiness, was really neerer then our selves, and that the same *punishment* was the more due to our selves, for intending it to him" (9). This
ability to reimagine a state of affairs so that it turns out to be the opposite

of what it first appeared to be is characteristic of Vane. Another striking example is when he provocatively asks whether it was "not less sin in the *Indians* to worship the *Sun, Moon,* and *Stars,* than in the *Spaniards* (professing *Christianity*) to worship their *Gold,* and to be so farre transported with love to that *Idoll,* as to sacrifice so many *millions* of men to it?" (5–6). The idolatrous native Americans (and Vane surely had Aztec blood sacrifices in mind) are in fact less guilty than the Spanish, who sacrificed millions of humans to their idol, gold.

It is surely at this juncture, if Coffey and others are to be believed, that Vane finally leaves Milton trailing in his wake. However, such relativism was not altogether beyond Milton. The complex interactions of pagan and Christian in *The History of Britain,* on which Milton was working in the mid-1650s, were susceptible to exactly this kind of treatment. Indeed, it is hard not to hear something of Vane in the remarkable statement with which Milton concludes his account of the Saxons and Britons in book 3 of *The History of Britain:* "Wherin we have heard the many miseries and desolations, brought by divine hand on a perverse Nation; driv'n when nothing else would reform them, out of a fair Country, into a Mountainous and Barren Corner, by Strangers and Pagans. So much more tolerable in the Eye of Heav'n is Infidelity profess't, then Christian Faith and Religion dishonoured by unchristian works" (*CPW,* 5:183). Open infidelity is for Milton, no less than for Vane, literally "more tolerable" than Christian hypocrisy.

Milton and Vane were thus closer to each other in religious attitudes than we might think, even on the vexed question of toleration—or lack of toleration—for Catholics. This is so for two reasons. One is that Vane was arguably less thoroughgoing in his commitment to the logic of toleration than has been assumed. But the other side of the equation is that Milton was less intransigent in some of his attitudes than it has recently been fashionable to suppose.

NOTES

1. Thomason's copy, E.1016(11), is dated March 3, 1659.
2. Cf. *CWJM,* 6:514. In the first edition, this assertion is preceded by a significant 325-word passage (6:512, 514) on the evils of imposing on the conscience that was cut from the second edition.

3. Cf. *CWJM*, 6:514.

4. A. H. Woolrych, "The Good Old Cause and the Fall of the Protectorate," *Historical Journal* 13, no. 2 (1957): 134.

5. Henry Vane, *The Healing Question propounded and resolved* (n. p., n.d.; Thomason's copy, E.879[5], is dated May 12, 1656), 3.

6. See Henry Vane, *The Proceeds of the Protector (so called) and his Councill against Sir Henry Vane, Knight* (London, 1656).

7. See now Martin Dzelzainis, "Harrington and the Oligarchs: Milton, Vane and Stubbe," in *Perspectives on English Revolutionary Republicanism*, ed. Gaby Mahlberg and Dirk Weimann (Farnham, Surrey: Ashgate, 2014).

8. Vane was elected to the council of state on February 14, 1649, which in turn resolved on March 13 to invite Milton to become its secretary for foreign tongues; he accepted two days later and was inducted on March 20. Ruth E. Mayers, "Vane, Sir Henry, the Younger (1613–1662)," in *ODNB*; J. Milton French, ed., *The Life Records of John Milton*, 5 vols. (New Brunswick, NJ: Rutgers University Press, 1949–58), 2:234, 236. On Milton and Vane, see Arthur Barker, *Milton and the Puritan Dilemma* (Toronto: University of Toronto Press, 1942), 205–13; Michael Fixler, *Milton and the Kingdoms of God* ([Evanston, IL]: Northwestern University Press, 1964), 185–96; and Feisal G. Mohamed, "Milton, Sir Henry Vane, and the Brief but Significant Life of Godly Republicanism," *Huntington Library Quarterly* 76, no. 1 (2013): 83–104. David Parnham, *Sir Henry Vane, Theologian: A Study in Seventeenth-Century Religious and Political Discourse* (Madison, NJ: Fairleigh Dickinson University Press, 1997), has surprisingly little to say on Milton.

9. Richard Baxter, *Reliquiae Baxterianae* (London, 1696), 75.

10. Edward Hyde, Earl of Clarendon, *Animadversions upon a book intituled, Fanaticism fanatically imputed to the Catholick Church, by Dr. Stillingfleet* (London, 1673), 61.

11. Fixler, *Milton*, 190n.

12. Christopher Hill, *The Experience of Defeat* (London: Bookmarks, 1994), 18; Blair Worden, *Literature and Politics in Cromwellian England: John Milton, Andrew Marvell, Marchamont Nedham* (Oxford: Oxford University Press, 2010), 363.

13. For a defense of Vane's style, see David Parnham, "Soul's Trial and Spirit's Voice: Sir Henry Vane against the 'Orthodox,'" *Huntington Library Quarterly* 70, no. 3 (2007): 365–66.

14. Violet Rowe, *Sir Henry Vane the Younger* (London: Athlone Press, 1970), 140–41.

15. John Coffey, "Persecution and Liberty Revisited: The Case for Toleration in the English Revolution," *Historical Journal* 41 (1998): 961–62, 969. For a valuable survey of the field with a comprehensive bibliography, see Alex-

andra Walsham, "Cultures of Coexistence in Early Modern England: Literature and Religious Toleration," *Seventeenth Century* 28, no. 2 (2013): 115–37.

16. See George Sikes, *The Life and Death of Sir Henry Vane, Kt.* (n.p., 1662), 93.

17. See Martin Dzelzainis, "The Politics of *Paradise Lost*," in *The Oxford Handbook of Milton*, ed. Nicholas McDowell and Nigel Smith (Oxford: Oxford University Press, 2009), 550–51, and "Milton and Antitrinitarianism," in *Milton and Toleration*, ed. Sharon Achinstein and Elizabeth Sauer (Oxford: Oxford University Press, 2007), 177–79.

18. See Carolyn Polizzotto, "The Campaign against *The Humble Proposals* of 1652," *Journal of Ecclesiastical History* 38 (1987): 569–81, and Blair Worden, "John Milton and Oliver Cromwell," in *Soldiers, Writers and Statesmen of the English Revolution*, ed. Ian Gentles, John Morrill, and Blair Worden (Cambridge: Cambridge University Press), 244–52.

19. See Roger Williams, *The Fourth Paper; The Bloody Tenent Yet More Bloody* (London, 1652; Thomason's copy, E.661[6], is dated April 28), *The Hirelings Ministry None of Christs* (London, Printed in the second Moneth, 1652), and *The Examiner Defended* (London, 1652; Thomason's copy, E.675[2], is dated September 14).

20. [Henry Vane], *Zeal Examined: Or, A Discourse for Liberty of Conscience in Matters of Religion. Upon an occasionall Question concerning the punishment of Idolaters* (London, 1652: Thomason's copy, E.667[15], is dated June 15). For the attribution to Vane, see Polizzotto, "Campaign," 579.

21. I have made my own transcriptions from Trinity College Library, R.3.4, Milton MS, p. 47, www.trin.cam.ac.uk/james/show.php?index=1394.

22. Trinity College Library, R.3.4, Milton MS, p. 48.

23. R. F. Hall, "Milton's Sonnets and His Contemporaries," in *The Cambridge Companion to Milton*, ed. Dennis Danielson, 2nd ed. (Cambridge: Cambridge University Press, 1999), 102.

24. See Martin Dzelzainis, "'In These Western Parts of the Empire': Milton and Roman Law," in *Milton and the Terms of Liberty*, ed. Graham Parry and Joad Raymond (Cambridge: D. S. Brewer, 2002), 60.

25. See Worden, *Literature and Politics*, 244. One objection is that from February 1651 the Council, unless it specified to the contrary, routinely excluded officials other than its secretary and his assistant from meetings; see Leo Miller, *John Milton's Writings in the Anglo-Dutch Negotiations, 1651–1654* (Pittsburgh, PA: Duquesne University Press, 1992), 5. This means that Milton might have witnessed discussions of the Blasphemy Act in 1650 but not of the Humble Proposals in 1652.

26. [Vane], *Zeal Examined*, sig. A2r; subsequent citations to this work are supplied parenthetically in the text by page number or, for the preface, signature

number preceded by "sig." For Vane's intervention, see *Journals of the House of Commons* 6:453 (August 9, 1650); my thanks to Blair Worden for this reference.

27. For David Loewenstein, however, this "positive reference to the Act remains a vexed and, arguably, a contradictory moment in [Milton's] radical religious writing"; David Loewenstein, "Treason against God and State: Blasphemy in Milton's Culture and *Paradise Lost*," in *Milton and Heresy*, ed. Stephen B. Dobranski and John Rumrich (Cambridge: Cambridge University Press, 1998), 180.

28. I shall confine my remarks to works Milton published during Vane's lifetime and leave out of account his late tract *Of True Religion* (1673). For a Roman Catholic response, see Martin Dzelzainis, "Milton's *Of True Religion* and the Earl of Castlemaine," *Seventeenth Century* 7 (1992): 53–69.

29. See Martin Dzelzainis, "John Milton, *Areopagitica*," in *A Companion to Literature from Milton to Blake*, ed. David Womersley (Oxford: Blackwell, 2000), 152–54.

30. Willmoore Kendall, "How to Read Milton's *Areopagitica*," *Journal of Politics* 22, no. 3 (1960): 461n.

31. S. R. Gardiner, ed., *Constitutional Documents of the Puritan Revolution 1625–1660*, 3rd, rev. ed. (Oxford: Clarendon Press, 1979), 230, 268.

32. Mark Goldie, introduction to John Locke, *A Letter Concerning Toleration and Other Writings*, ed. Mark Goldie, The Thomas Hollis Library (Indianapolis: Liberty Fund, 2010), xi.

33. For a comparable range of arguments used by Locke, see *Letter Concerning Toleration*, ed. Goldie, 49–52, 117–18, 122–25. However, Locke (like Vane but unlike Milton) also spelled out what this meant in terms of Catholic beliefs: "The Magistrate ought not to forbid the Preaching or Professing of any Speculative Opinions in any Church; because they have no manner of relation to the Civil Rights of the Subjects. If a *Roman Catholic* believe that to be really the Body of Christ, which another man calls Bread, he does no injury thereby to his Neighbour" (44).

34. Henry Stubbe, *Malice Rebuked* (London, 1659), 56; cf. [Vane], *Zeal Examined*, sig. A2v.

35. Henry Stubbe, *An Essay in Defence of the Good Old Cause, Or A Discourse concerning the Rise and Extent of the power of the Civil Magistrate in reference to Spiritual Affairs* (London, 1659), 133.

36. Anselm Cramer, "Preston, Roland (1567–1647)," in *ODNB*.

37. Stubbe, *Essay*, 139.

38. It is of course impossible to exclude the possibility that, on some points, the flow of influence was in the opposite direction—from Milton to Vane.

CHAPTER 4

ROMAN CATHOLICISM,
DE DOCTRINA CHRISTIANA,
AND THE PARADISE OF FOOLS

Thomas N. Corns

Much that Milton has to say about Catholicism comes from the core beliefs of Protestant and proto-Protestant theology, though he turns his attacks skillfully, at once invoking a historic and international tradition and subtly refining his own doctrine in distinction to that orthodoxy. In the English context, he generally enthuses about Lollardy and John Wycliffe's teaching, celebrating "that glimmering light which *Wicklef*, and his followers dispers't" and terming him "that Englishman honor'd of God to be the first preacher of a general reformation to all *Europe*."[1] Indeed, early Stuart theologians were more generally rediscovering the intellectual origins of the English Reformation. For example, Wycliffe on the follies of transubstantiation had been made available by Henry Jackson, better known as the editor of Richard Hooker and then a fellow of Corpus Christi College, Oxford.[2] The little pamphlet *Wickliffes Wicket, or a Learned and Godly Treatise of the* Sacrament, *Made by John Wickliffe*

(London, 1612) is offered as evidence of the prehistory of "the true doctrine of the sacraments with the now [*sic*] Church of England," clearly articulated "maugre the furious attempts of Papists."[3]

Milton at his intellectually most flamboyant shares common ground with the earthiness of Lollard martyrs in their analysis of Catholic doctrine. Thus, on transubstantiation, in a Norwich heresy trial of 1428 that would lead to a sentence of six floggings, the Lollard Margery Baxter, among a rich medley of anticlerical sentiment, has attributed to her the following doctrine: "You believe wrongly, since if every such sacrament were God and Christ's real body, then gods would be infinite in number, because a thousand priests and more confect a thousand such gods every day and then eat them, and once eaten emit them from their back side in filthy and stinking pieces. . . . Such a sacrament is ordained falsely and deceitfully by the priests in church."[4]

Milton is equally robust in tracking the host from the altar to the privy:

> If this flesh were his true flesh and were being eaten by all in the mass, as the Pontificians claim, then assuredly everyone—even the wickedest person, not to mention the mice and worms which often eat it—would be gaining eternal life from that heavenly bread. So what else can that living bread be which Christ says his flesh is, and his blood which [he says] is the true drink, other than the teaching about Christ's having been made man in order to pour forth his blood for us? Whoever takes in this teaching with true faith will live to eternity no less certainly than those who eat and drink amongst us sustain this mortal life for a little while—no indeed, much more certainly!—for thus Christ will remain in us, and we in him, as was quoted above. On the other hand, if we eat his flesh, it will not remain in us, but (to be utterly frank) after being digested in the stomach will finally be voided.[5]

Milton nursed a long interest in Lollardy and in the theology of John Wycliffe, perceiving the movement and the doctrinal critique as England's lost leadership of the European Reformation, hindered and frustrated by English Catholic bishops.[6] The grim reduction of transubstantiation to excretion recurs elsewhere and more tangentially in the Milton oeuvre, in a relatively rare passage of linguistic playfulness in *Paradise*

Lost, when Adam and Raphael eat together and Milton discusses the alimentary system of angels:

> So down they sat,
> And to thir viands fell, nor seemingly
> The Angel, nor in a mist, the common gloss
> Of Theologians, but with keen dispatch
> Of real hunger, and concoctive heate
> To transubstantiate; what redounds, transpires
> Through Spirits with ease. . . .
> Mean while at Table *Eve*
> Ministerd naked. . . .[7]

Though *transubstantiate* had some currency as a term for changing a material from one substance to another, its theological associations are clearly reinforced by the role of the naked Eve, ministering at table, like a priest at a communion table.[8] But the point of the passage is exactly the opposite of the theology of transubstantiation. Here a material substance is not subject to a mysterious transformation; rather, it obeys the laws of physics. Angels expend energy; angels need food; ingestion requires digestion; and digestion produces excretion of what is waste. Milton's materialist universe finds immediate expression in its assertion of the materiality of angels, but that carries a larger implication in the denial of a spiritual mystery.

A similar intellectual dynamic runs through the passage from *De Doctrina Christiana*. Of course, the communicant does not ingest literally the body of Christ, for to do so would necessitate the excretion of the undigested portion of that body, a gross concept that invalidates the assumptions of transubstantiation and the real presence of the godhead in the host. The related point about the status of the transubstantiated host if it were to be ingested by mice or worms has a sort of Lollard directness, but it originates in the ancient anxieties within Roman Catholic theology about the Eucharist, and particularly about how Christ's body is received when the host is eaten by an infidel or by an animal. One school argued that the nature of the reception was determined by the status of the recipient; the mysterious transformation works only for those in fit condition to receive it. Others, in the tradition of Albert the Great and Thomas

Aquinas, decline to insert in the mystery that additional component, conceding that whoever, whatever, eats the consecrated host in some sense eats Christ's body—a view that could breed extreme views. Thus "The Dominican Peter de La Palu (*c.* 1277–1342) . . . argued that the mouse who had swallowed the consecrated host must be caught and burned and his ashes washed down a *piscina,* the treatment accorded to old vestments, crumbs of the host and other sacred materials."[9] In a way, the Protestant tradition had little left to do to put into play what it perceived as the absurdities current in Catholic doctrine.

The passage allows Milton to draw a clear line of demarcation between that Protestant tradition and the Pontificians ("Pontificii") but also provides the vehicle for a somewhat heterodox perspective on the Son. Indeed, he seems to say, we Protestants are united in rejection of transubstantiation, preferring to regard the Eucharist as a symbolic celebration of the Atonement. But within that broad confederacy, he develops a distinctively limited notion of Christ's capacity and characteristics. In a way that Margery Baxter already understood, for Milton Christ cannot be in two places at once, and his "holy body" was, as a historical event in which belief is required by the faithful, physically transposed to heaven and "its supreme point of exaltation" at "the right hand of God the father" (*CWJM,* 8:763).

An attack on Catholicism precedes his fuller critique of Trinitarianism in his chapter on the Son of God, the fifth chapter of the first book of *De Doctrina Christiana.* An assertion of Protestant ground rules is his opening gambit:

> As I am going to discuss here the **Son of God and the Holy Spirit**, I have thought so arduous a task not one to be undertaken without a fresh preface. Truly, if I professed myself a nursling of the Roman Church, which demands implicit belief in all the heads of faith, then even though it denies that the doctrine of the Trinity as received today can be proved from any passage of scripture, I would nonetheless—through having been so thoroughly taught or at least accustomed—have acquiesced in its decree alone and its authority. But as things stand, since I am among those who acknowledge the word of God alone as their yardstick of faith, I freely present what

appears to me much more clearly evident from holy scripture than the received opinion is; and I do not see why anybody who proclaims the name of Protestant or Reformed, and the same yardstick of faith as I do, should be offended at me on that account, especially because I am not imposing any command on anyone, but merely proposing what I think more credible. (*CWJM*, 8:127)

On the assertion of the Protestant principle that doctrine should be founded solely on the interpretation of scripture, he leads his co-religionaries down an anti-Trinitarian and materialist path consonant with the limitations on the physical and historical Christ implicit in his critique of the Eucharist. His Christ is of a second order: "Surely if Christ's God and our God is the Father, and God is one, Who is God besides the Father?" Godhead requires a transcendence that a created entity cannot claim: "The Father alone is self-sufficiently God, because he who is not [self-sufficient] cannot be God." Christ's status is wholly derivative: "Whatever amount of Deity is assigned to the Son, the Son admits that he possesses it all by the Father's unique gift and favour." The infinity of the Father circumscribes the Son in a way that precludes co-essentiality: "Both the essence and the person of the Father are infinite; so the Father's essence cannot be shared with a second person, for in that case there could be two infinite people." He dismisses co-eternality: "*In the beginning*, he [John 1:1] says, not from eternity." With that comes a subordinate condition: "He who does not exist from himself, who did not beget but was begotten, is not the first cause but an effect; therefore he is not supreme God." Milton, though uncertain about significant aspects of the Father, is quite sure where the Son is: in heaven, at the Father's right hand, where he is to remain till his Second Coming.[10]

Milton's Christology contains much that is highly heterodox, and indeed elements that, in most earlier times, had provoked prosecution and severe punishment in Protestant states. Michael Servetus had been burnt at the stake in Calvin's Geneva for his anti-Trinitarianism. Nearer in time and place, the Long Parliament, in its Blasphemy Ordinance of May 1648, had imposed the death penalty for denial of the Trinity.[11] Quite how successful Milton's polemical strategy would have proved had *De Doctrina Christiana* seen publication in his lifetime defies confident assessment. But the gambit of playing to a broad spectrum of Protestantism by defining Catholic doctrine as distinctively erroneous, informs much of his more controversial propositions.

Consider, for example, his critique of the notion of purgatory. Rejection of a third eschatological component (besides heaven and hell) had been a distinctive belief in Reformation theology from the age of Luther, whose *Ninety-Five Theses* of 1517 rejects a cluster of related concepts, including the efficacy of prayer or indulgences in easing the passage of the soul in grace toward paradise. Milton dismisses the concept in these terms:

> And indeed the tale of purgatory in which—as the Papists spin that tale—sins are burnt away by flames, and cleansed and purged, is refuted by many other reasons but above all by Christ's *full* satisfaction. For, to pass over the fact that no such purgation-place is found in scripture, surely if Christ's blood has made full satisfaction for us and rendered us thoroughly pure from every stain, then nothing at all is left that fire could possibly purge. And let them know that "that fire," 1 Cor. 3: 13, 15, which they want to be understood as real fire, is not purgatory-fire but probatory fire prepared for testing vain teachers alone, whose teaching (whether flashy and phoney, or crude and uncouth) "the daylight"—that is, the light of truth—"will make clear." Like that "fire of afflictions" too, 1 Pet. 4: 12, it tests us in this life, [and] does not purge us in the next. Besides, all retribution after this life, all sense of either good or evil, is deferred to that judgement-seat of Christ, 2 Cor. 5: 10: *so that each one may be requited for the things that he did in the body, correspondingly to what he did, whether good or evil.* And surely if . . . the soul falls asleep with the body until the day of resurrection, by no other proof can the idea of purgatory be more strongly refuted. Nor, to those who are going to be saved, is any middle state except death given between "this earthly house" of this life and that "eternal home in the heavens," 2 Cor. 5: 1; 2 Tim. 4: 8: *the crown of righteousness is stored up for me, which the Lord, the just judge, will award to me on that day.* (CWJM, 8:535)

Note the dynamic of his argument. Milton takes his stand on his recurrent and thoroughly Protestant position: doctrine must be derived from the scriptures, not from tradition or from councils convened to augment or interpret the scriptures. Purgatory is not mentioned scripturally. A perfectly orthodox Protestant point, as can be easily exemplified. I select from William Whitaker's *An Answere to the Ten Reasons of Edmund Campion the Jesuit . . . Translated by Richard Stock* (London, 1606) a formal exposition of Protestant differences from Catholicism by a senior Protestant divine, writing in Latin in the early 1580s and translated in the early Stuart period by the clergyman who had baptized Milton and was rector of All Hallows, Bread Street, through Milton's childhood. Against Campion, Whitaker takes pretty much the same line as Milton: of purgatory and the Mass "neither the names nor the things themselves anywhere do appear [in the scriptures]. . . . What is Purgatorie more than a shamelesse merchandise of soules, and an intolerable contempt against the blood of Christ?"[12] Milton progresses to citation of the doctrine of the Atonement, with its associated Protestant inflection of solafideism, and wheels round to engage scriptural texts that have been—erroneously, he argues—invoked to support belief in a purgatorial process. Using a favored exegetical technique, he glosses the metaphor of 1 Corinthians with interpretation of the metaphor of 1 Peter.

Amid his own rehearsal of such wholly orthodoxy Protestant theology, Milton smartly inserts a heresy, albeit one to which Luther subscribed: mortalism. Milton refers back to his eschatological discussion in chapter 13 of the first book. Here he is at his most tentative. But he contextualizes that tentativeness with an argument he uses in *Of True Religion, Heresy, Schism, and Toleration* (to which we shall turn shortly), where he develops a distinction between saving faith and the legitimate scope for theological speculation: "Since this question [whether the body and soul separate at death] can be tossed about with no diminution of faith or piety, whether one were to maintain this or that opinion, I shall freely expound what I think I have learnt from almost countless passages of scripture—unless anyone supposes that truth should be imbibed from the schools rather than from the Sacred books" (*CWJM*, 8:443). Toss it about he indeed does, but he comes out strongly against separation and interim judgment and in favor of body and soul abiding together, in the sleep of the grave, until resurrection at the Second Coming. The case of Lazarus is a clinching argument, since to recall his soul from heaven would constitute no charity (*CWJM*, 8:453).

Though mortalism was a minority tradition in Reformation theology, it had occasioned significant controversy, for example in Calvin's attempted refutation of Luther's position on the topic. Moreover, in Milton's England, it had emerged as a scandalous position, most often associated with religious and indeed political radicals, for whom its materialist premises had an attraction. But Milton well knew how the doctrine was received among contemporary co-religionaries. His own rise to public notoriety, for the publication of *The Doctrine and Discipline of Divorce* (London, 1643; 2nd ed., 1644), advocating reform of divorce legislation, had occurred in step with the attacks on the most notorious English advocacy of mortalism, *Mans Mortallitie* ([Amsterdam?], 1643), by "R. O." (almost certainly the future Leveller Richard Overton). Recurrently, opponents of toleration bracketed the works together as evidence of the urgency of effective control of the press.[13] Indeed, such was the odium associated with mortalism that, like anti-Trinitarianism, it was listed among capital offenses in the Blasphemy Ordinance.[14]

Once more, dextrously, Milton has initiated a response to Catholic doctrine in terms taken from the core of Protestant orthodoxy, and in the process has insinuated a highly heterodox opinion of his own. He adopts the same approach in his wholly orthodox critique of the sacraments. He had, already, developed clearly and unambiguously his heterodox views on marriage and particularly on polygamy (justified by Old Testament example) and divorce and remarriage (also acceptable), in the latter case returning to those same arguments that had earned him notoriety in the mid-1640s (*CWJM*, 8:363–97). But he slips in another controversial perspective on matrimony when, following a wholly orthodox Protestant argument, which can be traced back to Luther, he dismisses marriage as a sacrament. Once more, Whitaker's example speaks from the core of the English Protestantism. The Roman Catholic position was and is that there are seven essential sacraments of the church: baptism, the Eucharist, confirmation, penance, extreme unction, ordination, and matrimony. Whitaker, in the standard Protestant response, asserts, "Dare you [Campion] appeale to Christ, whose Sacraments yee have banished with great reproch out of the Church, that ye might bring in certaine impure Sacraments not worthy to be named? we retaine those Sacraments which Christ hath commended to us: if there had been need of more, he would have left more. We have two Sacraments, *Baptisme, and the Lords Supper:* these

Christ did institute, . . . these the anncient Church acknowledged, and with these the later Church ought to have been contented."[15] Milton is completely aligned with this position: "As to the other things which the pontificians term sacraments . . . we perceive from the very definition of a sacrament that they are not truly and properly sacraments: if, that is, they were not divinely instituted; and if they do not contain a sign instituted by God to seal the covenant of grace" (*CWJM*, 8:763). This, as with Whitaker, is less of an argument and more of a process of exclusion through definition, requiring their satisfaction of the criterion that Christ instituted them. Indeed, a similar structure characterizes the discussion in the *Book of Common Prayer*, where the catechism defines sacraments in a limiting way that necessarily restricts the category to baptism and communion. Most of what follows as he works through the nonsacraments is rather pedestrian Protestant orthodoxy, but as he reaches matrimony a controversial opportunity arises. Although the Church of England, before 1653 and after 1660, had regarded the recognition and celebration of matrimony as its responsibility, the Marriage Act passed by the republican government required it to be observed as a civil process.[16] *A Directory for The Publique Worship of* God, *Throughout the Three Kingdoms of* England, Scotland, *and* Ireland (London: 1644 [i.e., 1645]), drafted by the Westminster Assembly of Divines along Presbyterian lines and endorsed by the Long Parliament as the statutory replacement for the *Book of Common Prayer*, had arrived at a compromise position on marriage. Its section on the solemnization of marriage begins stoutly: "Marriage be no sacrament, nor peculiar to the Church of God, but common to mankind, and of Publique interest in every Common-wealth." But it continues by reinstating matrimony as a church function: "Yet because such as marry are to marry in the Lord, and have speciall need of Instruction, Direction, and Exhortation, from the Word of God at their entring into such a new condition; and, of the blessing God upon them therein; we judge it expedient, that marriage be solemnized by a lawfull Minister of the Word."[17] What follows is a somewhat more austere liturgy for wedding ceremonies than the *Book of Common Prayer* had afforded. But in 1653 the republican government, of which Milton was a civil servant, took a sterner line as it passed the Marriage Act. This removed ecclesiastical involvement in matrimony. Thus Milton's second marriage, in 1656, probably took place in the Guildhall and was conducted by Sir John Dethicke, whose term as lord mayor of London had ended three days earlier. Dethicke was a civil magistrate. His third marriage, in 1663, took place in St. Mary Alder-mary and was conducted according to the *Book of Common Prayer*.[18]

As he works through his list of pseudosacraments, Milton takes his opportunity to deal blows to the Presbyterians and the Church of England's policy as it was followed before the *Directory* was adopted: "But as to **matrimony**, since it is something belonging to all people indiscriminately by the common law of nations (unless the term be understood as matrimony only of the truly faithful), it will assuredly have to be called a purely civil matter, not a sacred one, let alone a sacrament: so far is its celebration from being in any way the business of ministers of the church" (*CWJM*, 8:765). Milton begins with a formula that echoes that of the *Directory* before following it to an alternative conclusion, the position arrived at in 1653, rather than the abbreviated ceremonialism of 1645. Once more, the launchpad for the struggle within Protestantism is a broad, orthodox rejection of the Catholic position.

Arguably, the minority position to which Milton most frequently returned, from the early 1640s to his final prose writing, was tolerationism, the notion that heterodoxy in belief and practice should be allowed without church censure or sanction and without the intervention of the civil magistrate, and that matters of belief and conscience should not concern the state. At no point was the toleration he advocated without significant qualification and exception, and the structure of the argument remained quite stable despite its longevity through his career as controversialist. His interest in the topic had emerged somewhat tangentially even before his own writing on divorce had provoked the intolerance of powerful contemporaries. *The Reason of Church-Government* in part rehearses a repressive attitude toward radical sectaries, but it shows, too, an aspiration that a tolerant and newly reformed church could admit a wide diversity of Protestant opinion: "Noise it till ye be hoarse: that a rabble of Sects will come in, it will be answer'd ye, no rabble sir Priest, but a unanimous multitude of good Protestants will then joyne to the Church, which now because of you stand separated" (*CPW*, 1:787–88). Milton's *Areopagitica*, immediately stimulated by the hostile reception of his *Doctrine and Discipline of Divorce* (first ed., London, 1643), argues for the toleration of the expression of heterodox opinions (like his own). But it does so by distinguishing tolerable Protestant diversity from intolerable Catholic doctrine and discipline: "Yet if all cannot be one mind, as who looks they should be? this doubtless is more wholesom, more prudent, and more Christian that many be tolerated, rather then all compell'd." Then he clinches the point with the invocation of Catholic-Protestant distinctions: "I mean not tolerated Popery, and open superstition, which as it extirpats all religions and civill supremacies, so it self should be extirpat." He does, however, offer a tepidly irenic qualification: "provided first that all charitable and compassionat means be us'd to win and regain the weak and the misled" (*CPW*, 2:564–65). Catholics could perhaps be forgiven for a certain skepticism about Protestant compassion, given the wave of persecution that swept the territories under parliamentary control. Between 1641 and 1646 twenty-four Catholic priests were executed, sometimes with spectacular brutality, and there were frequent mob attacks on the Catholic community.[19] But the tactic is clear: Protestants don't agree on everything—and indeed why should they?—but they agree on enough to establish a saving faith and on the supremacy of scripture over tradition and received interpretation. Thus the pale of toleration is established by its distinction from Catholicism.

Milton published no controversial prose from the Restoration till 1673, when, reanimated by the easing of antidissenter sentiment and action and by the hostility to Catholicism provoked by the evident Catholicism of James, Duke of York and heir apparent, he dusted off the old argument in *Of True Religion, Heresy, Schism, and Toleration*. The three components—the essential unity of Protestantism, the diversity of belief within that faith community broadly defined, and the intolerable characteristics of Catholicism—are once more present. Thus "All Protestant Churches with one consent . . . maintain these two points, as the main Principles of true Religion: that the Rule of true Religion is the Word of God only: and that their Faith ought not to be an implicit faith, that is, to believe, though as the Church believes, against or without express authority of Scripture" (*CPW*, 8:419–20). He rather neatly reviews a spectrum of Protestant denominations, attributing to each a distinctive aberration from the general consensus:

> The Lutheran holds Consubstantiation; an error indeed, but not mortal. The Calvinist is taxt with Predestination, and to make God the Author of sin; not with any dishonourable thought of God, but

it may be over zealously asserting his absolute power, not without plea of Scripture. The Anabaptist is accus'd of Denying Infants their right to Baptism; again they say, they deny nothing but what the Scripture denies them. The Arian and Socinian are charg'd to dispute against the Trinity: they affirm to believe the Father, Son and Holy Ghost, according to Scripture, and the Apostolic Creed; as for terms of Trinity, Triunity, Coessentiality, Tripersonality, and the like, they reject them as Scholastic Notions, not to be found in Scripture. . . . The *Arminian* lastly is condemn'd for setting up free will against free grace; but that Imputation he disclaims in all his writings, and grounds himself largely upon Scripture only. (*CPW*, 8:424–26)

Note how each aberration from the mainstream is not argued for but acknowledged as tolerable because it is premised on scripture. As such, it is distinguishable from Catholicism. Indeed, it is not necessary or appropriate even to engage intellectually with Catholicism because it rests on papal authority, on councils, and on tradition: "Let them bound their disputations on the Scripture only, and an ordinary Protestant, well read in the Bible, may turn and wind their Doctors. They will not go about to prove their Idolatries by the Word of God" (*CPW*, 8:432).

The same approach to toleration pervades *De Doctrina Christiana.* Of course, toleration of minority positions to be found (though sometimes under persecution) in the Protestant tradition would have been the sine qua non for the publication of the tract, and Milton argues for it by the reiterated assertion that arguments from scripture alone are the bedrock of Reformation theology, a point made clearer by the differences between that assumption and the practices of the Catholic Church. At the very outset, he builds a narrative of the continuing reformation of the church and aligns his own endeavor with the sweep of history:

Seeing that from the beginning of the last century, ever since Religion began to be recalled in some measure to the purity of its origin from the continual corruptions which had stained it for over thirteen hundred years, so many books of instruction of purer Theology came forth, in which the heads of Christian Doctrine . . . seem to be contained, it is fair that I should in the first place declare why I have not stayed content with whatever such publication to date has (so far as is possible) been well-worked-out, or else why, if everyone hitherto has addressed the task unsuccessfully, I am not deterred from the same undertaking. (*CWJM*, 8:3)

The history of Western Christianity is represented as fractured around the inception of the Lutheran and Calvinist reformations, and Milton's own efforts belong firmly within that later process. Those who stand on the Protestant side are coworkers in a process of cleansing a faith polluted by the years of Catholic domination. At the same time, however, Milton works to make a space for his own contribution; while the Protestant endeavor has been purposeful, it remains incomplete, and his efforts, founded on the defining methodology of the Reformation, are "based exclusively on divine revelation," "the word of God itself alone," "the holy writings alone" (*CWJM*, 8:5, 7, 9). His program is implicitly tolerationist, in that it acknowledges that an incomplete reformation implies remaining uncertainties, despite the sureness of a saving faith at its core, and those uncertainties are to be engaged through scripture-based debate. But as he turns to consider the status of the Bible in more detail, in the thirtieth chapter of the first book, "On Holy Scripture," his emphasis changes subtly but tellingly. Once more he clears a firebreak between Protestant and Catholic practice; the former, as in apostolic times, rests on direct and individual access to the scriptures "by people of every kind and rank" (*CWJM*, 8:799), whereas the latter discourages the laity from reading the holy text. But he introduces another component in the search for personal enlightenment, the spirit within: "Every single one of the faithful has the right of interpreting the scriptures, of interpreting them for himself, I mean; for he has the spirit, the guide into truth, he has the mind of Christ" (*CWJM*, 8:805). Once more, a minority position has emerged from an exposition of a defining core doctrine of Protestantism. Promotion of the supremacy of the spirit within and its valorization over custom and even scripture was a recurrent characteristic of the radical wing of English Puritanism. Hill better than any has recognized the continuities between Milton's thought and that of the most radical groups. He observes, "This emphasis [on the spirit within] was common to Milton, Dell, Winstanley, Bunyan, Ranters and Quakers. . . .

Everything that is traditional is suspect just because it is traditional."[20] In *De Doctrina Christiana* Milton offers it as a necessary component in the evaluation of scriptural evidence, as something all Protestants must do as they turn from the monolith of Catholic belief and practice.

Of course, Milton's perspective on Catholicism and his close and valued relationship with identifiable Catholics require incorporation into a proper analysis of his thought and work. Yet in *De Doctrina Christiana* the simplicity of his analysis that I have identified is purposeful and focused. His intention is not "thundering upon the steel cap of Bellarmine."[21] Indeed, taking on such Catholic luminaries as Cardinal Roberto Bellarmino (1542–1621) probably belonged to the Elizabethan and early Jacobean phases of the English Reformation. Whitaker had attempted to answer him as well as to confute Campion, and Bellarmino was reputed to keep his picture above his desk, much as "Rommel was to keep an eye on Montgomery."[22] Milton himself remarked, "I observed that the stronghold of reformed religion was adequately fortified as regards the Pontificians" (*CWJM*, 8:7). Not until the years after Milton's death, during the Popish Plot and the Exclusion Crisis, did real anxiety about England returning to Rome animate the political nation, though concerns about the Duke of York constitute some of the immediate context for *Of True Religion*. As his recent editors note, his readership in *De Doctrina Christiana* is "the auditory of international Protestantism" (*CWJM*, 8:lv). Its principal agenda is the advocacy of minority opinions on mortalism, on divorce, on the status of the Son, and on toleration, and the advancement of an Arminian soteriology that remained deeply disputed in the Puritan wing of English Protestantism and in retreat in continental Europe, and particularly the United Provinces, despite its adoption among English church leaders of the Restoration period.

De Doctrina Christiana manifests a degree of polemical guile hitherto unsuspected in modern responses to the text. The identification of Milton's recurrent stratagem, of associating his views on issues that divide reformed thinkers with a sustained attack on the Catholic faith with which most Protestants would heartily concur, illuminates one of the most troublesome passages in *Paradise Lost*, his account in book 3 of the Paradise of Fools (lines 430–97). This section certainly challenges the high decorum of the preceding debate in heaven. Joseph Addison and Richard Bentley were particularly troubled by it, the latter disputing its Miltonic authenticity. More recent criticism has rallied to its defense. Alastair Fowler, for example, places it squarely in the tradition of Ludovico Ariosto's use of burlesque in an analogous passage in *Orlando Furioso*.[23] John N. King rightly identifies continuities with Milton's antiprelatical tracts, where he had adapted Ariosto in a sustained attack on Laudianism.[24] But no one in the commentary tradition sees its rehabilitation as straightforward. After the discourse of heaven comes:

> Embryo's and Idiots, Eremits and Friers
> White, Black and Grey, with all thir trumperie.
> Here Pilgrims roam, that stray'd so farr to seek
> In *Golgotha* him dead, who lives in Heav'n;
> And they who to be sure of Paradise
> Dying put on the weeds of *Dominic*,
> Or in *Franciscan* think to pass disguised . . .
> . . . .
> A violent cross wind from either Coast
> Blows them transverse ten thousand Leagues awry
> Into the devious air; then might ye see
> Cowls, Hoods and Habits with their wearers tost
> And flutterd into Raggs, then Reliques, Beads,
> Indulgences, Dispenses, Pardons, Bulls,
> The sport of Winds: all these upwhirl'd aloft
> Fly o're the backside of the World farr off
> Into a *Limbo* large and broad, since calld
> The Paradise of Fools. . . .
> (*PL* 3.474–80, 487–96)

King observes that Milton "returns to territory traversed by *Of Reformation* and *An Apology against Smectymnuus*."[25] Indeed so; but it is in an idiom well known to Luther himself. That hint of the scatological ("the backside of the world") would not have been out of place from the Ur-reformer's pen.

It remains aesthetically challenging, literally a descent from the sublime to the ridiculous, and one that, in its disturbing prolepsis, requires a slightly clumsy justification in terms of the narrative sequence; the region is "to few unknown / Long after, now unpeopl'd, and untrod" (*PL* 3.496–99). What has Milton to gain from the disruption in narrative and the risk to decorum?

The answer rests in the earlier debate in heaven, which contains Milton's fullest depiction in poetry of the Son of God in relationship to the Father as well as his most explicit poetic exposition of his doctrine of salvation; both, of course, are major preoccupations and sites of controversy in *De Doctrina Christiana*. Quite how heterodox are Milton's views on the Son remains opaque in the epic, though as Maurice Kelley well demonstrated, if the reader has the treatise open at his or her elbow, at least some of the anti-Trinitarianism can be discerned.[26] The doctrine of salvation, however, could scarcely be clearer. Milton allows for special provision extended to a tiny minority, the elect: "Some I have chosen of peculiar grace / Elect above the rest" (*PL* 3.183–84). For the rest of humankind, however, a synergy between grace and the free will of the individual believer is the route to salvation (*PL* 3.185–202). Predestination on the Calvinist model plays no part: "Man shall not quite be lost, but sav'd who will, / Yet not of will in him, but grace in me / Freely voutsaft" (*PL* 3.173–75).

In terms of censorship and personal safety, Milton could develop the broadly Arminian model with impunity. It was the doctrine of salvation widely held among senior members of the national church and by any career-minded Anglican clergyman of the Restoration period. But it has a problematic history, as a component in the fissures within the Church of England that played a significant part in the origins of the English Civil Wars.[27] Dissenters were surely an important target readership for the epic as part of that "fit audience . . . though few" whom Milton addresses (*PL* 7.31), and Arminianism, in terms of both its history and its anti-Calvinism, often remained at the least unpalatable among those who remained estranged from the national church. As in *De Doctrina Christiana*, Milton associates potentially divisive arguments, indeed potentially disappointing arguments, with an assertion of the common ground that unites all Protestants—in this case a rehearsal, in terms that Luther would have approved, of the absurdities of Catholicism, culminating in a satirical and rather violent flourish of the humiliation of its clergy.

NOTES

1. *Animadversions*, in *CPW*, 1:704; *Tetrachordon*, in *CPW*, 2:707.
2. Daniel Eppley, "Jackson, Henry (1585/6–1662)," in *ODNB*.
3. John Wycliffe, *Wickliffes Wicket, or a Learned and Godly Treatise of the* Sacrament, *Made by John Wickliffe*, ed. Henry Jackson (London, 1612), sig. *4r.
4. Quoted, translated, and discussed by Miri Rubin, *Corpus Christi: The Eucharist in Late Medieval Culture* (Cambridge: Cambridge University Press, 1991), 328. On Baxter, see Norman P. Tanner, "Lollard Women (*act. c.*1390–*c.*1520)," in *ODNB*. The deposition and sentence are transcribed in full in *Heresy Trials in the Diocese of Norwich, 1428–31*, ed. Norman P. Tanner, Camden Fourth Series, vol. 20 (London: Royal Historical Society, 1977), 41–51. Tanner suggests that Baxter "may have been on the lunatic fringe of Lollardy" (20).
5. John Milton, *De Doctrina Christiana*, in *CWJM*, 8:749, 751.
6. John Milton, *Of Reformation*, in *CPW*, 1:525, *Animadversions*, in *CPW*, 1:704, *Reason of Church-Government*, in *CPW*, 1:788, and *Areopagitica*, in *CPW*, 2:502 and 553.
7. *PL*, 5.433–39, 443–44. For a detailed discussion of the passage, see John N. King, *Milton and Religious Controversy: Satire and Polemic in "Paradise Lost"* (Cambridge: Cambridge University Press, 2000), 133–52.
8. *OED*, "transubstantiate," 1. a.
9. Rubin, *Corpus Christi*, 67–68. See also Jaroslav Pelikan, *The Christian Tradition: A History of the Development of Doctrine*, vol. 3, *The Growth of Medieval Theology (600–1300)* (Chicago: University of Chicago Press, 1978), 197–98.
10. Chap. 5 [On the Son of God], in *CWJM*, 8:127–229.
11. Christopher Hill, *The World Turned Upside Down* (1972; repr., Harmondsworth: Penguin, 1978), 179.
12. William Whitaker, *An Answere to the Ten Reasons of Edmund Campion the Jesuit . . . Translated by Richard Stock* (London, 1606), 278. On Stock, see Brett Usher, "Stock, Richard (1568/9–1626)," in *ODNB*, and Gordon Campbell and Thomas N. Corns, *John Milton: Life, Work, and Thought* (Oxford: Oxford University Press, 2008), 14–17. On Whitaker, see C. S. Knighton, "Whitaker, William (1547/8–1595)," in *ODNB*.
13. Campbell and Corns, *Milton*, 165–67.
14. Hill, *World Turned Upside Down*, 179.
15. Whitaker, *Answere*, 237.
16. "An Act touching Marriages and the Registring thereof [August 24, 1653]," in *Acts and Ordinances of the Interregnum*, ed. C. H. Firth and R. S. Rait (London: HMSO, 1911), 2:715–18.

17. *A Directory for The Publique Worship of* God, *Throughout the Three Kingdoms of* England, Scotland, *and* Ireland (London, 1644 [i.e., 1645]), 58.

18. Campbell and Corns, *Milton,* 268, 323.

19. John Coffey, *Persecution and Toleration in Protestant England, 1558–1689* (Harlow: Longman, 2000), 134–42.

20. Hill, *World Turned Upside Down,* 368.

21. *Animadversions,* in *CPW,* 1:731.

22. "Whitaker," in *ODNB.*

23. John Milton, *Paradise Lost,* ed. Alastair Fowler (1998; repr., London, Longman, 1999), 3.444–97n.

24. John N. King, "Milton's Paradise of Fools: Ecclesiastical Satire in *Paradise Lost,*" in *Catholicism and Anti-Catholicism in Early Modern English Texts,* ed. Arthur F. Marotti (Basingstoke: Macmillan, 1999), 198–217.

25. King, "Milton's Paradise of Fools," 201.

26. Maurice Kelley, *This Great Argument: A Study of Milton's "De doctrina Christiana" as a Gloss upon "Paradise Lost"* (Princeton, NJ: Princeton University Press, 1941), particularly chap. 4.

27. For the classic account, see Nicholas Tyacke, *Anti-Calvinists: The Rise of English Arminianism, c. 1590–1640* (Oxford: Oxford University Press, 1987).

CHAPTER 5

"HOW GIRD THE SPHEAR"?

Catholic Spain in Milton's Poetry

ANGELICA DURAN

In demonstrating the persistent anti-Catholicism in the prose works of
John Milton, scholars have demonstrated some aspects of its attendant
anti-Hispanism and in turn have redressed John Shawcross's assessment
in 1998 that "little has been written about Milton and Iberia."[1] Such a
redress seems imperative given the broad characterization of Milton as a
spokesperson for early modern English views of Spain: both the *Oxford
English Dictionary* and the *Century Dictionary and Cyclopedia* quote Milton's *Of Reformation of Church-Discipline in England* (1641) as an illumi-
nating example of the term *Hispaniolized* and its variants: "A Tympany
of *Spaniolized Bishops* swaggering in the fore-top of the State" (*CPW*,
1:587). While the *Century Dictionary and Cyclopedia* defines the term
Hispaniolized rather innocuously as "to make Spanish in character or sentiment," in practice, early modern English writers generally deployed the
term adversely to refer to the imperial depredations and close-minded
religiosity of their Catholic neighbors to the south, often in contrast to

the national and religious traits worthy of English citizens.[2] The Miltonic passage, like so many others in Milton's and his contemporaries' political works, merges the national ("*Spaniolized*") and the religious ("*Bishops*").

Such mergings and characterizations are rhetorically effective for the political arguments and immediate audiences of specific prose works. When writing prose with his "left hand," as he termed it in *The Reason of Church Government* (1642) (*CPW*, 1:808), Milton seethes at Spain as the conjoined hireling of the Roman Catholic Church.[3] In the work, Milton argues that a prelaty in the fashion of "*Italy* and *Spaine*" promotes "a num and chil stupidity of soul, an unactive blindnesse of minde"; and in his later *The Ready and Easy Way* (1660), he asks, "What liberty of conscience can we then expect from others far worse principl'd from the cradle, traind up and governd by *Popish* and *Spanish* counsels?" (*CWJM*, 6:515). Citizens raised in Catholic countries can hardly avoid Catholic error. Yet while Catholicism was concentrated in some geographic spaces it was not confined geographically or even institutionally; as Andrew Hadfield writes in a sensitive summary of Milton's prose, "For Milton Catholicism was a variety of customs and conventions rather than simply an institution."[4]

It is when writing with his right hand as a "poet soaring in the high regions of this fancies" that Milton creates works "so written to after-times, as they should not willingly let [them] die" (*CPW*, 1:808, 810). Thus his poetry is written for a different audience and with different aims. It is also in Milton's poems that we encounter the "regions" of Spain at times untethered from or differently associated with Roman Catholicism. Thus I focus here on Milton's poetic representations that prioritize Spain over Roman Catholicism at large. Such a parsing is indeed a hard task given that, for example, such anti-Catholic sentiment as the Paradise of Fools passage of *Paradise Lost* contains subtle reference to Spain, since the founder of the Dominican "Black" Friars is the Spanish priest Dominic de Guzman (*PL* 2.475).[5] Indeed, I use Raphael's caution about subjective interpretations as he sets out to respond to Adam's query about cosmography, "how gird the Sphear [?]" (*PL* 8.82), because it so vividly speaks to the interpretive "cycle and epicycle" that confront anyone seeking to construct valid interpretations of the "Sphear" of Milton's poetic representation: the difficulty of deciphering which ideas and characterizations the poetry itself triggers and which scholars may perhaps too insistently bring to their readings.

While I in no way claim that Milton's poems express Hispanophilia, I do claim that, in some poetic moments, Milton rearticulates what he has learned about Spain—its landscape, people, and ancient heritage—as an integral part of God's creation and as Christendom and that he integrates Spain as part of his larger vision of the fallen world rather than as a recalcitrant, specifically Catholic Other. Such an assessment may be as surprising to some as it is obvious to others. In what follows, I do not survey all of Milton's poetic representations of Spain but rather emphasize key instances from Milton's early, middle, and later poetry that most clearly evince how persistently Milton's sympathy with Spain as a fallen land and as a fungible nation of fellow fallen humans develops in the course of his poetry, an emphasis that I hope can be integrated with approaches to his prose representations, as well as other poetic ones, to obtain a fuller vision of the relation of Milton's poetry both to Spain and to its Catholicism.

SPAIN IN MILTON'S EARLY POETRY

It is clear from entries in the commonplace books of Milton and his English contemporaries that Spanish presence in England was generally associated with Catholic presence and the international relations fostered by the many-handed, politically active Roman Church. Annual commemorations of Guy Fawkes Day, the thwarted attack of November 5, 1605, on King James I and the English leadership at the House of Lords, was one mechanism for transmitting anti-Catholic and anti-Hispanic sentiment. Indeed, Milton's clearest sentiments of anti-Hispanism lie within his early poems, the six Gunpowder Plot poems, all "probably written for an academic celebration of the nation's deliverance from Catholic treachery on Guy Fawkes Day" during Milton's Cambridge days:[6] the four Latin epigrams, "On the Gunpowder Plot" ("In Proditionem Bombardicam") and three under the title "On the Same" ("In Eandem"); the related epigram "On the Inventor of Gunpowder" ("In Inventorem Bombardae"); and the Latin epic-in-miniature, "On the Fifth of November" ("In Quintum Novembris"). None of the epigrams mentions Spain. "In Quintum Novembris" does and is particularly consistent in using spatial terms to characterize neighboring Spain as a threat against the nearby

British Isles and as an underling in the Roman Catholic Church's international system.

Catholic Spain, Italy, and France, rather than specific human agents, harass Protestant England. The poem begins with a vista of the "widely expansive realms of Albion" (2–3). Even the name of Albion might recall violence in English-Spanish geographic encounters. In *History of Britain*, Milton notes that in pre-Christian times the namesake "Albion, the Giant" was supposed to have "rul'd it 44 years. Till at length passing over into *Gaul*, in aid of his Brother *Lestrygon*, against whom *Hercules* was hasting out of *Spain* into *Italy*, he was there slain in fight."[7]

"In Quintum Novembris" depicts a now-Protestant England as pitted against the devil, the "fierce tyrant" who finds aid from the "tamer of kings," the pope settled in Rome (7, 74).[8] Indeed, the evil spirit of faction comes to England from Continental shores: "And now there come into view the white land, its cliffs resounding to the noise of waves, and the country beloved of the Sea God, to which Neptune's offspring had in times past given his name" (25–27). The devil spurs the pope against England by reminding him first of international clashes between England and Spain. The devil enjoins the pope to recall the foiled Spanish Armada of 1588 during Queen Elizabeth I's reign: "ever mindful of the past, avenge Hesperias scattered fleet and the Iberian standards drowned in the wide deep, and the bodies of so many holy men nailed to the shameful cross during the recent reign of the Thermodontean maiden" (102–5). Rather than attempting Molochan "open Warr" (*PL* 2.50), the devil recommends a Beelzebubian "advantagious act" (*PL* 2.363), leaving in suspension the possibility that the citizens of two geographically proximate countries to England, "the fierce Gaul or the savage Iberian" ("In Quintum Novembris" 126), may invade.[9]

Milton published these Latin poems in his *Poems of Mr. John Milton* (1645) and *Poems, &c. upon Several Occasions* (1673).[10] They therefore participate in the nationalistic commemorations of the Fifth of November and perpetuate the xenophobia and eventual internecine anti-Catholicism that formed part of early modern English identity. As anti-Hispanism, however, they are rather tepid.

Early modern England's vituperative contributions to the Black Legend of Spanish atrocities in Europe and the Americas are stunning in their wit and dexterity.[11] In the long poem *The Unmasking of Murther, or a Briefe Declaration of the Catholike-intended Treason, Lately Discovered* (1606), "I.H." rails against "These Tygrish blood-sworne Jesuites, / Spanized British slaves."[12] The poem indicates Spain as the plot's breeding ground when introducing Robert Catesby's ally Thomas Winter, "who before had been imployed into *Spain*" (2). The poem's reference to the English plotter Winter as "Don Thomazo" indistinguishably Hispanizes or Italianizes him and the other plotters. Such a move is to be found in many other Gunpowder Plot poems, such as "Novembris Monstrum," with its reference to "Don Pluto" (25). While Milton's "In Quintum Novembris" includes one reference to the Spanish Armada's thwarted attack on England in 1588, *The Unmasking of Murther* recalls "*Rome's* Armado *Spain*" repeatedly and clearly characterizes the 1605 Plot as its delayed sequel. Samuel Clarke's variously republished *Englands Remembrancer: A True and Full Narrative of Those Two Never to Be Forgotten Deliverances: One from the Spanish Invasion in 88, the Other from the Hellish Powder Plot, November 5, 1605* (1657) represents Spain as subordinate to Rome, belittling "*Spayne*" as "envy's mother, Malice nurserie, / Squinting with both those eyes at her, that [] / This stripling Ile in strength the world outvie" (64).

The second verse of one of the most enduring ballads of the genre, "Remember, Remember the Fifth of November," focuses its verbal attacks on the Roman Catholic pope, a position not held by a Spaniard since Rodrigo Borgia, Pope Alexander VI (1431–1503, r. 1492–1503): "Burn him in a tub of tar. / Burn him like a blazing star. / Burn his body from his head. / Then we'll say ol' Pope is dead."[13] John Vicar's *Mischeefes Mysterie or Treasons Master-peece, The Powder-plot* (1617) maintains a similarly zealous stance but shifts the object of "hatred" from the papal person to papal doctrines in this passage:

> Preach and proclaime, with heart, tongue, pen & voice,
> With thanks and praise, each houre, month and yeare,
> Yea, teach thy childrens children to rejoice,
> For this so great deliuerance. And to beare
> > A deadly hatred, zealous detestation,
> > Of *Romes* false *Doctrines*, foule abhomination.[14]

The ending of Milton's "In Quintum Novembris" redirects its readers' attention even further: "But meanwhile the Heavenly Father pities his people from on high and obstructs the papists' cruel venture; they are captured and dragged off to severe punishments. But pious incense and grateful honours are offered up to God. All the crossroads rejoice as smoke rises from festive bonfires; crowds of young people dance, and in the whole year the arrival of no other day is marked with greater celebration than is the Fifth of November" (220–26). Rather than employing the imperative of "Remember, Remember" and *Mischeefes Mysterie* to foster present hostility, "In Quintum Novembris" summarizes the plotters' past punishments and focuses on God and on present thanksgiving. Milton's poem quickly moves the offenders offstage and leaves readers with recent memories of or in preparation for November Fifth revels. While "In Quintum Novembris" has been discussed in terms of the epic and tragic strategies Milton later uses in *Paradise Lost, Paradise Regained,* and *Samson Agonistes,* its ending can also be thought of in terms of the ending of *A Mask Presented at Ludlow Castle,* which prepares its audience for ensuing revels. As is particularly clear from a contrast of Milton's Gunpowder Plot poems to others', Milton draws attention to the schisms to which fallen humans are heir but does not strongly activate anti-Hispanic attitudes or target individuals.

Milton's "Third Elegy" ("Elegia Tertia," composed 1626) also keys in on Spain's geographical location, retaining it as an ancient locale in a dream vision of the blessed afterlife of the recently deceased Lancelot Andrewes, bishop of Winchester. The narrator represents the sun setting on the Spanish coast, the "Tartessian sea" (33), rather than an English coast, even though it too lies on the western edge of Europe, then complements this image with an image of another watery Spanish site in the narrator's dream of Andrewes's heavenly reward: "Silver streams wash the burgeoning plains, the sand is golden, richer than the Hesperian Tagus" (45–46). Ovid in his *Metamorphoses* had memorialized the golden sands of the river Tagus, the longest river of the Iberian Peninsula, that flowed through southern Spain into the Atlantic at Lisbon, in describing Phaethon's enthralling vistas during his ill-fated flight of the chariot of the sun: "The gold that Tagus carries in his sands / Ran molten in the flames" (2.251).[15] In contrast to Ovid, who describes blazing sands due to Phaethon's inexpert hand, Milton represents a landscape bathed "with crimson light just as when the mountain-slopes become red in the morning sun" (39–40) and the English bishop walking untroubled through flowery fields, whose beauty trumps ancient hubris and the violent effects on natural landscapes. Milton mythologizes the erstwhile Spanish and Portuguese locale as a site of profound beauty, the appropriate locale for Andrewes to "be forever free from cruel hardship" (64).[16] Perhaps it is easier for Milton to do so since the watery locale is far from England, in southern rather than northern Spain. In the event, it is a far cry from the extensive and obvious anti-Catholicism in Milton's allusion to the Roman Pantheon and St. Peter's Basilica in the description of the building of Hell's Pandemonium in *Paradise Lost* (1.710–17).

By the time the "Third Elegy" was republished in *Poems, &c. upon Several Occasions*, the river Tagus would have accrued more immediate associations for Milton and his English contemporaries. In March 1649, the site was the harbor that Admiral Robert Blake blockaded to threaten the nephew of King Charles I of England, Prince Rupert of the Rhine, who regularly attacked Commonwealth ships. But at the time of the poem's initial composition, it is possible that there was an underlying sense of conciliation between England and Spain in the image, since Andrewes's appointment as bishop of Winchester (1618–26) was viewed as based on his theological stances, which could bridge English-Spanish/Protestant-Catholic divides.[17]

SPAIN IN MILTON'S MIDDLE POETRY

Milton's two most widely read midcareer poetic works, *A Mask* (1634) and "Lycidas" (1637), evince as keen an awareness of the geographical proximity of England and Spain as do the two early Latin poems. Religious associations, however, are severely minimized in these occasional works. Further, Milton's poetic strategies, rather than eliciting discomfort toward external Others, focus on responsibility and threat from within.

Spain is directly referred to early on in *A Mask*, when the Attendant Spirit mentions Comus's promiscuous travels. In addition to fictive locales like Comus's eastern homeland of "*Circes* Iland," *A Mask* refers to "*Tuscan* Mariners," the "*Tyrrhene* shore," "th' *Indian* steep," and other environs (48, 49, 139). Comus is depicted as a non-native threat whose last stops before reaching the Welsh landscape are nearby France and Spain: "ripe, and frolick of his full grown age, / Roaving the *Celtick*, and *Iberian* fields, / [He] At last betakes him to this ominous wood" (59–61). These two locales are either the perfect places for Comus to pick up the undesirable habits that he then practices in Ludlow's "wilde Wood" (opening stage direction) or the unfortunate sites of his earlier forays.[18] The stage directions tell us that "Comus *enters . . . with a rout of Monsters, headed like sundry sorts of wild Beasts, but otherwise like Men and Women*," unfortunate if willing victims who comprise the "most [who] do taste through fond intemperate thirst" Comus's tempting liquor (stage directions after 92, 67). There is nothing to indicate that the monsters have immigrated with Comus. Thus Milton does not construct England as possessing a national virtue distinct from that of France or Spain. Further, neither France nor Spain is represented as the threat: Comus or a personal lack of temperance is.

The allusion to Spain in "Lycidas" is much stronger, when the narrator painfully imagines Edward King's body buffeted by the sea, perhaps "beyond the stormy *Hebrides*," or sleeping "Where the great vision of the guarded Mount / Looks towards *Namancos* and *Bayona*'s hold" (156, 161–62).[19] The two imaged locales—the Hebrides, the archipelago off Scotland, and St. Michael Mount, in Cornwall, from which can be seen the northwest district of Galician Spain—are invoked because they give a sense of just how "far away" the "sounding Seas" may have "hurld" King's corpse from the shipwreck in Anglesey (154–55). These places also give a sense of the natural ("stormy") and social ("guarded" and "hold") elements that mark not only King's storm-tossed body but also England's coast, and even its body politic, if we recall the many military actions that occurred at these two sites. Perhaps the most well-known literary representation of the Hebrides as the nexus point of external and internal military rebellion is in Shakespeare's *Macbeth*, in the Sergeant's description of the supplies the rebel Macdonwald received from the "Western Isles," to no avail against the (then) dutiful Macbeth.[20]

Milton's pastoral elegy "Lycidas" refers to many places, as does *A Mask*, but its mode and genre interact with such references quite differently, especially since the Ludlow drama was composed for a specific performance at a specific geographical place. The pastoral locale, the *locus amoenus*, is a persistent convention in the pastoral mode. As Paul Alpers notes, however, a distinctive feature of the setting of "Lycidas" is that there is "no traditional gathering of shepherds."[21] While Milton refers to Namancos and Bayona, Hebron, Galilee, Sicily, and other locales, he does not follow the pastoral convention of situating the readers or singers—or even the object of attention, King's buffeted body—in a bounded landscape or geographical space.[22] Lawrence Lipking notes that, in terms of geographical place, the poem is more unfixedly Miltonic than fixedly pastoral: "As usual Milton's maps cover time as well as space, identifying each site through its historic or legendary associations."[23] Indeed, in "Lycidas," the centrifugal forces of universalization are at least equal to and possibly greater than the centripetal forces of particularization. A. S. P. Woodhouse notes of the "perilous flood," which so pithily refers lamenting readers back to the Irish Sea where King died, that it refers finally to the whole world, bringing together "the excessively local and the excessively cosmic aspects."[24] The cultural shorthand of "flood" for Noah's biblical flood over "the face of the earth" (Gen. 7:4) is indeed present here, as it is so vigorously imagined "[b]eyond all bounds" nearly a quarter of a century later in *Paradise Lost* (11.828).

Such an unbounded representation of setting and geographical place culminates in the "fresh Woods and Pastures new" of the final line of "Lycidas" (193). Poetic representation culminates to speak predominantly to a human and universal rather than national or regional condition. Before (in the title) and during the poem (8, 9, and 10; 49 and 51; 166, 172, and 182), the very name Milton chooses for the poetic stand-in for the recently deceased Edward King, Lycidas, signals the larger context. It is the name Milton uses for this particular "Friend" (headnote) and the name used by the Sicilian writer of the Greek Theocritus, the Turkish writer of Greek Bion, the Gaulic-Roman writer of Latin Virgil, the Ibero-Roman writer of Latin Lucan, and now the Anglo-British writer of English Milton. Right after the last of the three clusters of the use of the name Lycidas and after the Noachian allusion, the "uncouth Swain" appears in a "Western bay" that is associated predominantly not with the "Irish Seas" but rather with a liminal space within an all-place (186, 191, headnote).

The larger engagement of "Lycidas" with geographic place must inform what we say about any place-names in the poem, Spanish ones being the most germane here. Editor John Carey notes of Namancos and

Bayona that "the two names represent the threat of Spanish Catholicism" and John Leonard more broadly, and more perspicaciously, links them to "the threat of Catholicism."[25] What is the degree of specifically Spanish threat? Lawrence Lipking views the threat as substantial: "Namancos and the castle of Bayona represent Britain's external enemy, lying in wait for a chink in the armor through which Catholic venom can pour."[26] Lipking's reading moderates Milton's well-used hyperbole by noting of the "genius of the shore" that, "like any border guard, it can shift in a moment from keeping out to keeping in and is never more effective than when its territorial claims can be presented as an extension of communal goodwill. Whether warding against Catholic Spain or melting with ruth at the internal breach that has struck home, Saint Michael stands for England."[27]

A number of poetic strategies represent the external threat as not an immediate one. First, mention of Spain is limited to two lines in a 193-line poem. Second, the use of ancient names rather than contemporary Galicia conjures Spain as an ancient enemy, not a present one, though these categories are not mutually exclusive. Third, Bayona has strong connotations of a contemporary Spain on the defensive, not the offensive. Bayona was the town that repelled the attacks of English vice-admiral Sir Francis Drake in 1585 and where King Philip II of Spain beat back pirates that were laying waste to the Galician coast in 1590. Then too, these two Spanish locales are paired with Scotland, just as in *A Mask* the Iberian fields are paired with French ones. Considered together, the pairings indicate a generalized external threat from nearby locales rather than a specifically Spanish one. Finally, as Lipking notes, Milton positions Lycidas's body potentially on England's shores looking toward Spain only to call on the "Angel now"—ambiguously Lycidas or the angel Michael—to "Look homeward . . . and melt with ruth" (163). As with *A Mask*, the more immediate threat is native. The poetic volta turns its back on the distraction of even the most persistent xenophobic threats.

The very lightness and paucity of Milton's representations of Spain in *A Mask* and "Lycidas" diminish their emotional force. The masque and pastoral elegy depict an entangled and entangling international context outside its borders and actively relocate attention to native environs, needs, and communities. Moreover, these Miltonic instances of evocation, then dismissal of Spain participate in the mid-seventeenth-century evolution of the English branch of the Black Legend, which shifted from representing Spain as a commanding threat to representing it as a waning power.

SPAIN IN MILTON'S LATE POETRY

Reaching valid interpretations of Milton's representations of Spain in *Paradise Lost, Paradise Regained*, and *Samson Agonistes* is complicated by their historical context, the complexity of their genres, and readers'— including critics'—stakes and commitments. R. A. Stradling has shown that, especially "between 1661 and 1663, Anglo-Spanish relations remained in a state of severe crisis, verging on war."[28] Thus English authors could count on even light allusions to Spain to ignite latent and smoldering Hispanophobia in some of their readers. The nature of Hispanophobia in England would likely have changed significantly during the second half of the seventeenth century, not only because of England's own governmental transformation but also because of Spain's significant imperial decline, especially as marked by its European territorial losses via the 1659 Treaty of the Pyrenees. Moreover, individual authors' own predispositions are hard to gauge. For example, there was no love lost between Milton and either the Restoration government of his homeland England or its longtime but weakening enemy Spain. Thus Milton may not have felt entirely antipathetic about Spain's support of the rebellious elements in Ireland that revealed the political imperfections of the restored English monarchy. It is a tension we see in Milton's self-designation as "John Milton, Englishman," yet his definition of "one's *Patria*" as "wherever it is well with" oneself (*CPW*, 8:4).

How to ensure that salient contexts inform but do not govern textual interpretation, especially with such complex genres as epic and tragedy? One way at least with *Paradise Lost, Paradise Regained*, and *Samson Agonistes* is to deal with the representations that directly refer to Spain specifically rather than to Catholicism more generally. By this careful wording, I seek to screen out representations in which the more general target of Catholicism is prioritized, as in the Paradise of Fools passage of *Paradise Lost* mentioned earlier. Even when these are excluded, it is clear that informed readers can readily associate Catholicism with Milton's representations of Spain; the task, however, is to determine how strong those associations are amid the representations of Spain in Milton's later works, which are truly stunning in their bittersweet beauty.

In the early books of *Paradise Lost*, geographical references to Spain exploit its nature as a borderland, and by extension, bellicose site. Early on in the epic is the Fontarrabia simile in which the narrator describes Satan preening over the puissance of his reawakened hellish warriors (1.585–87). Many editors note Milton's reference to *"Fontarabbia"* (1.587) as the locale of the climax of the French *Song of Roland*, forty miles from the scene of the battle of Roncevalles, at the Spanish Pyrenees where the Saracens massacred Charlemagne's rear guard. This simile displays the dazzling ability of literature to record resonances between the past and the present, the imaginary and the historical. Neil Harris explains of Milton's similes generally that "on the surface the Miltonic simile appears as a digression or a pleasant resting point in the narrative, but in reality it exploits the comparative device to express a split, conflictual viewpoint, in which the story being told belongs to one chronological and geographical context and the thing to which it is compared to quite another."[29] To that temporal and locational split I add the attendant split in sympathies. Milton conjures Fontarabbia only after he has guided readers to locales that draw a myriad of human emotions and international alliances:

> For never since created man,
> Met such imbodied force, as nam'd with these
> Could merit more then that small infantry
> Warr'd on by Cranes: though all the Giant brood
> Of *Phlegra* with th' Heroic Race were joyn'd
> That fought at *Theb's* [in Greece] and *Ilium* [in Turkey], on each side
> Mixd with auxiliar Gods; and what resounds
> In Fable or *Romance* of *Uthers* Son
> Begirt with *British* and *Armoric* [from Brittany] Knights;
> And all who since, Baptiz'd or Infidel
> Jousted in *Aspramont* [in Italy] or *Montalban* [in Gascony],
> *Damasco* [in Syria] or *Marocco* [in North Africa], or *Trebisond*
>   [on the Black Sea],
> Or whom *Biserta* [in Tunisia] sent from *Afric* shore

When *Charlemain* with all his peerage fell
By *Fontarabbia* [in northern Spain].

(1.573–87)

The final place-name of Fontarabbia is the most direct reference to Spain, but a complicated one. Already wresting readers back to the eighth century and northwest from Tunisia to the Spanish Basque town beside the estuary of the Bidasoa River, Milton explodes the transnational nature of the site in his choice of place-name: not the Spanish *Fuenterrabia* or French *Fontarrabie*, but the "italianate exonym."[30] Harris details other geographical "inexactitudes" related to the primary allusion of the site, to Charlemagne's legend and to "the siege and battle there in 1638, when French forces commanded by the Prince de Condé destroyed the town by shelling, but failed to overcome the stubborn resistance of its defenders" and of "the town's role in the late summer of 1659 as meeting place for what became known as the Treaty of the Pyrenees."[31] Many editions of *Paradise Lost* note the thwarted work of unification of Christian forces at this Spanish locale, whether of legend or recent history, whether that of Charlemagne or that of the similarly named English Charles I, and thus this passage's compression of the dangers of admiration that readers may have, indeed should have, for Satan's legions and any legions.

In another allusion in hell, the sympathy for Spaniards is decidedly greater, and equally complicated. The rebel angels respond to "thir great Sultan" like the "barbarous Sons [who] / Came like a Deluge on the South, and spread / Beneath *Gibralter* to the *Libian* sands" (1.348, 353–55). Milton exploits the location of the promontory of Gibraltar—again in the south, as in "Elegia Tertia"—Spain's closest point to Africa, separating from north to south Christendom and the African lands of infidels, and from west to east the Atlantic from the Mediterranean. He represents the dangers that Hispanic inhabitants repeatedly confronted as myriads convened at this seaport on their way to conquer other lands.[32] In A *Defence of the English People* (1651), Milton refers to "Diocletian and Maximianus," the co-emperors famous for their scorched-earth tactics as they moved from north to south, with Roman campaigns against Germanic tribes in the Rhine early in their reign (286–305 CE) and against Moorish pirates in Iberia and Mauretania later (*CPW*, 4.1:465). Milton perhaps seeks to trigger such a transhistoric, transnational sense in the slow-motion scene shortly after the attention-grabbing "Say, Muse" by restating the visual image of "thir great Sultan" as the auditory image of "thir great Emperors call" (*PL* 1.376, 378). We are put in a position to sympathize with those who witnessed or became the collateral damage of such a fearsome onslaught, which is to say, to sympathize with Spaniards.[33]

These two poetic examples refer to *Hispania*, called so starting roughly 200 BCE, before it emerged as the unified country *Spain* in the fifteenth century,[34] and concurrently as Catholic Spain rather than as part of the Christendom that preceded the Reformation. While a number of other representations of Spain in *Paradise Lost* deserve attention, I turn to those at the end of the epic, in Michael's prophecy in books 11 and 12, because they direct Adam on how to interpret future history, and by extension readers on how to read backwards into the epic's previous representations.

In relation to a Spain that was historically closer to Milton, the hemispheric view that the angel Michael reveals to Adam (11.379) is particularly problematic. Transitioning past Adam's ken, the narrator hypothesizes that Adam's

> Eye might there command wherever stood
> City of old or modern Fame, the Seat
> Of mightiest Empire, from the destind Walls
> Of *Cambalu* [capital city of Mongolian Cathay], seat of *Cathaian* Can
> And *Samarchand* by *Oxus* [in Uzbekistan], *Temirs* Throne,
> To *Paquin* [Peking/Beijing, China] of *Sinaean* Kings, and thence
> . . . from *Niger* Flood to *Atlas* Mount
> The Kingdoms of *Almansor*, *Fez* and *Sus*,
> *Marocco* and *Algiers*, and *Tremisen*;
> On *Europe* thence, and where *Rome* was to sway
> The World: in Spirit perhaps he also saw
> Rich *Mexico* the seat of *Motezume*,
> And *Cusco* in *Peru*, the richer seat
> Of *Atabalipa*, and yet unspoil'd
> *Guiana*, whose great Citie *Geryons* Sons
> Call *El Dorado*.

(11.385–90, 402–11)

The extension of the epic vista convention to include the entire globe contains a possible allusion to the Spanish Empire, which from King Charles V's reign (1516–56) through the seventeenth century was defined famously as "el imperio en el que nunca se pone el sol" (the empire on which the sun never sets) before the United Kingdom took over the slogan in the nineteenth century. Anglophone editors have not associated the vision with Spain's vast empire. The first two full Spanish translations of the epic, however, might be seen as indicating some Spanish religio-political discomfiture with the panoramic view. The 1812 Juan de Escóiquiz Spanish translation silently and entirely omits the lines from "Of mightiest Empire" until "but to nobler sights / *Michael* from *Adams* eyes the Filme remov'd" (11.387, 411–12).[35] The 1813 Benito Hermida Spanish translation omits lines 388 to 412 from the text but includes them in an endnote, noting the rationale for the omission to be to "better conserve the cohesion in the discourse" (para conservar mejor la union en el discurso).[36] As it turns out, readers are cautioned to take translator Hermida at his word, at least in part and perhaps in full, about this titillating omission, given that a similar endnote refers to the same omission in the 1805 Jacques Delille French translation.[37]

The explicit references to Spanish sites in this passage are lines 402 to 406, which juxtapose a Spain and North Africa conquered by the Muslim Almansor, a Europe governed by "Rome" or the Holy Roman Emperor, and parts of the Americas conquered under the aegis of the Catholic monarchs ("Reyes Católicos") Queen Isabella I of Castile and King Ferdinand II of Aragon.[38] This ambivalence is part of the moralizing vision of Michael's prophecy. The passage alludes, as might be expected, to the depredations of foreigners, like "*Geryons* Sons," Spaniards who named the Guianan "great Citie," likely Manoa. Simultaneously, it alludes to the English Sir Walter Raleigh, who explored Guiana near the Orinoco in 1595. Thus for Milton's original readers, this transatlantic territory would be associated with both foreign (Spanish) and native (English) agents, even though it was, at the time, the territory of Spain and had been that of Native Americans until shortly before.

Milton's vision here asks all readers to rethink the epic's earlier simile comparing the fallen Adam and Eve, in their makeshift leafy garments, to the Native Americans found by early modern American colonizers: "Such of late / *Columbus* found th' *American* so girt / With featherd Cincture, naked else and wilde / Among the Trees on Iles and woodie shores" (9.1115–18). The poetic line is ambivalent in terms of the nature of the relationship between Columbus and "th'*American*," requiring a great readerly *ecstasis* to stand outside of one's temporal identity and any national identity. In *Second Defence of the English People* (1654), Milton articulates a popular perception of Native Americans as idolatrous and therefore contemptible. Milton decries the superstitions wrought by the Roman Catholic Church, after the early church but before the Reformation, as "a barbarism fouler than that which stains the Indians, themselves the most stupid of mortals. The Indians indeed worship as gods malevolent demons whom they cannot exorcize" (*CPW*, 4.1:551). As J. Martin Evans's *The Imperial Epic* argues convincingly, Milton's epic depicts a wide range of attitudes towards American natives that do little to help readers secure allegiances in this ambivalent passage. What is clear is that the passage signals the famous initial encounter of Americans and Europeans in the Americas. By referring to the Spanish-funded but Genoan-born Columbus, the simile reinforces Spain's precedence in encounters in the Americas and its continuing transnational status, but as a leader rather than an underling to the Roman Catholic Church, as in some of the other passages discussed.[39]

The concentrated image contributes to the larger argument of this section of the epic, that so many individuals in human history will act unethically, leaving themselves and others without "rest or ease of Mind" and often with "high Passions, Anger, Hate, / Mistrust, Suspicion, Discord" (9.1120, 1123–24)—a lamentable consequence and one that readers are invited to prevent. The image capaciously presents the benevolent narrator investing this juncture of the epic's plot in the historical "Miltonic moment . . . , immediately before the plot [of American and European history] undergoes a dramatic change of course,"[40] and in doing so reminds readers of the opportunities for benevolence toward all Others.

Another, often overlooked, allusion to Spain occurs in the first part of the vision, in the geographical East "Of *Cambalu* . . . To *Paquin*," which also compounds the ethical and religious elements of Spain's maritime advances. One of the most visible organizations in restructuring the international reach of the Roman Catholic Church's Counter-Reformation was the Jesuit order, spearheaded by Ignatius of Loyola, or San Ignacio de Loyola as he was known in his homeland Spain, and therefore closely allied with Spain. From its founding in 1540, the Jesuits' strong missionary outreach made it the lightning-rod for Protestant concerns about the Roman Catholic Church's impact outside of Europe. Imperial extension is certainly embedded in the Oriental image of Satan gathering his rebel troops in the newly set up Pandemonium:

> High on a Throne of Royal State, which far
> Outshon the wealth of *Ormus* and of *Ind,*
> Or where the gorgeous East with richest hand
> Showrs on her Kings *Barbaric* Pearl and Gold,
> Satan exalted sat. . . .
>
> (2.1–5)

By 1555, Jesuit Eastern missionary outposts included Hormuz, the "island market in the [Persian] Gulf," along with Ethiopia, Indonesia, Japan, and India, the latter being the famed site of the especially successful work of the Spanish Jesuit St. Francis Xavier (1506–52).[41] John P. Donnelly summarizes the state of affairs succinctly: "The second half of the sixteenth century was a golden age of Catholic missionary work in Asia and the Americas. . . . During the first half of the sixteenth century the success of the Protestant Reformation in winning whole nations away from Rome made Catholics defensive and discouraged, but that changed gradually after 1550 as news of Catholic missionary work spread. . . . Catholicism was gradually sinking roots in Asia, Africa, and the Americas that would compensate for losses in Europe."[42] Milton was aware of the rhetorical force of alluding to Jesuits, given that they were so well known as Spanish missionaries and protectors of their form of Catholicism, not always appreciated by Rome.[43] The tactic Satan proposes to Beelzebub for the Demonic Council mirrors the perceived tactic of the Jesuits. Just as the Jesuits replaced the western European losses prompted by the Protestant Reformation with Asian, African, and American souls, the rebel angels seek to "confound" the inhabitants of the "new world" and seduce them to "our Party" (2.382, 403, 367).

The valence of the English royal image complicates our determination of the strength of the image's allusion to Spain and its Hispano-Catholic mission. Richard DuRocher brings to bear a variety of evidence—anecdotal, art historical, contextual, and literary—that aligns the Satan of this passage and King Charles II on the basis of "their shared mode of dress and imperial styles."[44] Barbara Lewalski erases the Spanish Catholic brokers of Asian commodities to Europe in her alignment of "the accoutrements of ostentatious splendor and absolutist tyranny commonly associated with Asiatic despots and sultans" and Milton's view of "the Stuart ideology of divine kingship."[45] Moreover, given that the simile subordinates all shows of earthly wealth to the infernal throne, it reproves all European countries where mercantile rather than spiritual Eastern riches were valued. The multivalent simile thus contributes to the emphasis on personal rather than national accountability in Michael's prophecy. I do not, for example, find Michael's prophecy to be a rebuke particular to the hard-hearted Israelites any more than to all of humanity who do not follow God after his First Coming. Indeed, the point of Michael's harrowing prophecy is to enable Adam, and by extension readers, to affiliate with potential Others in order to recognize personal error and seek to avoid it. The allusions to Spanish places thus function for readers in ways similar to Michael's caution to Adam and Eve shortly after he announces their expulsion from the place of Eden. Michael enjoins Eve against being "over-fond" of her "Native Soile" and Adam against building the "many grateful Altars" he imagines "rear[ing]" to demarcate some places as more "Divine," more important than others (11.289, 270 and 292, 323, 319). As Michael asserts, God is to be "found alike" in all places (11.350).

Place can indeed be a temptation, as *Paradise Regained* (1674) so pervasively indicates in its elaboration of the subtlety, complexity, and sheer beauty of the temptations of Spain, as place per se and as a figure of the Other. *Paradise Regained* is particularly important because it is set at the moment of the establishment of Christianity and revolves around the figure who established it. Given the setting of time and place in *Paradise Regained*, Milton represents the Hispania that would become Catholic Spain with the traits that Hispania contributed to Christendom's formation, including its shared status with that other outskirt precinct of the Roman Empire, Britannia. *Paradise Regained* extends the standard early modern English representations of Spain to convey imperialism as a perversion of the understandable desire of acquiring "marvelous possessions," to invoke Stephen Greenblatt's eminently relevant concept, and to flesh out the impulse to naturalize the exotic.[46] Correlatively, this nuanced complex of Hispanic associations calls attention to the enduring value of all God's creation, even a fallen one and even those elements that are culturally despised, as Spain was so often in early modern English writings.

Paradise Regained is set during the Roman Republic and Empire before the Roman Empire's association with Christianity, much less Roman Catholicism. The setting provides historical perspective and heightens the emotional import of imperialism, including that of the waning Spanish Empire and the waxing British Empire. During Jesus's lifetime, the Roman Empire was close to reaching its largest territorial extent, in the reign of Trajan (52–117 CE, born in Hispania Baetica) but was far from codifying religious unity in its evolution into the Holy Roman Empire (962–1806). Equally important, Milton's use of the setting highlights the flexibility of national affiliations and their discursive representations, as Britannia and Hispania were, then, two of the outskirt possessions that troubled the Roman Empire.

The first allusion to Spain in *Paradise Regained*, subtle yet foundational, perpetuates Spain's reputation for physical beauty and abundance. Directly preceding the temptation in book 2, Satan chastises Belial for suggesting that he "Set women in his [Jesus's] eye and in his walk" (2.153). Satan reasons against the use of concupiscence with Jesus by providing two examples of chaste restraint, by Alexander the Great and Publius Cornelius Scipio Africanus (the Elder, 236–183 BCE): "Remember that *Pellean* Conquerer, / A youth, how all the Beauties of the East / He slightly view'd, and slightly over-pass'd; / How hee sirnam'd of *Africa* dismiss'd / In his prime youth the fair *Iberian* maid" (2.196–200), after the fall of New Carthage, Cartagena, Spain.[47] Born in what would become Italy, Scipio was associated from a young age with Spain as much as Italy and Africa because of many factors, including his most renowned military victory at the Battle of Ilipa (near Seville, Spain) during the Second Punic War.[48] Successful in his military career, patient in his troubled maturity, Scipio was also famed for being chaste in his youth, like Milton's Jesus; both show their chaste mettle by resisting the positive national stereotype of the physical beauty of Spanish women, in Scipio's case, of the representative "fair *Iberian* maid."[49]

Despite his protestations, Satan is desperate enough by the time he reaches the temptation shortly after his dismissal of Belial's idea that he places before Jesus physically attractive women and men in a passage that extends Hispanic beauty from its women to its products. The narrator describes the seafood on the table from *"Pontus* and *Lucrine* Bay, and *Afric* Coast" and the "Ladies of th'*Hesperides*," along with other "Nymphs of *Diana's* train, and *Naiades*" (2.347, 357, 355). The bay near Naples, Lucrine Bay, was variously possessed by Spain, and the mythical gardens of the Hesperides were sometimes imagined to be in the south of Iberia. Milton forestalls essentializing evil to place in referring to England immediately thereafter, saying that these hellish imposters are "Fairer than feign'd of old, or fabl'd since / Or Fairy Damsels met in Forest wide / By Knights of *Logres*, or of *Lyones*" (2.358–60). Milton refers to Loegria in his *History of Britain* as the "common term for England south of Humber" (*CPW*, 5:17, 27). Jesus rejects the unstable foundation of Satan's temptations. First, Jesus recognizes that Satan has essentially commodified the people, useful materials, and foodstuffs of Hispania and Britannia into "pompous Delicacies" (*PR*, 2.390). This rejection would have been relevant in Milton's days, when Spanish and English imports from Asia, Africa, and the Americas were equally commodified and desired. Moreover, Jesus trumps the exoticism of Spain and other earthly locales with that of heaven: "I can at will, doubt not, as soon as thou, / Command a Table in this Wilderness, / And call swift flights of Angels ministrant" (2.383–85). Indeed, the table that the angels serve Jesus at the end of the poem is noticeably absent of earthly references. The angels "set before him spred / A table of Celestial Food, Divine, / Ambrosial, Fruits fetcht from the tree of life, / And from the fount of life Ambrosial drink" (4.587–90).

When Satan modifies the biblical temptation to eat in book 4, Jesus reconceives Spain's temptations into attractions, a subtle yet momentous shift. Satan provides Jesus with a ken of the Roman Empire reminiscent of Michael's vista for Adam in *Paradise Lost*. In *Paradise Regained*, Spain is included at the westernmost reach of the vision, as are France and England: "From *Gallia* [France], *Gades* [Cadiz, Spain] and the *British* West" (4.77). Jesus sardonically asks Satan why he did not also mention their respective products:

> sumptuous gluttonies, and gorgeous feasts
> On *Cittron* tables or *Atlantic* stone;
> (For I have also heard, perhaps have read)

Their wines of *Setia*, *Cales*, and *Falerne*,
Chios and *Creet*, and how they quaff in Gold,
Crystal and Myrrhine cups imboss'd with Gems
And studs of Pearls, to me should'st tell who thirst
And hunger still. . . .

(4.114–21)

A likely Hispanic element—the Atlantic stone of Mount Atlas—resides as just one of the Western commodities desired by many in Jesus's homeland of the Middle East, who show an Occidentalism equal to Orientalism.[50] This and many other sections of *Paradise Regained* recognize the complicated nature of transnationalism, appropriately enough in a text that has to do with truly catholic, or universal, salvation of "all mankind," "all the world," "all the earth" (1.3, 162, 218). Jesus recounts that he enters into the wilderness indeed because he has overcome his youthful ardor and his potential parochialism to "rescue *Israel* from the *Roman* yoke" (1.217). He exits ready to achieve a global state in which, whether "enshrin'd / In fleshly Tabernacle, and human form, / Wandring the Wilderness, whatever place, / Habit, or state, or motion," he expresses himself the "Son of God" (4.598–602). Milton's complex Hispanism-*cum*-humanism in *Paradise Regained* requires readers to avoid the temptation of making wholesale assessments of national identity and by extension national alterity.

With *Paradise Regained*, we are led to understand how far back interactions between Spain and England go and how far forward they can go. Such a simultaneous historical and forward-thinking vision is bolstered by the twinning of the publication of *Paradise Regained* with *Samson Agonistes*, whose setting in roughly 1000 BCE is again pre-Christian, pre-Reformation. The tragedy restricts itself by and large to the Middle Eastern and North African regions of the book of Judges: Gaza, Timna, Succoth, Penuel, Canaan, and so on. Iberia, however, figures briefly in an association with the delectable Other, Dalila. The Hispanic allusions capture the three main representations of Hispanic beauty and abundance, exoticism, and earthly might. In the captivating description marking Dalila's entrance, the Chorus depicts Dalila as a ship moving to either the Ionian Islands (modern Greece) or Cadiz on the southern Spanish coast, as she

Comes this way sailing
Like a stately Ship
Of *Tarsus*, bound for th'Isles
Of *Javan* or *Gadier*
With all her bravery on, and tackle trim,
Sails fill'd, and streamers waving,
Courted by all the winds that hold them play,
An Amber sent of odorous perfume
Her harbinger, a damsel train behind
(713–21)

In addition to exoticizing Dalila, the distant Tarsus (with its associations to modern Andalusia) indicates political power. The reference pays tribute to Iberia's early possession of technological maritime advances, so desired by the constrained Danite tribe.[51] As much as Iberia's maritime advances contributed to its early power, the Philistine monopoly on weapons contributed to Israel's subordination (Judges 5:8). It is a well-recognized tribute to the wily biblical Samson that he bypasses the restrictions on possessing metals of any kind by utilizing a jawbone as a sword (Judges 15:15) and a gate as a shield (Judges 16:3). *Samson Agonistes* compresses and intensifies the history of dominance through the possession of technologies into the married relationship of Samson and Dalila. The dominance of Dalila's nation over Samson's Danite tribe disables the ability of both to trust and to see, as is dramatically demonstrated by Dalila's freedom of external mobility, which the blind Samson so clearly does not possess.

This study of a few key Hispanic elements in Milton's poetry provides a brief glimpse of what Spain has been historically and can be imaginatively. It is a caution against reading complete antagonism toward Spain into Milton's works. Conversely, even *Paradise Regained* does not echo such irenic passages from the Christian Bible about forgiving one's brothers or sisters "seven times seventy times" (Matt. 18:21–35) or collapsing divisions so that there is "neither Jew nor Greek, there is neither bond nor free, there is neither male nor female" (Gal. 3:28). Yet the brief epic shows that Milton could conceptually incorporate positive elements of Spain, if not its Catholicism. Yet another "yet": Milton had to go very far back in time and space to do it, and he did so only sparsely. Especially in his late works, Milton's poetic representations of Spain, which one might expect to be vehicles for expressing censure, turn out instead to be touchstones for appreciating Milton's complex responses to national rivalries and religious strife, as well as his vision of a transnational republic of letters and his religious concepts of universal salvation. The critical disregard of representations of unity that include even enemy-Spain, which could complement the critical attention that focuses on dispiriting representations of conflict, enacts a disservice to Milton's poetry and to our understanding of all that Milton's works have to offer as productive meditations on and poetic articulations of the intertwined concepts and activities of empire and religion.

This essay is dedicated to John Shawcross (1924–2011).

NOTES

1. John Shawcross, "John Milton and His Spanish and Portuguese Presence," *Milton Quarterly* 32, no. 2 (May 1998): 41–52. Two works that display the range of Milton's anti-Catholicism are Cedric C. Brown's "'The Islands Watchful Centinel': Anti-Catholicism and Proto-Whiggery in Milton and Marvell," in *The Cambridge Companion to English Literature, 1650–1740*, ed. Steven N. Zwicker (New York: Cambridge University Press, 1998), 165–84; and John N. King's "Milton's Paradise of Fools: Ecclesiastical Satire in *Paradise Lost*," in *Catholicism and Anti-Catholicism in Early Modern English Texts*, ed. Arthur F. Marotti (New York: St. Martin's Press, 1999), 198–217.

2. For "Hispaniolized," see William Dwight Whitney and Benjamin Eli Smith, eds., *The Century Dictionary and Cyclopedia* (New York: Century, 1911), 5794; Christopher Highley, ed., *Catholics Writing the Nation in Early Modern Britain* (Oxford: Oxford University Press, 2008); and the attentive definition footnoted to the Miltonic line: "By 'Spaniolized' Milton means won over to the cause of Spain, hence sympathetic with Roman Catholic aims" (*CPW*, 1:587n54). For the frequency and uses of the Black Legend, see Margaret R. Greer, Walter D. Mignolo, and Maureen Quilligan, eds., *Rereading the Black Legend: The Discourses of Religious and Racial Difference in the Renaissance Empires* (Chicago: University of Chicago Press, 2007). George Borrow's highly popular *The Bible in Spain* records the persistence in the general Anglophone population of the characterization of Spain as Rome's vassal: "Creo que durante

casi dos siglos España fué La Verduga de la malvada Roma, el instrument es-
cogido para llevar a efecto los atroces planes de esa potencia" (I believe that
during nearly two centuries Spain was the executioner of evil Rome, the instrument selected to effect the atrocious plans of that power). George Henry
Borrow, *La Biblia en España*, 3 vols., translated (from English into Spanish)
by Manuel Azaña (Madrid: Jiménez-Fraud, 1921), 1:40. All translations from
Spanish to English are mine unless otherwise indicated.

3. For Milton's prose writings on international and religious alliances, see
Robert Fallon, *Milton in Government* (University Park: Pennsylvania State University Press, 1993). For Milton's recognition of strands of early modern Ca-
tholicism as geographically tethered, specifically to Ireland and Spain, including
its New World empire, see Elizabeth Sauer, "Toleration and Translation: The
Case of Las Casas, Phillips, and Milton," *Philological Quarterly*, 85. nos. 3/4
(2006): 271–91; for connections specifically to France and Spain, see Paul
Stevens, "Milton's 'Renunciation' of Cromwell': The Problem of Raleigh's
'Cabinet-Council,'" *Modern Philology* 98, no. 3 (2001): 363–93; see also
Joan S. Bennett, "Catholicism," in *Milton in Context*, ed. Stephen B. Dobranski
(New York: Cambridge University Press, 2010) 237–47.

4. Andrew Hadfield, "Milton and Catholicism," in *Milton and Toleration*,
ed. Sharon Achinstein and Elizabeth Sauer (Oxford: Oxford University Press,
2007), 191.

5. The fact that this light reference to a Spaniard appears amid references
to the founder of the White Friars, usually said to be the French crusader St.
Berthold, and the founder of the Gray Friars, the Italian preacher St. Francis
of Assisi, bolsters my subsequent argument that Spain is not singled out as a
unique Other.

6. "In Quintum Novembris," headnote, in John Milton, *The Complete
Poems*, ed. John Leonard (New York: Penguin, 1998); *CWJM*, 3:156–59, 166–
81. See also Angelica Duran, "'John Milton, Englishman,' and His Spanish,
International, and Global Reception," in *Milton through the Centuries*, ed.
Gábor Ittzés and Miklós Péti (Budapest: Károli Gáspár University of the Re-
formed Church in Hungary, 2012), 188–205.

7. John Milton, *The History of Britain* (London, 1670), 4.

8. The year was remarkable in having three popes: Clement VIII (Floren-
tine Ippolito Aldobrandini; January 1–March 5), Leo XI (Roman Alessandro
Ottaviano de Medici; April 1–27), and Paul V (Roman Camillo Borghese; from
May 16).

9. *Hesperia* refers variously to Italy and Spain. For example, Martin Lasso
de Oropesa sidenotes in his Spanish translation of Lucan that "Hesperia magna,
es Italia. y Hesperia minor, Hespaña" (Hesperia Major is Italy, Hesperia Minor
Spain). Lucan, *La historia que escrivo en Latin el poeta Lucan* (Antwerp, ca.
1540), 52.

10. John Milton, *Poems of Mr. John Milton both English and Latin* (London: Humphrey Moseley, 1645); John Milton, *Poems, &c. upon several occasions* (London: Tho. Dring., 1673).

11. A useful resource is Walter Maltby's *The Black Legend in England: The Development of Anti-Spanish Sentiment, 1558–1660* (Durham, NC: Duke University Press, 1968).

12. I. H., *The Diuell of the Vault, Or, The Unmasking of Murther, Or, a Briefe Declaration of the Catholike-complotted Treason, Lately Discovered* (London, 16[06]), [2]. See also E. M. A. D. O. C. [*sic*], *A.B.C.D.E. Novembris Monstrum, or, Rome Brought to Bed in England with the Whores Miscarying* (London, 1641).

13. See James Sharpe's *Remember, Remember: A Cultural History of Guy Fawkes Day* (Cambridge, MA: Harvard University Press, 2005).

14. John Vicar, *Mischeefes Mysterie or Treasons Master-peece, The Powder-plot* (London, 1617), 100.

15. See also Catullus's Poem 26 and Juvenal's Satire 3. Tagus provides early modern English poets with rich fodder. Richard Crashaw's poem "Saint Mary Magdalene, or the Weeper" also utilizes the golden Tagus as an epitome of earthly beauty. Upon the composition of Milton's poem in 1626, Portugal still remained Spanish territory. Portugal gained its independence from Spain in 1640.

16. A speculation worth noting is the homely representation of Andrewes engaging in one of his favorite hobbies of walking and actually resting, since, in his "appointment as chaplain to the godly third earl of Huntingdon, lord president of the north, . . . he accompanied the earl, preaching widely and with success for the conversion of recusant Catholics" (*ODNB*).

17. Peter E. McCullough, "Lancelot Andrewes's Transforming Passions," *Huntington Library Quarterly* 71, no. 4 (2008): 573–89; Peter E. McCullough, "Lancelot Andrewes," in *ODNB*.

18. See George Harper's argument for the two-handed engine representing France and Spain in "Milton's 'Two-Handed Engine,'" *Times Literary Supplement*, June 16, 1924.

19. The first allusion to possible Spanish threat is not specifically geographically related and is subtle to the point of being perhaps untenable but deserves mention. Adding to a chilling image of sheep starved on unproductive English soil is "the grim Woolf with privy paw [that] / Daily devours apace" (128–29). The analogy is clear enough: the "corrupted clergy" of England enable the Catholic Church, symbolized commonly as a wolf, to walk off with some of its citizens (headnote). In her Miltonic bestiary, Karen Edwards notes that "the figurative wolf in Milton's works consistently represents those with Romish allegiances or inclinations, promoters of superstition, arch-hypocrites, and rapacious predators" ("Wolf," *Milton Quarterly* 43, no. 4 [2009]: 277). She does not extend the wolf's association to the founder of the Jesuit order, St.

Ignatius Loyola, whose castle is in today's Basque region of Spain. His family coat of arms includes two gray wolves. The Jesuit Loyola University Chicago (est. 1870) adopted the gray wolf, "LU Wolf," as its mascot: "Lou Wolf is the mascot for the university. He was inspired by the coat-of-arms of St. Ignatius of Loyola, from whom Loyola derives its name, which depicts two wolves standing over a kettle" ("About Us: Our Traditions: LU Wolf," Loyola University Chicago, February 28, 2017, www.luc.edu/sto/aboutus/ourtraditions /luwolf/). The likelihood that Milton was tapping into this specifically Spanish image is worth mentioning but minimal given his economy of poetic images.

20. William Shakespeare, *The Riverside Shakespeare*, ed. G. Blakemore Evans (Boston: Houghton-Mifflin, 1984), 1:2. For a thought-provoking discussion of literary representations of England as archipelego, see John Kerrigan's *Archipelagic English: Literature, History, and Politics, 1603–1707* (Oxford: Oxford University Press, 2008).

21. Paul Alpers, *What Is Pastoral?* (Chicago: University of Chicago Press, 1996), 93.

22. Ibid., 24.

23. Lawrence Lipking, "The Genius of the Shore: Lycidas, Adamastor, and the Poetics of Nationalism," *PMLA* 111, no. 2 (1996): 210.

24. A. S. P. Woodhouse and Douglas Bush, eds., *A Variorum Commentary of the Poems of John Milton* (London: Routledge, 1972), 2:212.

25. John Milton, *Milton: The Complete Shorter Poems*, 2nd ed., ed. John Carey (New York: Longman, 2007), 254n162; Milton, *Complete Poems*, ed. Leonard, 658n162.

26. Lipking, "Genius of the Shore," 210.

27. Ibid., 213.

28. R. A. Stradling, "Spanish Conspiracy in England, 1661–1663," *English Historical Review* 87, no. 343 (1972): 271.

29. Neil Harris, "Milton's Toponomastic Epic: The Fontarabbia Simile in *Paradise Lost*." Special thanks to Charles Ross for sharing the unpublished version of the essay, from which I quote.

30. Ibid., 17.

31. Ibid., 21.

32. This promontory point of crossing is again alluded to in a reference to the "Gorgon" (*PL* 2.628).

33. Such sympathy can be found elsewhere in early modern literature: "In the context of an English fashion for exotic 'Turkish' plays at the time— Marlowe's *Tamburlaine* 1 and 2, Peele's *The Battle of Alcazar, Selimus*—Kyd specifically associates Iberia with the world of the East, suggesting both the special vulnerability of Spain to Ottoman rapacity, and its enduring identification with Islam" (Barbara Fuchs, "Sketches of Spain: Early Modern England's 'Orientalizing' of Iberia," in *Material and Symbolic Circulation between Spain*

and England, 1554–1604, ed. Anne J. Cruz [Aldershot: Ashgate, 2008], 68). The north-to-south deluge also pays homage to Hispania's history. The Roman Empire lost power over the Iberian territory because the Visigoths drove the Germanic Suevi, Vandals, and their recruits there as they protected their lands in Gaul in 409 before they themselves conquered it in 412.

34. The *OED* cites 1275 as the year of the first use of *Spain* (from Laymon's *Brut*).

35. The missing section would have appeared in the Escóiquiz translation on 434 (*El paraíso perdido,* trans. Juan de Escóiquiz [1812; repr., Barcelona: Administración Nuevo San Francisco, 1883]) and the Hermida translation on 2:199 (John Milton, *El paraíso perdido,* trans. Benito Ramon de Hermida Maldonado [Madrid: Ibarra, 1814]).

36. Milton, *Paraíso perdido,* trans. Hermida, n270.

37. The passage is indeed absent from the French Delille translation (John Milton, *Paradis perdu,* 3 vols., trans. Jacques Delille [Paris: Giguet et Michaud, 1805]). It would have occurred at 3:186. It is not uncommon for translations of Milton's works to omit passages that have also caused Anglophone critics consternation or given editors and annotators the burden of providing substantial notes. John Leonard describes Samuel Johnson's, T. S. Eliot's, and William Empson's disapprobation, as well as E. M. W. Tillyard's defense, of this passage on the basis of style (*Faithful Labourers: A Reception History of "Paradise Lost," 1667–1970,* vol. 1, *Style and Genre* [Oxford: Oxford University Press, 2013], 52, 194–95, 198, 200–201). Among the appropriately lengthy annotations to this passage are Patrick Hume's (*Annotations on Milton's Paradise Lost* [London, 1695], 298–300).

38. On Almohad Emir Abu-Yusuf Ya'qub al-Mansur (1184–99), see Gordon Campbell and Roger Collins, "Milton's *Almansor,*" *Milton Quarterly* 17, no. 3 (1983): 81–82.

39. This simile is set up with the proximate, preceding references to another peoples and lands, the "Indian herdsman" (9.1108) and "Amazonian targe" (9.1111). The presence and instability of national alliances perhaps also inheres in the image for Milton's original audience, which would have been aware that Spanish king "Philip's decision to prevent the co-operation of England and France in the supply of troops and materials to Lisbon involved equipping Genoese pirates . . . hired to infest peninsular waters and prey indiscriminately on English shipping" (Stradling, "Spanish Conspiracy," 272).

40. J. Martin Evans, *The Miltonic Moment* (Lexington: University of Kentucky Press, 1998), 2.

41. Milton, *Complete Poems,* ed. Leonard, 728n22; *PL,* 864n11. Responding to and strengthening English interest in Spanish missionary work in Asia is John Dryden's *The Life of St. Francis Xavier,* published by Jacob Tonson in the same year he published his illustrated *Paradise Lost* (London, 1688).

42. John Patrick Donnelly, *Ignatius Loyola: Founder of the Jesuits* (New York: Pearson Longman, 2004), 95.

43. In the 1650s, Milton retrospectively explained his return to England from his European tour by blaming Jesuits, but English ones: "As I was on the point of returning to Rome, I was warned by merchants that they had learned through letters of plots laid against me by the English Jesuits, should I return to Rome, because of the freedom with which I had spoken about religion" (*CPW*, 4.1:619).

44. Richard DuRocher, "The Emperors' New Clothes: The Royal Fashion of Satan and Charles II," in *Paradise Lost: A Poem Written in Ten Books: Essays on the 1667 First Edition*, ed. John T. Shawcross and Michael Lieb (Pittsburgh, PA: Duquesne University Press, 2007), 12–14.

45. Barbara Lewalski, "Milton and Idolatry," *Studies in English Literature, 1500–1900* 43, no. 1 (2003): 222, 223.

46. Stephen Greenblatt, *Marvelous Possessions: The Wonder of the New World* (Chicago: University of Chicago Press, 1991).

47. The note for this passage in *Milton's Paradise Regained: With Select Notes Subjoined* (London: T. Bensley et al., 1796) reads, "The continence of Scipio Africanus at the age of twenty-four, and his generosity in restoring a beautiful Spanish lady to her husband and friends, are celebrated by Polybius, Livy, Valerius Maximus, and various other authors. *Newton*" (394). In his Spanish translation of *Paradise Regained*, Cayetano Rosell includes one of only six footnotes in book 2 to this line about "Escipion el Africano" (John Milton, *El paraíso perdido por John Milton, seguido de El paraíso recobrado del mismo autor*, trans. Cayetano Rosell [Barcelona: Montaner y Simon, 1873], 320). See David Quint's analysis of the pervasiveness of Rome in Milton's works. For his insights into an offhand yet powerful allusion to Scipio, see his "Milton's Book of Numbers: Book 1 of 'Paradise Lost' and Its Catalogues," *International Journal of the Classical Tradition* 13, no. 4 (2007): 528–49.

48. For John Dryden's use of the figure of Scipio in *Annus Mirabilis* and in relation to Spain, see Stella P. Revard, "Charles, Christ, and the Icon of Kingship," in *Visionary Milton: Essays on Prophecy and Violence*, ed. Peter E. Medine, John T. Shawcross, and David V. Urban (Pittsburgh, PA: Duquesne University Press, 2010), 227–28.

49. Milton's youthful Italian sonnets and "Canzone" are set in Italy and likely draw on national stereotypes of the physical beauty of Italian women but do not directly repeat the stereotype. In his Latin "Elegia Prima," Milton's refutation of the famed physical beauty of Greek, Persian, Syrian, Italian, and Trojan women indicates that he is introducing uncommon praise for "the prime glory of British maidens" (73; Floria virginibus . . . prima Britannis).

50. For a thorough description of the various sources of "*Cittron* tables or *Atlantic* stone," see Henry Todd's notes in John Milton, *The Poetical Works of*

John Milton with Notes of Various Authors, Six Volumes (London: Rivington et al., 1826), 4:229.

51. See also the "Tartessian waves" of Milton's "Elegia Quinta." Tartessus was one of the earliest civilizations in Hispania, recorded by Herodotus, Strabo, and Pliny in his *Natural History*. As I have noted elsewhere (see *The Age of Milton and the Scientific Revolution* [Pittsburgh, PA: Duquesne University Press, 2007]), Milton's rendition of the Samson story includes the governing Philistines' withholding of resources and technology from the Israelites. Editor Merritt Hughes's footnote emphasizes the instability of even denotative meaning: "Josephus . . . seems to have identified *Tarsus* on the River Cydnus in Cilicia with the Tarshish of the Old Testament. Tarshish was a port on the Guadalquivir in Spain" (*John Milton: Complete Poems and Major Prose* [New York: Odyssey, 1953], 568, 715n). For a fuller discussion, see the entries for "Tarshish" and "Tarsus" in John McClintock and James Strong, *Cyclopaedia of Biblical, Theological, and Ecclesiastical Literature* (New York: Harper, 1894), 10:218–22.

CHAPTER 6

"COELUM NON ANIMUM MUTO"?

Milton's Neo-Latin Poetry and Catholic Italy

Estelle Haan

Milton's *Elegiarum Liber*, the first half of his *Poemata* published in *Poems of Mr John Milton Both English and Latin* (1645), concludes with a series of eight Latin epigrams: five bitterly anti-Catholic pieces on the failed Gunpowder Plot of 1605, followed by three encomiastic poems hymning the praises of an Italian soprano, Leonora Baroni, singing in Catholic Rome. The disparity in terms of subject matter and tone is self-evident yet surprising in an epigrammatic series that runs sequentially, unmarked by, say, a printer's dividing line evident elsewhere in the *Poemata*.[1] These pieces may indeed be unified by meter, but they are otherwise poles apart. The gunpowder epigrams denigrate Rome as a "Beast" (2.2; Belua) dwelling upon seven hills;[2] they describe her as "profane" (2.8; profana) and attack her religious fraternity (symbolized by filthy Franciscan cowls [2.7; "fœdos . . . cucullos"] meriting an explosion up to the heavens),[3] her ownership of "brute gods" (2.8; brutos . . . Deos), and her misguided doctrine of purgatory (3.1; "Purgatorem animae . . . ignem").[4] By contrast, the Leonora epigrams present the city as a cultured hub of inclusivity, the welcome host of a Neapolitan soprano. In providing the setting for a human song that both enthralls its audience and attests to the presence of a divine power, Rome (described as situated by "the Tiber's lovely waters" [3.5; amoenâ Tibridis undâ] and as offering a favorable reception to Leonora [3.7; "Romulidûm studiis . . . secundis"]) now epitomizes something other than brute idolatry, clerical habit, or doctrine. And for the poet this facilitates an interrogation of theological (especially Catholic) doctrines.

That this seeming polarity is attributable to something other than the eclectic *varietas* afforded by the neo-Latin epigram is suggested by the second half of the *Poemata*: the *Sylvarum Liber*. This is nowhere more evident than in the contrast between the anti-Catholic "In Quintum Novembris," pertaining to Milton's Cambridge years,[5] and "Mansus" and "Epitaphium Damonis," both of which are associated, albeit in different ways, with his Italian sojourn. The gunpowder epic traces the origins of a Catholic conspiracy back to Satan himself and satirizes the Franciscan order, the pope (described as a "secret adulterer" [75; secretus adulter] and a "Babylonian priest" [156; antistes Babylonius]), the Vatican, and associated Catholic ritual. "Mansus," on the other hand, sings the praises of a staunchly Catholic poet, patron, and biographer, while "Epitaphium Damonis" nostalgically depicts Florence as a *locus amoenus*, the setting for an allegory of a Protestant Englishman's applauded performance of his Latin verse before Catholic academicians.

"Coelum non animum muto, dum trans mare curro" (I change the climate, not my mind, while I race across the sea), wrote the homeward-bound Milton in the autograph book of Camillo Cardoini at Geneva on June 10, 1639.[6] The inscription, preceded by the closing lines of *A Mask*, adapts a verse by Horace.[7] The phrase, Campbell and Corns believe, may proclaim Milton's "unwavering Protestantism,"[8] now inscribed in a Calvinist hub. But the Latin poems that Milton "patch[ed] up" in the course of his Italian journey suggest that this was an *animus* that could indeed acclimatize to religious and cultural difference.[9] Central to that acclimatization, as this chapter will argue, is Milton's quasi-Catholic self-fashioning. Thus "Mansus" offers a poetic autobiography of sorts, a self-inscribed *vita* colored by intertextually kaleidoscopic links with two

Catholic poets of Renaissance Italy and their patron; "Ad Leonoram" 1 both invokes and interrogates Catholic doctrine before a Catholic audience, only to view the whole through the lens of a neo-Platonic hermeticism that may refreshingly transcend religious difference. Finally, "Epitaphium Damonis," composed upon Milton's return home, seems to highlight the potential interconnectedness of Protestant England and Catholic Italy through the Anglo-Italian identity of its deceased subject and through a pseudomonasticism suggested by the poem's possible engagement with the hagiography of a Catholic saint. Perhaps Continental travel and the physical encounter with the symbols, personages, and institutions of the other have engendered in the Milton of the Italian journey a tolerance,[10] or, more accurately, the manipulation of a seeming tolerance to serve poetic and cultural ends.

The possibility of Milton's "Catholic" self-fashioning must also, however, be read in conjunction with, and as originating in, an essential paradox, for, as Susanne Woods remarks, "Milton in Italy was an oxymoron in search of the higher resolutions of a paradox: a Protestant in the center of Catholicism."[11] Inevitably religious tensions ensued. In *Defensio Secunda* he announces, albeit with hyperbolic pride, that when abroad he had decided that he would not introduce spontaneously the subject of religion but that when interrogated about faith he would dissimulate nothing, irrespective of the consequences.[12] In the company of the Catholic Manso, he seems indeed to have refused to conceal his opinions when discussion turned to religion ("quod nolebam in religione esse tectior" [because I was unwilling to be more discreet about the subject of religion]). And it was on this account that Manso apologized for his inability to show him greater hospitality in Naples even though it was his wish to do so.[13] And yet the excessive pride characterizing Milton's retrospective account of his patriotic defense of the faith, so to speak, is hardly surprising in a self-defense.[14] When it comes to highlighting religious difference Milton possesses a self-awareness that is matched only by his literary self-consciousness.

In a Latin letter (April 20, 1647) to the Florentine Carlo Dati, Milton promises to send him and his fellow academicians the Latin part of the 1645 volume and says he would have done so already had he not feared that its antipapal content ("ea quæ in Pontificem Romanum aliquot paginis asperius dicta sunt" [those rather harsh comments, in some of the pages, against the pontiff of Rome]) might not be too pleasing to their ears.[15] He is, in the words of John Hale, "skat[ing] on thin ice."[16] He hopes that his Italian friends will pardon his freedom of speech as indeed they were accustomed to do (he is quite confident that at least Dati will).[17] But at the same time, as if to heal the potential wound, he announces that he is reading "with pleasure" (libenter) Dati's description of Florentine ceremonies held in honor of the deceased King Louis XIII of France.[18] The reference is to the *Esequie della Maestà Christianiss. di Luigi XIII descritte da Carlo Dati* (Florence, 1644), a work that in fact exudes Catholicism. It does so not only in its ekphrastically detailed description of, for example, "La nobil Chiesa di San Lorenzo"—its naves, altar, ornaments, inscriptions—but also in its celebration of the king as someone who proved to be "fervente in protegere la Religione Cattolica."[19] Milton's description of this act of reading as *libenter* is quite fascinating even if it is marked by the courtesy characteristic of humanist epistolary correspondence. Dati's reply, dated October 22 / November 1, 1647, is polite but firm.[20] He will exclude from his anticipated general admiration of the *Poemata* those pieces that show contempt for his own religion.[21] And he will indeed excuse but not applaud these, even though they are uttered from the lips of a friend. In any case, they will not be an obstacle to his reception of the others, if only Milton can excuse his (Dati's) liberty of expression (*WJM*, 12:310). From his subsequent letter to Milton, dated November 24 / December 4, 1648, we learn that he has indeed received not one but two copies of the *Poemata*. Here Dati's silence about the potentially offensive antipapal pieces speaks volumes. He chooses instead to describe the collection as "most erudite poetry, which, although small, contains infinite value."[22] It is tempting to conclude that manifestations of erudition between erstwhile fellow academicians have the ability to engender a shared humanism that is also perhaps a shared literary ecumenism.

CATHOLIC VOICES IN "MANSUS"

Certainly when it comes to literary expression, it is evident that potential religious differences can be bridged by good-humored tolerance. The-

ological tension between Milton and the Catholic Neapolitan Giovanni
Battista Manso may have reared its head in private conversation or perhaps in a more formal setting: that of the Accademia degli Oziosi, a
learned body intrinsically linked to Catholicism and the rigidity that
might ensue (its statutes, for example, forbade "per riverenza" the recita-
tion of any material pertaining to theology or to Holy Writ).[23] In its initial years the Oziosi had held its meetings in the convent of San Maria
delle Grazie,[24] and in 1615 it took possession of the abandoned monastery of St. Dominic.[25] As founder of this academy, as well as of several
charitable organizations, Manso may well have earned a prestige whereby,
as Sean Cocco suggests, he could "skirt the edges of orthodoxy,"[26] but his
influence in Catholic Neapolitan circles cannot be overemphasized. His
devout Catholicism had already manifested itself in his published hagiography (1611) of Saint Patricia, which presented her miracles as historical fact,[27] and later in his unabashed attribution of the preservation
of Naples from the erupting Vesuvius (December 16–17, 1631) to the
miraculous relics of San Gennaro. In an extant letter he describes the
miracle eloquently and in some detail: the procession bearing the saint's
relics, his own role as privileged among the crowd, the cardinal taking the
saint's blood from the tabernacle, raising the vessel to the erupting moun-
tain, and making the sign of the cross, and the subsequent bowing of
the cloud of fire, as if in veneration of the holy relics.[28] The formality
of a Catholic ritualistic procession, indeed the veracity of the Eucharist and of sainthood, had been the target of Miltonic ridicule in "In
Quintum Novembris."[29] But that any tension between the English Protestant and his Neapolitan host was ultimately regarded by both parties as
good-humored is suggested by Manso's two-line "written Encomium" of
Milton,[30] and Milton's accomplished reply: the one-hundred-line poem
"Mansus." Manso, echoing the words of Gregory the Great upon seeing
pagan youths who had been brought to Rome for sale, states that if Milton's *pietas* could only match his *mens, forma, decor, facies,* and *mos,* then
he would be, not an "Angle," but an "Angel."[31] Milton seems to turn
the whole upon its head in his self-fashioning in the concluding lines of
"Mansus" as a radiantly blushing angel,[32] looking down from heaven,
smiling, and applauding himself.

TWO SMILING POETS: MARINO AND MILTON

That act of smiling draws the discerning reader back to the earlier description in "Mansus" of a Catholic poet, Giambattista Marino: "Vidimus arridentem operoso ex aere poetam" (16; We have seen the poet smiling from elaborate bronze). The line is of particular interest given the frustratingly odd silence in the Miltonic corpus with regard to the breathtaking art and sculpture of Catholic Italy that the then sighted poet doubtless beheld. Upon Marino's death in 1625 Manso had commissioned a bronze bust of the poet, which is not without its own "angelic" connotations: the workmanship of Bartolomeo Viscontini of Milan, it was placed in Manso's domestic chapel of St. *Angelo* a Foro.[33] According to De Lellis, Manso also erected in the same chapel a magnificent cenotaph with an inscription commemorating him as "distinguished, presented and encircled with the laurel as a result of the applause of the whole world" (Laurea ab omnium Orbis Terrarum plausu; / Insignito, Impertito, Redimito).[34] Milton's reference is thus likely testimony to his visiting a Catholic church, Manso's domestic chapel of St. Angelo a Foro, and viewing the bust and probably the inscription. The latter possibility is further strengthened by the potential appropriation of the inscription's "laurea . . . insignito" in Milton's envisaged memorial to his own deceased self ("Nectens . . . Parnasside lauri / Fronde comas" ["Mansus" 92–93; binding my hair . . . in the leaf of Parnassian laurel] and of "Orbis Terrarum plausu" in "æthereo plaudam mihi lætus Olympo" ["Mansus" 100; with joy will I applaud myself on heavenly Olympus]). Milton the *Anglus*, Milton the possible *Angelus*, is aspiring to receive posthumous honors already won by the Italian Marino in St. Angelo.

Milton also expresses the poignant wish that perhaps someone (like Manso?) would see to it that his limbs, relaxed in livid death, would be gently laid in a "small urn" ("Ille meos artus liventi morte solutos / Curaret parvâ componi molliter urnâ" ["Mansus" 89–90]). Contemporary accounts record that it was Manso who made sure that Marino's body would be interred in the cemetery of the Church of the Holy Apostles in Naples.[35] The positioning of the adverb *molliter* literally inside Milton's "small urn" is worth emphasizing in that the adjective *mollis* occurs earlier in "Mansus" as a virtual synonym for Marino himself.[36] Highlighting the awe-inspiring effects of Marinism upon Italy by a poet who was "sweetly-speaking" (9; dulciloquus) and "verbose" (11; prolixus), Milton continues: "*Mollis* & Ausonias stupefecit carmine nymphas" (12; In his smoothness, he stunned the Ausonian nymphs with his strains). The use of adjective as substantive here serves to equate both Marino and *mollis*. Perhaps the placing of *molliter* within Milton's small urn can be read as an aspiration to receive burial rites "in a manner that is *mollis*/Marino." Indeed, Marinism itself, the baroque movement inaugurated by that *mollis poeta*, is, as I have argued elsewhere, inventively showcased in the *Latinitas* of Milton's poem.[37]

"DIALOGUES OF FRIENDSHIP": TASSO, MANSO, MILTON

Marino is not the only Catholic poet to find a place in "Mansus." The poem seems to conduct a literary "dialogue of friendship" with two other Catholic writers. It is worth remarking that its very title lacks the customary prepositional *Ad* with an accompanying accusative of the addressee characteristic of the titles of Milton's other Latin poems to Italians (who are further complemented by a present participle), such as "Ad Salsillum . . . ægrotantem" and "Ad Leonoram . . . canentem." In this respect it invites comparison with the simply entitled *Il Manso*, even if the latter is qualified by a subtitle: *Overo dell'amicizia dialogo*.[38] The author of this work, which had seen publication at Naples in 1596, was Torquato Tasso. For Tasso (and indeed for Milton) Manso's very name serves as the work's title, a name regarded by the Italian poet as synonymous with friendship. As if in acknowledgment of that synonymity, Milton's accompanying headnote not only describes Manso as "Tassi amicissimus" (an extremely good friend of Tasso), but also mentions the dialogue in question, and the fact that it was to Manso that it was addressed: "Ad quem Torquati Tassi dialogus extat de Amicitiâ scriptus" (There is extant a *Dialogue on Friendship* written by Tasso and addressed to him). And the poem proper alludes to friendship on no fewer than three separate occasions (15, 63, 78). Milton, moreover, seems to draw upon Tasso's brief prose paraphrase identifying and describing the dialogue's "Interlocutori." There Manso is said to be one who has been trained in both warfare and letters ("è non-dimeno nelle belle, e buone lettere ammaestrato"),[39] and he is praised for "l'acume dell'ingegno."[40] Milton presents him as a man greatly distinguished among Italians for his genius, his literary studies, and military prowess (headnote; "vir *ingenii* laude, tum literarum studio, nec non & bellicâ virtute apud Italos clarus in primis est"), one who possesses an "ingenium . . . vigens" (77; a flourishing intellect) and an "adultum mentis *acumen*" (77; a mature sharpness of mind [emphasis mine]). Milton may be summarizing Manso's talents, but the terms in which he chooses to do so are Tassonian.

Milton's headnote continues by drawing the reader's attention to the fact that in the *Gerusalemme Conquistata* Tasso actually praised Manso by name, a point also highlighted in the poem proper ("& æternis inscripsit nomina chartis" [8; and he inscribed your name in his eternal pages]).[41] It even cites the relevant lines.[42] These points are also singled out in the opening pages of Manso's *Vita di Torquato Tasso* (Venice, 1621),[43] which contains a somewhat self-conscious description of Manso as "a close friend of Tasso, as is attested by his verse and prose in many passages and especially the *Gerusalemme* and the *Dialogue on Friendship*, which he entitled *Il Manso*."[44] Elsewhere in the work Manso describes the nature of a friendship, whose sacred laws Tasso observed and exemplified by his deeds, and also by his dialogue on the subject.[45] He was in short a "fidelissimo amico."[46] In fact, it is the essential reciprocity of the Manso/Tasso, patron/poet relationship that lies at the heart of the Miltonic quest for *amicitia* as articulated later in the poem ("Mansus" 78–84). And as Milton announces his projected national epic, an *Arthuriad*, he longs for a prototype of Manso, that *amicus* (78) who knows how to "decorate" poets.[47] *Decorâsse* (79) recalls the etymologically related noun *decus* attributed earlier in the poem to Tasso himself (50). It is hardly without significance that the ensuing lines should combine the bellicose and the chivalric in a Tassonian manner. The projected epic's theme (epitomized here by the Knights of the Round Table and the military exploits of King Arthur leading British resistance to Germanic invaders) conforms, as Douglas Bush has noted, to the principle established by Renaissance epic theory and practice that the heroic poet (of which Tasso and Ariosto were acclaimed the prime exemplars) should deal with the early history or legends of his own country.[48] In its quasi-Italian quest for patronage, "Mansus" proffers an advertisement for a projected epic uttered by an English poet in a Tassonian voice.

It is a voice that may also be heard in the poem's most enigmatic lines (54–64). Preceding what is in all likelihood an allegorical representation of the Accademia degli Oziosi (59–64) are two rather puzzling verses, which have been described by Anthony Low as "by far the most complex and subtle thus far in their use of classical allusion."[49] They amount to a proud proclamation that "it will be said that Cynthius dwelt of his own accord in your [i.e., Manso's] home" ("Mansus" 54–55; Dicetur tum sponte tuos habitâsse penates / Cynthius). Bush remarks: "Milton is saying that Apollo (i.e. poetry) voluntarily dwelt in Manso's house."[50] While Cynthius is indeed a name for Apollo (derived from Mount Cynthus, the god's birthplace), the occurrence of this name in combination with the contracted perfect *habitâsse* (emphasis mine) may punningly allude to Tasso's strong bond of friendship with Cardinal *Cinzio* (emphasis mine) Passeri Aldobrandini,[51] the dedicatee of *Gerusalemme Conquistata*, a bond that is particularly evident in their last moments together as described by Manso. It was Cardinal Cinzio who had invited Tasso to come to Rome to be crowned poet laureate at the Campidoglio. Tasso arrived in the city in November 1595, only to learn that the ceremony would have to be postponed because of inclement weather and the cardinal's illness.[52] Only five months later (April 1596) Tasso, himself now ill, retreated to the monastery of St. Onofrio, where he would die in the very month named for the rescheduled laureate ceremony. Crucially, Cinzio came to visit Tasso ("andò a visitarlo") on his deathbed and gave the dying poet a papal benediction ("& à recargli in nome del Pontefice la sua santa benedittione").[53] According to Manso, the dying Tasso stated that this would serve as his "laureate coronation," his triumph in a "celestial Campidoglio."[54] "Mansus" too has a deathbed scene, albeit an envisaged one: that of Milton himself, who longs for someone who would stand before his bed with tear-drenched eyes (87; "Ille mihi lecto madidis astaret ocellis"). It will be enough for Milton to say to him as he stands there, "Take me to your care" (88; Astanti sat erit si dicam sim tibi curæ). That *sat erit*, when viewed alongside the dying Tasso's words, seems to betray a reticent simplicity. But the ensuing lines envisage a Miltonic coronation that is essentially ekphrastic: his features sculpted in marble (91; "nostros ducat de marmore vultus"), his hair bound with Paphian myrtle or Parnassian laurel (92–93; "Nectens aut Paphiâ myrti aut Parnasside lauri / Fronde comas"). And, as with Tasso, the envisaged triumph is a celestial one, even if the ultimate applause is ironically self-applause ("æthereo plaudam mihi lætus Olympo" [100; With joy will I applaud myself on heavenly Olympus]).

LEONORA, GUARDIAN ANGELS, AND
NEO-PLATONIC HERMETICISM

Applause, or more specifically Catholic applause, governs the appropriately entitled *Applausi Poetici Alle Glorie della Signora Leonora Baroni* (Bracciano, 1639),[55] a multilingual collection of encomia of Leonora Baroni, something of an Italian diva in her day and, it would seem, much more. Daughter of the famed Adriana Baroni (herself the recipient, in 1628, of a volume of encomiastic verse in her honor), Leonora was not only an outstanding soprano but also a polished instrumentalist, singing sometimes to her own accompaniment, sometimes to that of her mother (on *lira*) and her sister Caterina (on harp).[56] She was also a gifted composer of over thirty arias.[57] Despite or perhaps because of the extravagant nature of the poems included in the *Applausi*, religious analogies are virtually nonexistent. Perhaps the contributors are displaying that cautious conservatism articulated in the volume's prefatory letter, which quite tellingly points out to the reader that the encomiasts of Leonora have not had the intention of detracting from "the observation that is due to the true Catholic and Roman religion."[58] Praise of human song should be regarded, not as a form of idolatry, but as mirroring on earth (but not usurping) angelic praise of God. The volume's frontispiece seems to seek to achieve a similar reconciliation between the celestial and the terrestrial. Here the coat of arms of the family of de Melo/Moura (the volume is dedicated to Marquess Eleonora de Melo) is held aloft, not, as in the family crest, by two military, spear-wielding warriors, but by two winged angels. Beneath, there stand two Muses: one classical and laureate, gazing in wonderment at a new earthly Muse, who holds a viol and treads underfoot the Muses' customary instruments—in all likelihood Leonora herself as a tenth Muse.[59] This figure, human yet mythological, classical yet contemporary, is the object of gazes both angelic and Roman.

MILTON AMONG THE CATHOLIC UMORISTI

That Milton's three Leonora epigrams, datable in all likelihood to his return visit to Rome, did not appear in the published collection is largely inconsequential in that it is highly unlikely that they were ever intended to appear there.[60] What is of significance, however, is the possibility that several of the *Applausi* poems may have been circulating in Rome in manuscript at the time of his visits to that city. Milton's awareness of the contemporary vogue in Rome of hymning Leonora in verse seems to be attested by the very existence of his own epigrams, which, while indeed suggesting that he has heard the soprano firsthand, also note that she has been "adorned by the favorable enthusiasm of the sons of Romulus" ("Ad Leonoram" 3.7; Romulidûm studiis ornata secundis). This acknowledgment may extend beyond the responses of those members of a Roman audience actually listening to her performance to embrace an essentially literary reaction—the latter reading rendered possible by the twofold meaning of *studium* as "enthusiasm" and "intellectual activity."[61] In fact, an academic context seems very likely. Leonora was the only female member of the Roman Accademia degli Umoristi, a highly reputable academy, many of whose members penned several of the encomia eventually included in the *Applausi*.[62] The Umoristi were particularly hospitable to foreign visitors, as John Evelyn eloquently describes.[63] Although by contrast Milton's attendance remains unattested, there is a strong possibility that here, as in the Florentine Accademia degli Svogliati and the Accademia degli Apatisti, he participated in their activities or at least had the pleasure of listening to the musical performances and intellectual debates that graced their meetings.[64] Worthy of mention also is the fact that Giovanni Salzilli, to whom Milton addressed a Latin poem ("Ad Salsillum"), which has been studied by Freeman and Haan in relation to the Roman Accademia dei Fantastici (of which Salzilli was a member), and a volume produced by that body, was also, like Leonora, a member of the Umoristi.[65] The fact that this academy unites two separate addressees of Milton's Latin poetry is worth emphasizing.

What remains virtually indisputable with regard to Milton is a point aptly noted by Campbell and Corns: that the three Leonora epigrams "were written for the benefit of Milton's Roman friends, not for the lady herself"[66]—an instance perhaps of those poems he "patch[ed] up" while in Italy (*CPW*, 1:809–10) and in all likelihood showed/recited to Italian fellow academicians. For the Umoristi, as perhaps for Milton, this talented soprano served as a vehicle for interrogating the effects of music upon the sensibilities of the listener, engendering an intellectual discourse shared among peers.[67] Significantly for the Protestant Milton, these were Catholic peers. Foremost among the Umoristi's elite membership were several cardinals, including Cardinal Giulio Rospigliosi (the future pope Clement IX), Francesco Barberini (who owned a personal copy of the *Applausi*), and his brother Antonio Barberini.[68] Milton certainly met Cardinal Francesco Barberini in Rome at another musical event held to inaugurate the recently completed theater of the Palazzo Barberini at the Quattro Fontane,[69] and he was even granted a private audience the following day. This is attested by his Latin letter to Lukas Holste (who since 1636 had been Francesco's librarian, and would in 1641 be appointed Vatican librarian).[70] Here Milton asks Holste to greet the "Eminentissimum Cardinalem" in his name ("meo nomine"), carefully using the cardinal's formal title,[71] and proceeds to extol his "magnæ virtutes, rectique studium," which embrace not only his patronage of the arts but also his "summissa animi celsitudo." This extravagant praise of a cardinal who, after all, had been one of the ten judges in the trial of Galileo, is particularly striking.[72] And among the contributions to the *Applausi* is a Latin poem by Holste himself.[73] A convert to Catholicism since late 1624, Holste even conducted Milton on a guided tour of the literary treasures of the Vatican Library and gifted to him one of his own published editions.[74] Campbell and Corns perceptively remark that "the common interest in Hellenic scholarship seems to have been more powerful than the religious differences."[75] What is certainly apparent is that Milton is doing much more than simply moving in erudite circles. As if temporarily sloughing any sense of religious alterity, he seems to rejoice in being physically present in the very hub of Catholicism, which his letter presents in superlative terms ("its most choice collection of books" [conquisitissimam Librorum supellectilem]).[76] Thus, as if in a reinvention of the *anabasis*/*katabasis* motifs, Milton "ascends" into the Vatican ("cum . . . in Vaticanum ascenderem"),[77] his physical motion almost mirroring the aspirations of the library's ancient Greek manuscripts edited by Holste, which, as they await publication and hence a delivery into the world, resemble, Milton says, the souls in Virgil's Elysium (*Aeneid* 6.679–80) awaiting rebirth (*WJM*, 12:40).[78] Whether in the Vatican Library or in the theater of the Palazzo Barberini or possibly in the Accademia degli Umoristi itself, the Protestant Milton is taking his place quite literally alongside the Catholic literati of Rome. To what extent might this also work on a literary level given that his Leonora epigrams have at their time of composition an audience/readership that is academic, Italian, Roman—indeed Catholic to the very core?

LEONORA AMONG THE ANGELS

Read alongside the poems in the *Applausi*, two of Milton's three Latin epigrams (nos. 2 and 3) seem to assume a literary place that is at times comfortable, even conventional, certainly less extravagantly effusive.[79] Andrew Dell'Antonio has highlighted "the quasi-interactive 'dialogic' interplay of the poems in the *Applausi*."[80] Central to this is the association of Leonora with images and personages that are mythological rather than religious or specifically Catholic. Milton's third Latin epigram, like several of the *Applausi* poems, equates her with the Sirens famous for the alluring power of their song ("liquidam Sirena" ["Ad Leonoram" 3.1; clear-voiced Siren]),[81] and presents her as a second Parthenope exchanging a less attractive Naples for the serenity of Rome.[82] Indeed, this allusion finds a close *Applausi* parallel in Fulvio Testi's salutation: "Fastosetta Sirena / Che da Partenopei liti odiosi / Sù la Romana arena / Se' venuta à turbar gli altrui riposi."[83] However, Milton's much-neglected first Leonora epigram is an altogether different, even daringly defiant piece,[84] which, as if in breach of the theological discretion that would govern the published collection, articulates Catholic doctrine. But it does so only to interrogate it, and, as argued below, to recast it in the language of hermeticism, perhaps as a means of bridging the divide between Catholicism and Protestantism.

Comparison of "Ad Leonoram" 1 with the multilingual encomia in the *Applausi* reveals in Milton's case a poem that is ostensibly more "Catholic" than those contained therein. Its opening acknowledgment of the belief that an angel has been allotted to each individual ("Angelus unicuique suus (sic credite gentes) / Obtigit æthereis ales ab ordinibus" [1–2;

Each individual [believe this, you nations], has been allotted a winged angel from the heavenly ranks]), "a fancy" according to David Masson, seems, as Robert West suggests, to exemplify Milton's use of "the Catholic idea" of the guardian angel.[85] By contrast, rarely in the *Applausi*, a volume of some 267 pages, is an angelic context invoked. And even when it is, the treatment is peripheral and highly conventional. Thus, for Domenico Benigni, Leonora's "mouth breathes forth an angelic sound";[86] for Fulvio Testi, Leonora is "my little angel," whose song, soaring heavenwards, enables its audience to forget earthly things;[87] for Vincenzo Marescotti, her music replicates angelic harmony controlling the motions of the spheres themselves.[88] But West's conviction that Milton's use of the idea is nothing more than "a fanciful compliment to Leonora's voice" is the consequence of an overly simplistic reading.[89] Milton in Rome is himself speaking in a voice that is carefully tuned and instantly recognizable to his Catholic audience.

While the polarization between Catholic and Protestant theology concerning angels has been somewhat exaggerated, belief in guardian angels allocated to *individuals* (as opposed to places or communities) was, as Joad Raymond notes, on balance a Catholic tenet.[90] That Milton is discussing the individual's angel is highlighted by *unicuique* (1).[91] But his seeming acknowledgment of Catholic doctrine is tellingly couched in language of ambiguity ("sic credite gentes"). Raymond notes two possibilities afforded by Milton's phraseology: "He could be suggesting that the belief in tutelary angels is one held by Leonora's audience at Rome, distancing himself from the belief; or the imperative *credite* might encourage the belief ('believe me')."[92] However, another reading is possible when the lines are examined in the context of the poem as a whole. Milton proceeds to proclaim that Leonora possesses a glory (3; "gloria major") that is greater than that of individual angelic custodianship: "Nam tua præsentem vox sonat ipsa Deum" (4; For your very voice sounds out the presence of God). This is then followed by the suggestion that it is either God or the "mens tertia" (5) of a now empty heaven that secretly winds its way (6; "serpit agens") through her throat. "Serpit agens" is repeated (7) (the Miltonic syntax likewise entwining itself across the hexameter and pentameter lines) in language that is both corporeal and spiritual,[93] as this force teaches that mortal hearts can gradually become accustomed to an immortal sound.[94] And the theology changes from the Catholic to the pantheistic: "For if indeed God is all things and diffused through all things it is in you alone that he speaks; the rest he possesses in silence" (9–10; Quòd si cuncta quidem Deus est, per cunctaque fusus, / In te unâ loquitur, cætera mutus habet). Charles Lamb remarks that in "thus apostrophis[ing] a singing-girl" Milton "came not much short of a religious indecorum," reading "something very like blasphemy in the last two verses."[95] But rather than blasphemy, this is a theological riddle in which a Catholic tenet is voiced, questioned, and given an esoteric interpretation.

THE *MENS TERTIA* OF NEO-PLATONIC HERMETICISM

Milton's enigmatic *mens tertia* has been variously interpreted as the sphere of Venus, one of the seraphim, the last of three musical categories as described by Boethius, the music of the spheres, or the Holy Spirit (as depicted by Saint Paul).[96] That the allusion is indeed to the Holy Spirit is attested by a hitherto unnoticed parallel in a hermetic work by a certain sixteenth-century Franciscan, Hannibal Rosselli. A member of the Order of Capuchin Friars Minor, and professor of theology at the Bernardine monastery on Castle Hill, Cracow, Rosselli penned a huge six-book commentary on the *Pymander* and *Asclepius* of Hermes Trismegistus.[97] Familiarity with the *corpus hermeticum*, in which "fantastic, magical and theurgical elements were mixed in plentifully," was greatly facilitated by the appearance in 1471 of Ficino's Latin translation entitled *Pimander*, the name of the first treatise in the collection.[98] The translation was hugely popular in Renaissance Italy. This and the commentary tradition that it engendered would have found a natural home in the Neoplatonic academies of Florence and Rome.

Rosselli's commentary was published between the years 1584 and 1590. In book 3, *De Ente, Materia, Forma, et Rebus Metaphysicis*, dedicated to Ferdinando de Medici, he interprets the hermetic *deus est mens*[99] as a divine substance ("Divina substantia") that has three types of descent ("tres habet descensus"): the first is God most high ("altissimus deus"); the second is the mind of the creator ("mens artificis"); the third in the order of descent, the "anima mundi," is named "mens tertia" by Trismegistus and specifically identified as the Holy Spirit:

> Deinceps est anima mundi, quae à Trismegisto *mens tertia* vocatur
> in primo Pymandri dicens: Pymandrum cum suo verbo peperisse
> aliam mentem, *qui est ignis sanctus, & spiritus numen.*

> ———

> [Next is the *anima mundi*, which is termed the *mens tertia* by Tris-
> megistus in the first *Pymander*, where he says that Pymander with
> his word gave birth to another *mens* that is holy fire and the divine
> power of the spirit.]

Indeed, Rosselli meticulously explicates the doctrine ("Pater igitur est
prima mens, filius secunda, *tertia spiritus sanctus*" [And so the first mind
is the Father, the second the Son, the third the Holy Spirit]).[100] In short
deus est mens denotes a trinity, whose "mens tertia" is explicitly equated
with the Holy Spirit ("spiritus sanctus").[101]

For the humanist hermeticist Lodovico Lazzarelli that Holy Spirit
was essentially a spirit within. If Rosselli used the *corpus hermeticum*
as an "interface between Christian and Platonic thinking," Lazzarelli's
Crater Hermetis (1505) offered a "Christianized compendium of the Hermetic texts."[102] Presented in the form of a dialogue between Lazzarelli
and King Ferdinand of Aragon, this work, through inventive admixture
of the poetic and the prosaic, reinvented hermeticism as a mixing bowl
("crater") filled with mind ("mens") sent down to earth by God. Now
for the first time Pymander was explicitly identified as Jesus Christ,[103]
whereby, as Jill Delsigne notes, "the human being . . . [is] ensouled by
God himself rather than a lesser angel or demon."[104] Lazzarelli conflates
this with Pentecost, when the Holy Spirit descended upon the apostles, dwelling within them and giving them the power to speak in other
tongues.[105] Thus does the "mens" enable the individual to become the
temple ("aedes") of the *Spiritus Sanctus*.[106]

Central to Milton's conception of Leonora is the emphasis on her
voice as resonating the presence of God ("Nam tua præsentem vox sonat
ipsa Deum" [4; For your very voice sounds out the presence of God]).
This is developed in the poem's closing couplet, which seems to seek a
reconciliation between the pantheistic and the quasi-Pentecostal. On the
one hand, "Si cuncta quidem Deus est, per cunctaque fusus" (9) seems to
embrace "the optimist gnosis" of hermeticism whereby "the universe is

impregnated with God";[107] on the other, Leonora herself may be endowed with a quasi-Pentecostal gift whereby God speaks in her alone, holding all else in silence (10; "In te unâ loquitur, cætera mutus habet").

"Christianus ego sum o Rex: et Hermeticum simul esse non pudet" (I am a Christian, Your Majesty, and at the same time I am not ashamed to be a Hermeticist), proclaims Lazzarelli.[108] Termed by James Ellison the "international language of tolerance and ecumenism," hermeticism provided, in the words of Frances Yates, "a panacea for the religious situation of Europe."[109] Perhaps this was replicated on a microcosmic level in the case of the Protestant Milton in Catholic Italy, who could now appeal to a "*prisca theologia*, a divine wisdom that was more ancient than denominational difference."[110] In a sense, then, hermeticism, like Latin, constituted a universal language.

"EPITAPHIUM DAMONIS": WHAT'S IN A NAME?

Language, and more specifically the nuances attendant upon the etymology of proper names and associated epithets, may also act as a means of bridging religious divides. Composed upon his return to England, Milton's "Epitaphium Damonis," a pastoral lament on the premature death of his close friend Charles Diodati, is careful to depict its Protestant subject as both *Anglus* and *Thuscus*.[111] Thus the poem's headnote points out that Charles was descended on his father's side from the Tuscan city of Lucca but was in every other respect an Englishman,[112] a point reinforced in the poem proper ("& Thuscus tu quoque Damon, / Antiquâ genus unde petis Lucumonis ab urbe" [127–28; and you too Damon were Tuscan, deriving your family from the ancient city of Lucca]). Milton's description of Lucca as an *antiqua urbs* may look back to Virgil's depiction of the falling city of Troy (*Aeneid* 2.363; "urbs antiqua ruit multos dominata per annos") from which Aeneas had to flee in exile. Exile likewise dogged the distinguished Diodati clan, who were in fact unable to worship in Lucca. "The family's heroic part in the struggles of Italian Protestantism" is notably evident in a series of emigrations (1555–85) as they sought refuge in Geneva.[113] It is worth pausing to consider the first of such refugees to reach Geneva: Charles's grandfather, who interestingly was also the first of the clan to be named Carlo.[114] Born to the celebrated Michele Diodati, at a time when, according to a persistent family tradition, Charles V was lodging in Michele's palace, Carlo was purportedly godson to the emperor himself. Even Pope Paul III is said to have officiated at his baptism.[115] If the tradition is true, then Carlo Diodati, Charles's paternal grandfather and namesake, bore an original allegiance to the papacy itself, even if in later years he would convert to Protestantism. Whether or not Milton was aware of this is impossible to determine (Dorian argues that his Latin poems "suggest his close familiarity with the history of the Diodati family").[116] In any case, it is interesting to note that the Charles of "Epitaphium Damonis" (as if perhaps following in his grandfather's footsteps) is specifically described as one who worshipped the *prisca fides* and possessed an associated *pietas* ("Si quid id est, priscamque fidem coluisse, piúmque" [33; if it means anything to have respected the ancient faith and to have been pious).[117] Having matriculated as a student of theology at the Academy of Geneva on April 16, 1630, Charles, like Carlo, resided, albeit for a brief period, in that city,[118] before changing his career path from the church to medicine. His signature on the matriculation list describes him as "Carolus Deodatus Anglus natu" (Charles Diodati, English by birth).[119]

"Thuscus tu Quoque"

Throughout the "Epitaphium," however, the Protestant *Anglus* is also *Thuscus* in intratextual ways that enable Diodati/Damon to sit comfortably (like Milton?) among Catholic academicians. This is achieved through the role of mirror imaging in a poem united by the Anglo-Italian identity of its deceased subject, by the interdenominational possibilities that this affords, and by the fact that Milton was in Italy at the time of his friend's death. For if Charles is "Thuscus . . . quoque" (127), he is to some extent equatable with Florence itself, the "Thusca . . . urbs" (13) and that city's academicians (126; "pastores Thusci").[120] His possession of "cultos . . . lepores" (56) is mirrored by "Charis, atque Lepos" (127) in the allegorical representation of Florentine academies and the performance of their members (Milton included). And he can even take his place alongside ekphrastic depictions of two books gifted to Milton by the Catholic Manso (198–99; "Tu quoque in his . . . / Tu quoque in his certe es").[121] In fact, names both lost and recovered are central to a poem about identity and the quest for, and acknowledgment of, identity. Thus the "sine nomine virtus" (21) of a Diodati initially envisaged as bereft of celestial reward is countered by the acclaimed "nomina" (of Milton and perhaps of Diodati too)[122] that Carlo Dati and Antonio Francini have taught their beech trees (136; "Quin & nostra suas docuerunt nomina fagos"), and ultimately by the "divinum nomen" (210) punningly possessed by the "god-given" *Deodatus*, envisaged in the poem's soaring conclusion.

That Milton had the poem printed separately, probably for the purpose of sending to Dati and fellow academicians in Florence, is attested by Bradner's discovery in the British Museum of an anonymous separately printed edition (ca. 1640).[123] Milton's letter to Dati (1647) reveals that the poem did reach Italy,[124] and it draws attention to the piece's "emblematic" section on the academies themselves.[125] But it also seems to suggest an equation between Charles Diodati and Carlo Dati, now addressed in the fondest of terms as "mi Carole" (*WJM*, 12:52). As Hale aptly notes: "The affectionate address is unprecedented—he does not address even Charles Diodati like this."[126] Indeed, as Milton describes his state of perpetual solitude ("ut in perpetua fere solitudine versari mihi necesse sit" [*WJM*, 12:46; so that I must of necessity pass my time virtually in unremitting loneliness]), he does so in terms not far removed from the *Argumentum* to the "Epitaphium" itself ("se, suamque solitudinem . . . deplorat" [he laments himself and his loneliness]).[127] And it could be argued that his lament about the absence of those who have been separated from him by either death ("mors") or distance ("distantia") may be read as embracing both the deceased Charles and the far-distant Carlo.[128] The letter's potential alignment of the two losses is further suggested by the telling juxtaposition of Milton's heartfelt sorrow at leaving Florence with his overwhelming grief at Diodati's death.[129]

Sanctus Deodatus

But the "Epitaphium," unlike the Latin letter, can offer some form of *consolatio* through recourse to the etymological signification of the name Diodati. This had earlier been highlighted in a neo-Latin epigram by John Owen addressed to Charles's father, Theodore Diodati.[130] Likewise

John Florio, signaling the latter's assistance in his translation of Montaigne's *Essays*, described him as "one Maister *Theodoro Diodati*, as in name, so indeede Gods-gift to me."[131] Nicolas Du Mortier notes that holy men who bear the name Diodati are possessed of an abundance of divine favor at birth, wholehearted devotion to God in life, and the greatest of glory in death.[132] In both of his extant Greek letters to Milton, Charles Diodati translates his name into the Greek for "god-given" (*theósdotos* or *theódotos* respectively), which he juxtaposes with a transliteration of Milton's name into Greek,[133] while Milton in *Epistolae Familiares* 6 and 7 invokes him in a Latinized version of the Greek form of his name: "Theodate" (*WJM*, 12:18; 12:26).

In the closing lines of the "Epitaphium," the "divine name" (210) is one by which the "heaven-dwellers" (211) will know Damon. In all of this, Diodati is potentially equatable with a certain "Sanctus Deodatus" (born ca. 590, bishop of Nevers and abbot of St. Jointures),[134] details of whose life are preserved in a *Vita* composed in about the ninth or tenth century by a monk of St. Dié, and are augmented in the eleventh century by a certain Valcandus, abbot of Mayenne.[135] Milton's possible engagement with a Catholic hagiographical tradition is hardly incongruous in a poem that, as noted above, he sent to Dati and his Florentine fellow academicians.

The *Vita* presents Deodatus as a man who progressed from virtue to virtue (*PLat*, 151:612; "de virtute in virtutem . . . eundo"), remarkable for embracing sanctity, charity, wisdom, knowledge, and fear of God. His appointment as bishop of Nevers is viewed as divinely bestowed in reward for his "giving of himself completely to God" in accordance with the signification of his name (*PLat*, 151:612; "a Deo [cui se totum dederat] iuxta nominis sui exemplar donatus est pontificia Nivernis"). That progression ("eundo") from virtue to virtue seems to find its antithesis in the anguished questions posed in the "Epitaphium" with regard to the fate of Damon's/Diodati's *virtus* ("tua sic sine nomine *virtus / Ibit*, & obscuris numero sociabitur umbris?" [21–22; Is this how your virtue will pass away without a name, and be united to the company of the unknown shades?] and "nam quò tua candida virtus?" [200; for where would your innocent virtue go?]). After all, he too had cherished the ancient faith (33; "priscam . . . fidem coluisse") and had been pious (33; "piúmque"), but unlike the saint, who died in the fullness of his years, he had a *vita* that was prematurely cut short.

Deodatus's founding of the monastery of Jointures was the consequence of his resolve to live a life of solitude. Here he formed a friendship with a certain monk named Hidulphus. Both were neighbors in the desert ("in eremo . . . vicini facti") and would visit each other's monasteries, staying awake throughout the night in deep conversation, which was central to the preservation of their love.[136] So too is conversation at the heart of the Milton/Diodati friendship as depicted in the "Epitaphium," a friendship likewise contracted by neighbors (*Argumentum*; "ejusdem viciniæ Pastores"). But now Thyrsis can only wonder who will teach him to beguile night's length (46; "longam fallere noctem") with sweet conversation (47; "Dulcibus alloquiis"). Indeed, his consequential solitude (*Argumentum*; "suam . . . solitudinem"; and 58; "solus . . . solus") and traversal of lonely places (8, 58) are both pseudo-Petrarchan and quasi-eremitic in essence.[137]

In his latter years Deodatus left his abbey at St. Jointures and retired in solitude to a monastery, where he became mortally ill. The *Vita* describes how Hidulphus was warned in a divine vision to hasten to his friend's bedside, to beseech him not to forget him, to confer on him the last rites, to close his eyes in death, and to see to his funeral. Hidulphus fulfilled all of these injunctions in accordance with the will of God.

> Super hoc facto et tam sancti viri obitu, dilectissimus eius Hidulphus in visu noctis divinitus commonetur, ut ad eum properaret quantocius; decebat enim ut amicus amico ad Deum praecedenti extremum valediceret, sui non oblivisci devote supplicaret, commendationem ecclesiasticam faceret, viaticum praeberet; os et oculos, manus et pedes eius rite componeret, funus eius, debita veneratione procuratum, deduceret, atque in sepulcro cautissime collocaret. Quae cuncta, Deo volente, a Domino Hidulpho constat circa piissimum Patrem Deodatum impleta.[138]

> [About this fact and about the death of so holy a man, his most beloved Hidulphus received divine warning in a vision at night: that he should hasten to him as quickly as possible; for it was befitting that

a friend should bid his final farewell to a friend going before him on to God, that he should devoutly beseech him not to forget him, that he should bestow upon him the commendation of the church, offer him the last sacraments, duly tend to his face and eyes, his hands and his feet, arrange and conduct his funeral with due veneration and place him with the greatest care in a tomb. All of which things in regard to the most pious Father Deodatus were, it is clear, fulfilled by Dom Hidulphus in accordance with the will of God.]

Thyrsis, however, far from receiving a divine dream-vision, has been indulging in idle daydreams about the pastoral activities of his already deceased friend (143–46). Hidulphus found Deodatus still alive ("quem adhuc vivum reperit"), and Deodatus in turn was renewed at the sight and rejoiced in God for revealing his imminent death to his friend and deigning that he should see to his funeral (*PLat*, 151:627; "eum ad suum funus curandum destinare est dignatus").[139] Crucially, where Hidulphus was present at Deodatus's bedside and was thus privileged to bid his final farewell, to hold his hand, to close his eyes in death, and to beg him to remember him, Thyrsis was significantly absent, thereby failing on precisely all four counts:

> Ah certè extremùm licuisset tangere dextram,
> Et bene compositos placidè morientis ocellos,[140]
> Et dixisse vale, nostri memor ibis ad astra.
> ("Epitaphium Damonis" 121–23)

> [Ah, at least if I could have been permitted to touch your right
> hand for the last time and gently close your eyes as you peacefully
> died, and could have said, "Farewell: remember me as you journey
> to the stars."]

The *Vita* also records Deodatus's final request that Hidulphus look after his flock (*PLat*, 151:627). This he would indeed fulfill (*PLat*, 151:628). Thyrsis can only profess his neglect of his *oves* (66–67), forcefully signaled in the poem's pulsating refrain: "Ite domum impasti, domino jam non vacat, agni" (Go home unfed, lambs, your master has no time for you now).

In the end Hidulphus managed to fulfill all of Deodatus's burial requests (*PLat*, 151:627), publicly praying over his dear friend's body as it was committed to the earth (*PLat*, 151:628). By contrast the stark realism of Milton's "Nec dum aderat Thyrsis" (12; and Thyrsis was not yet present) says it all: his absence from London at the moments of Diodati's death and burial is the antithesis of Hidulphus's privileged presence. Unable to see to the burial of his friend, he has instead been sightseeing among the ruins of a "buried Rome" (115; Romam . . . sepultam), an antiquated metropolitan substitute for the human burial that he missed. The language is pejorative and immediately contradicted by fond reminiscences of everything Italian. The *Vita* concludes in the "Veneratio . . . Deodati" (*PLat*, 151:629) by Hidulphus and the monastic community (*PLat*, 151:629–30). Damon/Diodati is promised posthumous honors "inter pastores" (30), who will rejoice in paying their vows (30; "vota") to him and in singing his praises (30–32). Ultimately these honors are transmuted into the heavenly blessings enjoyed by Diodati in reward for a past life now presented (in pseudomonastic terms?) as pure (204; "purus") and celibate ("nulla tori libata voluptas" [213; you never tasted the pleasures of the marriage-bed]).

If Diodati can attain a "sainthood" of sorts, so too can Milton as neo-Latin poet assume a surprisingly comfortable stance, both literally and metaphorically, alongside the poets, patrons, and academicians of Catholic Italy. It is a stance facilitated by a shared sense of humanism, by a manipulated tolerance evincing an alertness to Catholic doctrine and audience, and perhaps ultimately by Catholic self-fashioning. As such it invites us to revisit the seeming religious intransigence of "Milton's unchanging mind" eternally self-inscribed in that autograph-book in Geneva.[141]

NOTES

I am very grateful to my husband, Tony Sheehan, for his help in identifying Italian sources cited in this chapter.

1. Contrast, for example, the clear dividing line between the seven Latin elegies and their ensuing retraction or, in the *Sylvarum Liber*, between "Ad Salsillum" and "Mansus."

2. The language is evocative of Rev. 13:1. All quotations of Milton's shorter poems are from *CWJM*, vol. 3; all translations are mine.

3. Cf. *PL* 3.489–90 (of the Paradise of Fools): "then might ye see / Cowles, Hoods and Habits with thir wearers tost." All quotations are from *PL*.

4. On possible links between this epigram and King James's ridicule of purgatory in *A Premonition* prefixed to the second edition (1609) of his *Apology for the Oath of Allegiance*, see Walter MacKellar, "Milton, James I and Purgatory," *Modern Language Review* 18 (1923): 472–73; Estelle Haan, introduction to Phineas Fletcher's *Locustae vel Pietas Iesuitica*, ed. Estelle Haan (Leuven: Leuven University Press, 1996), xxv–xxix.

5. On the essentially anti-Catholic nature of the gunpowder epic tradition in which Milton's "In Quintum Novembris" assumes an impressive place, see Estelle Haan, "Milton's *In Quintum Novembris* and the Anglo-Latin Gunpowder Epic," *Humanistica Lovaniensia* 41 (1992): 221–50; Francis Herring, "Pietas Pontificia," ed. Estelle Haan, *Humanistica Lovaniensia* 41 (1992): 251–95; Michael Wallace, "In Serenissimi Regis Iacobi . . . Liberationem," ed. Estelle Haan, *Humanistica Lovaniensia* 42 (1993): 368–401; Haan, introduction to Fletcher, *Locustae*, xvi–lx. See also David Quint, "Milton, Fletcher and the Gunpowder Plot," *Journal of the Warburg and Courtauld Institutes* 54 (1991): 261–68; R. F. Hardin, "The Early Poetry of the Gunpowder Plot: Myth in the Making," *English Literary Renaissance* 22 (1992): 62–79; Dana F. Sutton, "Milton's *In Quintum Novembris, anno aetatis 17* (1626): Choices and Intentions," in *Qui Miscuit Utile Dulci: Festschrift Essays for Paul Lachlan MacKendrick*, ed. Gareth Schmeling and Jon D. Mikalson (Wauconda: Bolchazy-Carducci, 1998), 349–75; John K. Hale, "Milton and the Gunpowder Plot: *In Quintum Novembris* Reconsidered," *Humanistica Lovaniensia* 50 (2001): 351–66. Among useful general studies of Milton's anti-Catholicism are Raymond D. Tumbleson, "Of True Religion and False Politics: Milton and the Uses of Anti-Catholicism," *Prose Studies* 15 (1992): 253–70; Andrew Hadfield, "Milton and Catholicism," in *Milton and Toleration*, ed. Sharon Achinstein and Elizabeth Sauer (Oxford: Oxford University Press, 2007), 186–99.

6. The autograph book is now held in the Houghton Library in Harvard (MS Sumner 84).

7. ". . . if Vertue feeble were, / Heav'n it self would stoop to her" (*A Mask* 1021–22). Horace, *Epistles* 1.11.27: "Coelum non animum mutant qui trans mare currunt."

8. Gordon Campbell and Thomas N. Corns, *John Milton, Life, Work, and Thought* (Oxford: Oxford University Press, 2008), 126.

9. Cf. *Reason of Church Government*: "But much latelier in the privat Academies of *Italy* . . . other things which I had shifted in scarsity of books and conveniences to patch up amongst them, were receiv'd with written Encomiums, which the Italian is not forward to bestow on men of this side the Alps" (*CPW*, 1:809–10).

10. See, among others, John Coffey, *Persecution and Toleration in Protestant England, 1558–1689* (Harlow: Longman, 2000); Alexandra Walsham, *Charitable Hatred: Tolerance and Intolerance in England, 1500–1700* (Manchester: Manchester University Press, 2006); Achinstein and Sauer, *Milton and Toleration.*

11. Susanne Woods, "'That Freedom of Discussion Which I Loved': Italy and Milton's Cultural Self Definition," in *Milton in Italy: Contexts, Images, Contradictions*, ed. M.A. Di Cesare (Binghamton, NY: Medieval and Renaissance Texts and Studies, 1991), 9–18, 9. For further discussion of the paradoxical elements of Milton's Italian journey, see Estelle Haan, "England, Neo-Latin and the Continental Journey: Linguistic and Textual Itineraries," in *Political Turmoil: Early Modern British Literature in Transition, 1623–1660*, ed. Stephen B. Dobranski (Cambridge: Cambridge University Press, forthcoming 2018).

12. *Defensio Secunda.* All quotations from Milton's Latin prose works are from *WJM.* The present reference occurs at *WJM,* 8:124.

13. *Defensio Secunda* (*WJM,* 8:124).

14. See Diana Treviño Benet, "The Escape from Rome: Milton's Second Defense and a Renaissance Genre," in Di Cesare, *Milton in Italy,* 29–49.

15. *Epistola Familiaris* 10 (*WJM,* 12:44–53, 50).

16. John K. Hale, *Milton's Languages: The Impact of Multilingualism on Style* (Cambridge: Cambridge University Press, 1997), 90. Hale points out that *asperius* "may mean either 'rather harshly' or 'too harshly'—let Dati take his pick."

17. *Epistola Familiaris* 10 (*WJM,* 12:50). On the Milton/Dati correspondence, see Estelle Haan, *From Academia to Amicitia: Milton's Latin Writings and the Italian Academies* (Philadelphia: American Philosophical Society, 1998), 53–80.

18. *Epistola Familiaris* 10 (*WJM,* 12:50).

19. See Carlo Dati, *Esequie della Maestà Christianiss. di Luigi XIII descritte da Carlo Dati* (Florence, 1644), 5–9, 42.

20. *WJM,* 12:296–313. Dati's letter, probably the holograph, but possibly his file copy, is extant among the John Milton Papers of the New York Public Library in the Manuscripts and Archives Division: MssColl 2011.

21. "Eccetto però in quelle che sono in disprezzo della mia Religione" (*WJM,* 12:310).

22. "Due copie delle sue eruditissime Poesie . . . perche quantunque piccolo racchiude in se valore infinito" (*WJM,* 12:312).

23. "Vietando che non si debba leggere, alcuna materia di Teologia, ò della Sacra Scrittura." See Carlo Padiglione, *Le leggi dell' Accademia degli Oziosi in Napoli ritrovate nella Biblioteca Brancacciana* (Naples: F. Giannini, 1878), 19. On the Oziosi in general, see Haan, *From Academia to Amicitia,* 118–29.

24. Michele Maylender, *Storia delle Accademie d'Italia* (Bologna: Licinio Cappelli, 1926–30), 4:183.

25. Ibid., 4:186.

26. Sean Cocco, *Watching Vesuvius: A History of Science and Culture in Early Modern Italy* (Chicago: University of Chicago Press, 2013), 53.

27. Giovanni Battista Manso, *Vita, virtù, e miracoli principali di S. Patricia Vergine* (Naples, 1611).

28. "Lettera del Signor Giov. Battista Manso, Marchese di Villa, in materia del Vesuvio," *Archivio Storico per le Provincie Napoletane*, vol. 14, fasc. 3 and 4 (Naples 1889), 503. Cf. Cocco, *Watching Vesuvius*, 68.

29. Describing a papal procession on the eve of the feast day of St. Peter, "In Quintum Novembris" depicts the pope as "triple-crowned" (55; Tricoronifer), carrying his "gods made of bread" (56; panificos . . . Deos) (cf. George Buchanan, "Franciscanus" [740: "de pane ut numen faciant"]), and borne aloft upon the papal sedan (56–57). The candle-lit procession consists of "a very long line of mendicant friars" (58; mendicantum series longissima fratrum). These would include the orders of the Franciscans, Dominicans, Carmelites, and Augustinian Hermits. The disparaging reference to sainthood and to Catholic feast days in honor of saints is significantly addressed to the pope by Satan in Franciscan disguise: "Welcome the support of the gods and goddesses and all those divinities that are celebrated in your feast-days" (129–30; divos divasque secundas / Accipe, quotque tuis celebrantur numina fastis).

30. The phrase is Milton's. See note 9 above.

31. See Bertram Colgrave and R. A. B. Mynors, eds., *Bede's Ecclesiastical History* (Oxford: Oxford University Press, 1969), 132–34. For an earlier version of the story, cf. Paulus Diaconus, *S. Gregorii Magni Vita*, PLat, 75:50. For fuller discussion, see Anthony Low, "*Mansus*: In Its Context," *Milton Studies* 19 (1984): 105–26, 106–7, and Haan, *From Academia to Amicitia*, 130–36.

32. "& totâ mente serenùm / Ridens purpureo suffundar lumine vultus" ("Mansus" 98–99; and smiling with complete serenity of mind, my face will be suffused with blushing radiance). Cf. (of Raphael) "with a smile that glow'd / Celestial rosie red" (*PL* 8.618–19). Manso's *Erocallia* (Venice, 1628), 687–88, discusses the nature of the angelic *facies* and angelic possession of a natural radiance that matches their intellect. This may have been one of the books gifted by Manso to Milton and ekphrastically described in "Epitaphium Damonis" 191–97; see Michele De Filippis, "Milton and Manso: Cups or Books?," *PMLA* 51 (1936): 745–56. For fuller discussion, see Haan, *From Academia to Amicitia*, 134–36.

33. Cf. Francesco de Pietri, *Dell'historia Napoletana* (Naples, 1634), 210: "Nella Cappella dell' *Angelo* sotto il Palagio del Monte di Manso è il vivo Capo di metallo del Poeta Gio. Battista Marino Napoletano di rara maestria, opera di Bartolomeo Viscontini Milanese." Cf. Carlo De Lellis, *Parte seconda o'vero sup-*

plimento a Napoli sacra di D. Cesare D'Engenio Caracciolo (Naples, 1654), 78: "Si vede in questa Capella [sc. dell' Angelo] l'effigie al naturale del Principe della Lirica Italiana poesia, dico del Cavalier Gio: Battista Marino." Emphasis is mine.

34. De Lellis, *Supplimento*, 78. Cited also in Franciscus de Magistris, *Status Rerum Memorabilium Tam Ecclesiasticarum, Quam Politicarum, ac etiam Aedificiorum Fidelissimae Civitatis Neapolitanae* (Naples, 1678), 296.

35. See, for example, De Lellis, *Supplimento*, 78: "riposandosi il corpo del Cavalier Marino nel Cimeterio della Chiesa di SS. Apostoli."

36. Cf. Virgil, *Eclogue* 10.33: "o mihi tum quam molliter ossa quiescant." As noted by Robert Coleman, ed., *Vergil: Eclogues* (Cambridge: Cambridge University Press, 1977), 284, the adverb *molliter* occurs only here in Virgil.

37. See Estelle Haan, *Both English and Latin: Bilingualism and Biculturalism in Milton's Neo-Latin Writings* (Philadelphia: American Philosophical Society, 2012), 126–29.

38. Text is that of *Il Manso, Overo dell' amicizia dialogo del Sig. Torquato Tasso al Molto Illustre Sig. Gio. Battista Manso* (Ferrara, 1602).

39. Ibid., 2.

40. Ibid.

41. Cf. Tasso's encomium of Manso, in which he states that Manso's name is inscribed by the gods not only in one thousand pages but also in beautiful metal or in stone (*Poesie Nomiche* (Venice, 1635), 257; "E'l nome vostro in bel metallo, o in pietra / Scriver si dee, non solo in mille carte").

42. "Fra cavalier magnanimi, è cortesi / Risplende il Manso"; *Gerusalemme Conquistata* 20.142 (Rome, 1593).

43. "Mansus" 20–21, alludes to Manso's *Vita* of Tasso and to his now lost *Vita* of Marino.

44. "Stretto amico del Tasso, come i costui versi, e le prose in molti luoghi, e spetialmente la Gerusalemme, e'l Dialogo dell' amicitia, ch' egli intitolò il Manso, feciono fede." Text is that of Manso, *Vita di Torquato Tasso* (dedicated to Cardinal Antonio Barberini) (Rome, 1634), 4.

45. Ibid., 248: "Quindi è ch'egli fù così leale osservatore delle sacre leggi dell' Amicitia."

46. Ibid., 249.

47. On the projected *Arthuriad*, cf. "Epitaphium Damonis" 162–71.

48. Douglas Bush, *A Variorum Commentary on the Poems of John Milton*, vol. 1, *The Latin and Greek Poems* (New York: Columbia University Press, 1970), 279. Just three years later in *Reason of Church Government* Milton would discuss "that Epick form whereof the two poems of *Homer*, and those other two of *Virgil* and *Tasso* are a diffuse, and the book of *Job* a brief, model" (*CPW*, 1:813).

49. Low, *"Mansus,"* 114. On the allegorical representation, see Haan, *From Academia to Amicitia*, 149–64. Cf. the allegory of Florentine academies in "Epitaphium Damonis" 125–38, most likely the *illis paucis versiculis, emblematis ad morem inclusis* ("those few little verses incorporated in emblematic fashion"), mentioned by Milton in his letter to Carlo Dati (April 20, 1647; *WJM*, 12:48). See Haan, *From Academia to Amicitia*, 56.

50. Bush, *Variorum Commentary*, 1:276.

51. Cf. the *Mansus/mansuetus* pun in line 60 and the possible *mansuetæ/ Manse tuæ* anagram in line 1.

52. See Manso, *Vita di Torquato Tasso*, 225–29.

53. Ibid., 235.

54. Ibid.

55. Edited by Francesco Ronconi, this 267-page volume contains poems in Italian, Latin, Greek, Spanish, and French.

56. See *Il Teatro delle Glorie della Signora Adriana Basile* (Venice, 1628); Alessandro Ademollo, *La Bell' Adriana ed altre virtuose del suo tempo alla corte de Mantova* (Citta di Castello: Lapi, 1888).

57. See Frederick Hammond, *Music and Spectacle in Baroque Rome: Barberini Patronage under Urban VIII* (New Haven, CT: Yale University Press, 1994), 86. Unfortunately, none of Leonora's compositions survive. On Leonora in general, see Alessandro Ademollo, *La Leonora di Milton e di Clemente IX* (Milan, 1885); Eugene Schuyler, "Milton's Leonora," *Nation* 47 (October 18, 1888): 310–12; *The New Grove Dictionary of Music and Musicians*, ed. Stanley Sadie (London: Macmillan, 1980), 2:171–72; *Dizionario biografico degli Italiani* (Rome: F. Scarano, 1964), 6:456–58; Haan, *From Academia to Amicitia*, 99–117; Cristina Galassi, "La virtuosa Eleonora Baroni in un ritratto di Fabio della Corgna," *Kronos* 13 (2009): 177–83. On the representation of Leonora in the *Applausi* volume, see Amy Brosius, "'*Il suon, lo sguardo, il canto*': Virtuose of the Roman Conversazioni in the Mid-Seventeenth Century" (Ph.D diss., New York University, 2009), 328–50.

58. Ronconi, *Applausi*, A5v ("Lettor Cortese"): "perche non è frà questi Autori chi habbia havuta intentione di allontanarsi punto dall' osservanza, che si deve *alla vera Cattolica, e Romana Religione.*" Emphasis is mine.

59. On Leonora as a tenth Muse, see Alfonso Pallavicini in Ronconi, *Applausi*, 12.

60. Contrast Margaret Byard, "'Adventurous Song': Milton and the Music of Rome," in Di Cesare, *Milton in Italy*, 305–38, 322–23: "the three Latin epigrams he wrote and intended for a volume of poetry dedicated to her." As for the date of their composition, Milton's allusion to Tasso's madness because of his love for another Leonora ("Ad Leonoram" 2.1–2) favors the return visit, by which time he had met in Naples Giovanni Battista Manso, author of the

Vita di Torquato Tasso discussed above. It was Manso who promulgated the story of Tasso's insanity in consequence of his love for Leonora d'Este (one of three Leonoras of whom, Manso claims, Tasso was enamored). See *Vita di Torquato Tasso*, 44–67; Haan, *From Academia to Amicitia*, 110–12.

61. *Oxford Latin Dictionary* (Oxford, 1968), *studium*, s.v. 2: "enthusiasm, eagerness (for)"; s.v. 7: "intellectual activity, esp. of a literary kind, or an instance of it, study."

62. On Leonora's membership of the Umoristi, see her sonnet "Alli Signori Accademici Humoristi con occasione, che fù ricevuta nella loro Accademia," in *L'Idea della Veglia* (Rome, 1640), 220. See also Haan, *From Academia to Amicitia*, 102; Hammond, *Music and Spectacle*, 86; Andrew Dell'Antonio, *Listening as Spiritual Practice in Early Modern Italy* (Berkeley: University of California Press, 2011), 84. For an example of an encomium of Leonora penned by a member of the Umoristi, see Lelio Guidiccioni (Ronconi, *Applausi*, 196).

63. John Evelyn records that on February 17, 1645, he "was invited (after dinner) to the Academie of the *Humorists*, kept in a spacious Hall, belonging to Signor Mancini, where the Witts of the Towne meet on certaine daies, to recite poems, & prevaricate on severall Subjects &c." He notes that "the best part of the day we spent in hearing the Academic exercises." See *The Diary of John Evelyn*, ed. E. S. de Beer (Oxford, 1955), 2:364–65; Haan, *From Academia to Amicitia*, 102–3.

64. Attendees are listed in Maylender, *Storia*, 5:375–81. The list, however, is far from definitive. The absence of Milton's name should be viewed alongside the omission of the name Leonora Baroni (a member) and that of John Evelyn (who was in attendance in 1645). On the latter, see previous note. On Milton's participation in the Florentine Accademia degli Svogliati, see Haan, *From Academia to Amicitia*, 10–28. The minutes of the Svogliati attest to Milton's performances on three occasions, most notable of which is that of September 6/16, 1638: "Furono lett' alcune compositioni e particolarmente il Giovanni Miltone Inglese lesse una poesia Latina di versi esametri multo erudita" (Biblioteca Nazionale Centrale, Florence, MSS Magliabecchiana, MSS Cl. IX, cod. 60, fol. 48). On Milton's participation in the Accademia degli Apatisti, see Haan, *From Academia to Amicitia*, 29–37. Anton Francesco Gori (1691–1757) records Milton's attendance at the Apatisti under the year 1638 (Biblioteca Marucelliana, Florence MS A.36, fol. 53r).

65. On Salzilli's membership of the Umoristi, see Maylender, *Storia*, 5:379; on "Ad Salsillum," see James A. Freeman, "Milton's Roman Connection: Giovanni Salzilli," *Milton Studies* 19 (1984): 87–104; Haan, *From Academia to Amicitia*, 81–98. Salzilli contributed fifteen Italian poems to the *Poesie de' signori Accademici Fantastici di Roma* (Rome, 1637), 148–69.

66. Campbell and Corns, *Milton*, 123.

67. See Dell' Antonio, *Listening as Spiritual Practice*, 84–86.

68. On the membership of Rospigliosi and the two Barberini cardinals, see Maylender, *Storia*, 5:377 and 378. The Umoristi also included the celebrated musicologist Giovanni Battista Doni. Francesco Barberini's copy of the *Applausi* is in the Biblioteca Apostolica Vaticana, Stamp. Barb. JJJ.VI.67.

69. The musical event was in all likelihood the performance (on February 17/27, 1639) of a comedic pastoral opera *Chi soffre, speri* (libretto by Cardinal Giulio Rospigliosi; music by Virgilio Mazzocchi and Marco Marazzoli). See Haan, *From Academia to Amicitia*, 104. Cf. Alessandro Ademollo, *I teatri di Roma nel secolo decimosettimo* (Rome, 1888), 25–34; J. S. Smart, "Milton in Rome," *Modern Language Review* 8 (1913): 91–92; G. L. Finney, "Chorus in *Samson Agonistes*," *PMLA* 58 (1943): 649–64, 658 (revised in her *Musical Backgrounds for English Literature, 1580–1650* [New Brunswick, NJ: Rutgers University Press 1962], 228–30); John G. Demaray, *Milton's Theatrical Epic: The Invention and Design of Paradise Lost* (Cambridge, MA: Harvard University Press, 1980), 129; Margaret Murata, *Operas for the Papal Court, 1631–1668* (Ann Arbor, MI: UMI Research Press, 1981), 32–34, 164–66, 182–86; Frederick Hammond, "Bernini and the 'Fiera di Farfa,'" in *Gianlorenzo Bernini: New Aspects of His Art and Thought*, ed. Irving Lavin (University Park: Pennsylvania State University Press, 1985), 115–25; Hammond, *Music and Spectacle*, 235–36; Emily Wilbourne, *Seventeenth-Century Opera and the Sound of the Commedia dell'Arte* (Chicago: University of Chicago Press, 2016), 92–129.

70. See John Milton, *Epistola Familiaris* 9 (*WJM*, 12:38–45), in which he describes how Cardinal Francesco Barberini sought him out at the door, almost seized him by the hand, and escorted him inside to the performance. Milton proceeds to relate that Holste facilitated a private audience with Francesco the following day (*WJM*, 12:40). As Campbell and Corns, *Milton*, 123, note: "There is no record of what was said at the meeting, which may have been entirely formal." Milton's holograph letter to Holste has survived (Vat. Barb. Lat. 2181, fols. 57–58v).

71. "Si Eminentissimum Cardinalem quantâ potest observantiâ meo nomine salutes" (*WJM*, 12:44). Cf. H. J. Todd, *Some Account of the Life and Writings of John Milton* (London, 1826), 38.

72. See Campbell and Corns, *Milton*, 123. Whether Milton was aware of this fact remains a mystery. In *Areopagitica*, recalling his Italian sojourn, he would famously claim: "There it was that I found and visited the famous *Galileo* grown old, a prisner to the Inquisition, for thinking in Astronomy otherwise then the Franciscan and Dominican licencers thought" (*CPW*, 2:538). The claim, although much contested, is probably true. The meeting could have been facilitated by Galileo's illegitimate son, Vincenzo, who is included in a letter from Carlo Dati to Milton as among those who send him their affectionate greetings: "I Signori Frescobaldi, Coltellini, Francini, Galilei et altri infiniti

unitamente le inviano affetuosi saluti" (*WJM*, 12:314), and might have oc-
curred either at Galileo's villa in Arcetri or in Florence. See Campbell and
Corns, *Milton*, 112–13. Cf. Neil Harris, "Galileo as Symbol: The 'Tuscan
Artist' in *Paradise Lost*," *Annali dell' Istituto e Museo di Storia della Scienza di
Firenze* 10 (1985): 3–29.

73. Ronconi, *Applausi*, 201–3.

74. On Holste's role as an important avenue to both Catholic and Protestant scholars seeking access to the Barberini and Vatican libraries, see F. J.
Blom, "Lucas Holstenius (1596–1661) and England," in *Studies in Seventeenth-
Century English Literature, History and Bibliography*, ed. G. A. M. Janssens and
F. G. A. M. Aarts, Costerus 46 (Amsterdam: Rodopi, 1984), 25–39, 25. For
the argument that the volume gifted to Milton was Holste's *Demophili Demo-
cratis et Secundi Veterum Philosophorum Sententiae Morales* (Rome, 1638) (a slim
volume containing Holste's Latin rendering of the axioms of the later Pythago-
reans), see Leo Miller, "Milton and Holstenius Reconsidered: An Exercise in
Scholarly Practice," in Di Cesare, *Milton in Italy*, 573–87, 574. However, the
Pythagorean imagery and language of Milton's letter (see note 78 below) and
its inclusion of several specific Greek words discussed by Holste in an earlier
published work suggest that the volume in question was more likely Holste's
substantial edition of *Porphyrii Vita Pythagorae* (Rome, 1630). See Estelle Haan,
"That Puissant City": John Milton's Roman Sojourns 1638–1639 (Philadelphia:
American Philosophical Society, forthcoming 2018). Milton's description of the
gift as *duplex* alludes to the fact that the volume is bilingual: Greek with facing
Latin translation.

75. Campbell and Corns, *Milton*, 123. One might add that the special
affinity (evident in the warmth of Milton's Latin letter) may have been en-
hanced by the fact that Holste himself had spent time in England (1622–24)
working in the Bodleian Library (admitted June 27, 1622, and working there
until December of that year, on which see Blom, "Lucas Hostenius," 27) for
a planned edition of Greek geographers, which, however, like many of his
projects, did not see fruition. Holste collected the autograph of John Rouse (to
whom Milton would later address a Latin ode). Also, as noted above, Holste
was a Catholic convert, but had been one only since 1624.

76. On the ability of the Vatican library to impress English visitors, cf.
Evelyn, *Diary*, ed. De Beer, 2:300: "[18 Jan. 1645]: This Library is doubtlesse
the most nobly built, furnish'd, and beautified in the World, ample, stately,
light & cherefull, looking into a most pleasant Garden: The walls & roofe are
painted; not with Antiqu<e>s, & Grotesc's (like our Bodlean at Oxford) but
Emblemes, Figurs, Diagramms, and the like learned inventions found out by
the Wit, & Industry of famous Men, of which there are now whole Volumes
extant."

77. Contrast Milton's allegorical equation of the Vatican with Virgil's underworld in "In Quintum Novembris," 139–59.

78. Among other hitherto unnoticed aspects of Milton's letter that find a possible parallel in the Virgilian underworld are the motifs of being received ("recepisti"; "accipiuntur"; cf. *Aeneid* 6.315, 393, 412–13; 693) and admitted ("admisso"; cf. *Aeneid* 6.330), while his description of the cardinal's virtual grasping of his hand ("pene manu prehensum") may recall Aeneas's plea to the ghost of Anchises: "da iungere dextram" (*Aeneid* 6.697), a plea that was unfulfilled (*Aeneid* 6.700–702). The letter's potential recourse to both *anabasis* and *katabasis* would, moreover, be highly appropriate given the Pythagorean nature of the likely book gifted by Holste to Milton, on which see note 74 above.

79. Contrast Charles Lamb's rather blinkered viewpoint: "I am afraid some of his addresses (*ad Leonoram* I mean) have rather erred on the farther side" ("Some Sonnets of Sir Philip Sidney," in *The Works of Charles and Mary Lamb*, ed. E. V. Lucas [New York, 1903], 2:214). Milton's poems, however, do not mention Leonora's beauty or chastity forever lauded by the *Applausi* poets (e.g., Berlingiero Gessi in Ronconi, *Applausi*, 31–38).

80. Dell'Antonio, *Listening as Spiritual Practice*, 86.

81. Cf. "ò bella Sirena" (19), "questa Sirena" (118), "vaga Sirena" (121), "la dolce Sirena" (129 and 185), "fastosetta Sirena" (157), "pudica Siren" (201). See Haan, *From Academia to Amicitia*, 114–16.

82. "Illa quidem vivitque, & amœnâ Tibridis undâ / Mutavit rauci murmura Pausilipi" ("Ad Leonoram" 3.5–6; In fact she is alive and has exchanged the murmurings of the raucous Posillipo for Tiber's lovely waters).

83. Ronconi, *Applausi*, 157. Cf. Lucas Holste: "pulchrae Parthenopes canora proles" (*Applausi*, 201; songful offspring of the beautiful Parthenope).

84. Epigram 1 was dismissed by Cowper as less accomplished than epigrams 2 and 3: "I have translated only two of the three poetical compliments addressed to Leonora, as they appear to me far superior to what I have omitted" (*The Poetical Works of William Cowper*, ed. H. S. Milford [London: Henry Frowde, 1911], 598).

85. David Masson, ed., *The Poetical Works of John Milton* (London: Macmillan, 1882), 3:305, describes the lines as "a fancy in which I discern something characteristic of Milton." Robert H. West, *Milton and the Angels* (Athens: University of Georgia Press, 1955), 132.

86. Ronconi, *Applausi*, 138: "Quindi angelico suon spira la bocca."

87. Ibid., 156: "Se l'Angioletta mia tremolo, e chiaro / A le stelle, onde scese, il canto invia, / Ebra del suono, in cui se stessa oblia, / Col Ciel pensa la Terra irne del paro." In a letter dated March 24, 1634, Testi had proclaimed of Leonora's musical talents: "Se gli angeli cantano in paradiso, bisogna credere che cantino com'ella fra." See Fulvio Testi, *Lettere*, vol. 2, *1634–1637*, ed. M. L. Doglio (Bari: Laterza, 1967), 129–30n660. Cf. André Maugars's praise (in 1639) of Leonora's song, which "me surprit si fort les sens et me porta dans un tel ravissement, que j'oubliay ma condition mortelle, et creuz estre desia parmy

les anges" (*Response faite à un curieux sur le sentiment de la musique d'Italie, escrite à Rome le premier Octobre 1639*, ed. Ernest Thoinan [Paris: A. Claudin, 1865], 37–38).

88. Ronconi, *Applausi*, 260: "S'al moto armonioso / De l'angelo movente / Ogni sfera si volge."

89. West, *Milton and the Angels*, 132.

90. Joad Raymond, *Milton's Angels: The Early Modern Imagination* (Oxford: Oxford University Press, 2010), 232: "Belief in individual guardian angels marked a clear, though not absolute, difference between Protestants and Roman Catholics."

91. Cf. *A Mask* 212–20, in which the Lady asserts her belief that "the Supreme good" (217) "Would send a glistring Guardian if need were / To keep my life and honour unassail'd" (219–20).

92. Raymond, *Milton's Angels*, 235.

93. Interestingly, Milton's phrase, while lacking classical precedent, finds a parallel in the *Electrica* (Rome, 1767) of Giuseppe Maria Mazzolari (alias Josephus Marianus Parthenius), an Italian Jesuit and professor of rhetoric in Florence and Rome. Proclaiming in book 5 the inspirational power of *furor philosophicus*, he states: "Adeo vis ignea totis / Serpit agens se se venis, et pectore gliscit." Text is that of *Josephi Mariani Parthenii Electricorum Libri VI* (Rome, 1767), 186. Y. A. Haskell, *Loyola's Bees: Ideology and Industry in Jesuit Latin Didactic Poetry* (Oxford: Oxford University Press, 2003), 235, while not noticing the possible echo of Milton, remarks: "[Mazzolari's] description of the *furor philosophicus* in terms of a *vis ignea* might seem playfully to flirt with the idea of an electrical (i.e. material) spirit."

94. Cf. Milton, "At a Solemn Musick" 17–18: "That we on Earth with undiscording voice / May rightly answer that melodious noise."

95. Lamb, *Works*, ed. Lucas, 2:214.

96. On *mens tertia* as Venus, see Thomas Keightly, ed., *The Poems of John Milton* (London, 1859), ad loc; as one of the seraphim, Diane K. McColley, "Tongues of Men and Angels: *Ad Leonoram Romae Canentem*," *Milton Studies* 19 (1984): 127–48, 139–42; as a Boethian category, Boethius, *De Musica* 1.2: "tertia est musica, quae in quibusdam consistere dicitur instrumentis," and S. K. Heninger, *Touches of Sweet Harmony: Pythagorean Cosmology and Renaissance Poetics* (New Haven, CT: Yale University Press, 1974), 101–4; as the music of the spheres, Haan, *From Academia to Amicitia*, 108–9; as the Holy Spirit, Bush, *Variorum Commentary*, 1:149, who cites "the third heaven" of 2 Cor. 12.2.4.

97. The Protestant John Dee records that on April 19, 1585, "I took Ghostly counsel of Doctor Hannibal, the great Divine, that had now set out some of his Commentaries upon Pymander, Hermitis Trismigisti," and that on the following day "I received the Communion at the Pernardines [*sic*], where

that Doctor is a Professor." See *A True and Faithful Relation of What Passed for Many Yeers Between Dr. John Dee … and Some Spirits* (London, 1659), 397. Hermes Trismegistus is the "Ter magnus Hermes" of Milton's "De Idea Platonica" 33 (where he is described as "trino gloriosus nomine" [32; boasting in a threefold name] and as "arcani sciens" [33; skilled in mysteries]), and the "thrice great *Hermes*" of "Il Penseroso" 88.

98. Samuel Mintz, "The Motion of Thought: Intellectual and Philosophical Backgrounds," in *Backgrounds to Seventeenth-Century Literature*, ed. C. A. Patrides and Raymond B. Waddington (Manchester: Manchester University Press, 1980), 138–69, 152. See *Mercurii Trismegisti Liber de Potestate et Sapientia Dei e Graeco in Latinum Traductus a Marsilio Ficino Florentino ad Cosmum Medicem Patriae Patrem. Pimander Incipit* (Treviso, 1471). Among other translations or editions of the *corpus hermeticum* was the Italian translation of Tommaso Benci (1548) and a Latin rendering by Francesco Patrizzi (1591). It was not until 1650 and 1657 that John Everard's famous English translation would see print.

99. The Greek original has *noûs ho theòs*. See Gustav Parthey, ed., *Hermetis Trismegisti Poemander* (Berlin: Nicolai, 1854), 4.

100. *Pymander Mercurii Trismegisti cum Commento Fratris Hannibalis Rosseli Calabri, Ordinis Minorum Regularis Observantiae, Theologiae & Philosophiae, ad S. Bernardinum Cracoviae Professoris. Liber III: De Ente, Materia, Forma, et Rebus Metaphysicis* (Cracow, 1586), 364. Emphasis is mine.

101. *"Aliquando est spiritus sanctus, & omnes tres una mens*, quia nimirum unus intellectus, una sapientia atque natura" (ibid., 365). Cf. *Mercurii Trismegisti Liber*, trans. Ficino, fol. 2v: "Mens autem deus: utriusque sexus fecunditate plenissimus. vita et lux cum verbo suo mentem alteram opificem peperit: qui quidem deus ignis atque *spiritus numen.*" Emphasis is mine.

102. Valery Rees, *From Gabriel to Lucifer: A Cultural History of Angels* (London: I. B. Tauris, 2013), 69; M. J. B. Allen, *Synoptic Art: Marsilio Ficino on the History of Platonic Interpretation* (Florence: Leo S. Olschki, 1998), 28.

103. Lodovico Lazzarelli, *Lodovici Lazareli Poete Christiani ad Ferdinandum Regem Dialogus Cui Titulus Crater Hermetis* (Paris, 1505), 60v: *Ipse qui in Hermetis mente Pimander erat in me christus* IHESUS. Cf. *Laudabo itaque christum* IHESUM *sub Pimandri nomine* (*Crater Hermetis*, 80).

104. Jill Renée Delsigne, "Sacramental Magic and Animate Statues in Edmund Spenser, William Shakespeare, and John Milton" (PhD diss., Rice University, 2012), 122.

105. Cf. Acts 2:3–4: "And there appeared unto them cloven tongues like as of fire, and it sat upon each of them. And they were all filled with the Holy Ghost, and began to speak with other tongues, as the Spirit gave them utterance" (*KJV*).

106. Lazzarelli, *Crater Hermetis*, 74v.

107. Mintz, "Motion of Thought," 152.
108. Lazzarelli, *Crater Hermetis*, 61–61v.
109. James Ellison, "*The Winter's Tale* and the Religious Politics of Europe," in *New Casebooks: Shakespeare's Romances*, ed. Alison Thorne (New York: Palgrave Macmillan, 2003), 171–204, 189; Frances Yates, *Giordano Bruno and the Hermetic Tradition* (London: Routledge and Kegan Paul, 1964), 179.
110. Delsigne, *Sacramental Magic*, 120.
111. For discussion of the poem's engagement with classical pastoral, see Janet Leslie Knedlik, "High Pastoral Art in *Epitaphium Damonis*," *Milton Studies* 19 (1984): 149–63; Gordon Campbell, Imitation in *Epitaphium Damonis*," *Milton Studies* 19 (1984): 165–77; Victoria Moul, "Of Hearing and Failing to Hear: The Allusive Dialogue with Virgil in Milton's *Epitaphium Damonis*," *Canadian Review of Comparative Literature* 33 (2006): 154–71; Philip Hardie, "Milton's *Epitaphium Damonis* and the Virgilian Career," in *Pastoral Palimpsests: Essays in the Reception of Theocritus and Virgil*, ed. Michael Paschalis (Herakleion: Crete University Press, 2007), 79–100. For possible links with neo-Latin writers, see T. P. Harrison, "The Latin Pastorals of Milton and Castiglione," *PMLA* 50 (1935): 480–93; L. V. Ryan, "Milton's *Epitaphium Damonis* and B. Zanchi's Elegy on Baldassare Castiglione," *Humanistica Lovaniensia* 30 (1981): 108–23; Stella P. Revard, "Milton's *Epitaphium Damonis*: The Debt to Neo-Latin Poets," *The European Legacy: Toward New Paradigms* 17 (2012): 309–16; Estelle Haan, "Pastoral," in *A Guide to Neo-Latin Literature*, ed. Victoria Moul (Cambridge: Cambridge University Press, 2016), 163–79.
112. "Carolus Deodatus ex urbe Hetruriæ Luca paterno genere oriundus, cætera Anglus."
113. D. C. Dorian, *The English Diodatis* (New Brunswick, NJ: 1950), xii, 7.
114. Cf. ibid., 8.
115. MS *Libro di ricordi degnissimi delle nostre famiglie* (MS Supp. 438, Bibliothèque Publique et Universitaire, Geneva), fol. 76r.
116. Dorian, *English Diodatis*, 115.
117. The phrase may look back to the lament for the prematurely deceased Marcellus at *Aeneid* 6.878: "heu pietas, heu prisca fides." R. G. Austin, ed., *P. Vergili Maronis Aeneidos Liber Sextus* (Oxford: Clarendon Press, 1977), 271, remarks that "*prisca* (with *pietas* as well as with *fides*) suggests the purity of 'old-fashioned' ways." Interestingly, descriptions of Marcellus by both Velleius Paterculus (2.93.1) and Seneca (*Ad Marciam* 2.3) highlight youthful qualities of virtue, cheerfulness, and genius likewise attributed to Diodati by Milton in "Epitaphium Damonis."
118. "Matricula Studiosorum S. Theologiae in Genevensi Academia ab Anno MDCXII," MS Fr. 141c (Inv.345), fol. 9v, in Bibliothèque Publique et Universitaire de Genève. See Dorian, *English Diodatis*, 130–31; Gordon Camp-

bell, "Charles Diodati," in *ODNB*. Geneva was the birthplace of Charles's father Theodore and the residence of his uncle Jean Diodati, an esteemed Protestant theologian.

119. Dorian, *English Diodatis*, 131. Diodati's signature is no. 301 in the list.

120. Diodati as "Thuscus" may also evoke a certain Tuscus, poet and contemporary of Ovid (cf. Ovid, *Ex. Pont.* 4.16.20). See Haan, "Pastoral," 175–77.

121. See note 32 above.

122. See Haan, *Both English and Latin*, 103.

123. BL C57.d.48. See Leicester Bradner, "Milton's *Epitaphium Damonis*," *Times Literary Supplement*, August 18, 1932, 581; H. F. Fletcher, "The Seventeenth-Century Separate Printing of *Milton's Epitaphium Damonis*," *Journal of English and Germanic Philology* 61 (1962): 788–96; J. T. Shawcross, "The Date of the Separate Edition of Milton's *Epitaphium Damonis*," *Studies in Bibliography* 18 (1965): 262–65; Haan, *From Academia to Amicitia*, 55–56. See also *CWJM*, 3:clx–clxi, 550–56.

124. "Siquidem ad vos carmen illud pervenit, quod ex te nunc primum audio" (*WJM*, 12:48).

125. "Illis paucis versiculis, emblematis ad morem inclusis" (*WJM*, 12:48).

126. Hale, *Milton's Languages*, 89.

127. Cf. "Jam solus agros, jam pascua solus oberro" ("Epitaphium Damonis" 58; But in solitude I wander now through fields, in solitude now through pastures); "solus" ("Epitaphium Damonis" 141).

128. "Illos jam pene omnes, aut morte, aut iniquissimâ locorum distantiâ invideri mihi" (*WJM*, 12:46; They are now almost all withheld from me either by death or by a spatial distance most unfair). Cf. Milton's wistful recollection of his cultivation of so many friends and companions "in a single city [Florence], albeit a very distant one" (*WJM*, 12:48; unâ in urbe, longinquâ illâ quidem).

129. "Testor illum mihi semper sacrum et solenne futurum Damonis tumulum; in cujus funere ornando cum luctu & mœrore oppressus" (*WJM*, 12:48; I call to witness that tomb of Damon which I will forever hold sacred and solemn, in the honoring of whose death I have been overwhelmed by grief and sorrow).

130. *Ioannis Audoeni Epigrammatum Libri Tres* (London, 1606), ed. J. R. C. Martyn (Leiden, 1978), 2:83: "Ad Theo-dorum Deo-datum, Medicum: Nomine tu Graio Theodorus es atque Latino; / Arte potens Phoebi, Ter-Theodorus eris."

131. John Florio, trans., *The Essays or Morall, Politike and Millitarie Discourses of Lo: Michaell de Montaigne* (London, 1603), A3r (Preface).

132. Nicolas Du Mortier, *Etymologiae Sacrae Graeco-Latinae seu e Graecis Fontibus Depromptae* (Rome, 1703), 634: "Sancti hoc nomine nuncupati, summâ largitate in eorum natali Universo à Deo dati, totis cordium medullis

in vità Deo dediti, maximâ gloriâ in morte Deo redditi, eius beatitudinis ineffabili felicitate participes sunt effecti."

133. *WJM*, 12:292–95; J. M. French, ed., *The Life Records of John Milton*, vol. 1, *1608–1639* (New York: Gordian Press, 1966), 98, 104.

134. The saint's name does not occur in Dorian's Appendix II: "The Name Diodati," in *English Diodatis*, 328–29.

135. See *Vita Sancti Deodati Valcandi Mediani*, in *PLat*, 151:605–34.

136. *PLat*, 151:624: "vicini facti non dormitaverunt, sed alacriter vigilaverunt erga custodiam amoris mutui atque sinceri . . . quibus . . . maxima iucunditas esset simul semper conversari et esse . . . [noctem] insomnes totam in sanctis colloquiis et divinis laudibus solebant expendere."

137. On the "Epitaphium Damonis" as pseudo-Petrarchan, see Haan, "Pastoral," 173–77.

138. *PLat*, 151:627.

139. *PLat*, 151:627.

140. Cf. Castiglione, *Alcon* 84: "ne manibus premerem morientia lumina amicis."

141. See E. S. Le Comte, *Milton's Unchanging Mind: Three Essays* (Port Washington, NY: Kennikat Press, 1973).

CHAPTER 7

MARIAN CONTROVERSIES AND MILTON'S VIRGIN MARY

JOHN FLOOD

It is not unusual to argue that in *Paradise Regained* Milton was of Mary's party, as the poem represents her as humble, faithful, and intelligent as well as identifying her closely with Jesus. However, whereas the poet could have relied on what his audience knew of Satan in advance of reading *Paradise Lost*, Mary's case was a good deal more complicated. Unlike Satan, Mary came with more mixed associations because of differences in belief between Roman Catholics and Protestants. Although she is theologically and artistically subordinate to her son in *Paradise Regained*, Mary has a prominent role, and it is curious that Milton shows little if any anxiety about how such a controversial character was to be deployed. A few words here or there would have clarified confessional issues without trespassing on the poem, but, as will be seen, these qualifications never appear.

A number of fundamental complications face the enterprise of considering *Paradise Regained* in the light of Marian Catholicism, and these must be addressed. It can, for example, be objected that in the seventeenth century there is no such thing as a monolithic Catholic position on Mary and that to talk of one is an oversimplification. In Milton's time this is clearest in the case of the Immaculate Conception, which was only solemnly defined in 1854. In the seventeenth century it was particularly controversial, to the extent that the phrase "Immaculate Conception" was outlawed by the Dominican-controlled Roman Inquisition between 1627 and 1644.[1] In 1661, at the request of Philip IV of Spain, Alexander VII issued *Sollicitudo Omnium Ecclesiarum*, a brief recognizing the popularity of the belief and the fact that "almost all Catholics already embrace it," while at the same time he noted that it had given rise to "great offense to God, scandals, quarrels, and discords."[2] Simultaneously, Alexander confirmed *Grave Nimis* (1483), a constitution of Sixtus IV that leaned toward an endorsement of the Immaculate Conception but forbade any of the participants in the debate from branding their opponents as heretics or sinners.[3] In effect, then, while appeasing Philip IV, the pope delayed making a definitive opinion in favor of a doctrine that had been rejected by authorities including St. Augustine, Peter Lombard, and Albert the Great in a debate that played out during the latter half of the seventeenth century.[4] This division of opinion, most obvious between the Franciscans (who supported the doctrine) and the Dominicans, was a source of satisfaction to reformers such as John Foxe who were otherwise deeply disturbed by the scandal that "the people was taught nothing els almost in the pulpits all this while, but how the virgine Mary was co[n]ceiued immaculate, and holy wythout Originall sinne, and how they ought to call to her for helpe, whome they wyth special termes do cal the way of mercy: the mother of grace: the lover of pietie: the comforter of mankind: the continuall intercessour for the salvation of the faithfull: and an advocate to the king her sonne, which never ceasseth."[5] The Immaculate Conception was the most obviously divisive aspect of Catholic Marian belief. Given Mary's prominence, she was more rather than less likely to be a source of differing viewpoints, as is already evident in the patristic era. Nevertheless, the broad brush stroke of "Catholic devotion" can be serviceable in the light of a discussion of Milton's Mary.

Another possible oversimplification, and one that is more important to the matter at hand, is defaulting to an association between Mary and the Roman Catholic as opposed to the Protestant churches. Reformers too had a Marian tradition, and a student of Milton should turn to this before thinking of Catholicism, the church to which he was so openly hostile. Diarmaid MacCulloch argues that the "prehistory" of the reformers' attitudes to Mary "lies in the mind of Desiderius Erasmus."[6] Although throughout his life Erasmus wrote devotional works to celebrate the Virgin (including a Mass for Our Lady of Loreto), he was critical of the way "the ordinary run of men attribute more almost [to Mary] than to her son."[7] In *The Praise of Folly* he lampooned the manner that this misguided devotion expressed itself: "What a huge flock of people light candles to the virgin mother of God, even at noon, when there is no need!"[8] His skepticism regarding Marian relics—necessarily of a special kind because of the Assumption—expressed itself in terms that would later be taken up by the reformers: "O Mother most like her Son! He left us so much of his blood on earth; she left us so much of her milk that it's scarcely credible a woman with only one child could have so much, even if the child had drunk none of it."[9] Erasmus's biblical scholarship was also important for its influence on reformed views of Mary. He pruned back scriptural references linked to her from outside the Gospels: she had been erroneously associated with the bride of the Song of Songs and with the figure of Wisdom in Ecclesiasticus (Sirach), whereas both of these actually referred to the church. Furthermore, he showed that Ezekiel 44:2 ("This gate shall be shut, it shall not be opened, and no man shall enter in by it; because the Lord the God of Israel hath entered in by it, therefore it shall be shut") and Isaiah 7:14 ("Behold, a Virgine shall conceive and beare a Sonne") were not testaments to the perpetual virginity of Mary (a doctrine he in fact disbelieved, but on nonscriptural grounds).[10] Erasmus's interpretation of the Gospels also deviated from Roman Catholic orthodoxy. Following the lead of Lorenzo Valla, in his New Testament of 1519 he substituted "gratiosa" (gracious one) for the Vulgate's "gratia plena" (full of grace) in Luke 1:28, thereby setting the precedent for the Geneva Bible's "freely beloved" and the Authorized Version's "highly favored," and avoiding the possibility that the Virgin herself was to be seen as a potential fount of grace.[11] He also denied that Luke 2:51 (in which, having been found in the Temple, the twelve-year-old Jesus returned home with his parents and "was subject unto them") implied that Mary still had authority over Christ in heaven.[12] Overall, Erasmus's emphasis was on the spiritual rather than the corporeal: "It would have been of no use even to the Virgin Mary to have borne Christ of her own flesh if she had not also conceived his spirit through the Holy Spirit."[13]

Jaroslav Pelikan warned that it is a mistake to emphasize the negative elements of Protestant Mariology at the expense of the positive ones.[14] By this he meant that Protestant writers did not merely subtract things from traditional devotion to Mary; they also created spaces in their theological systems for her. It is perhaps significant that Pelikan was the general editor of the standard English translation of Luther's works because although Luther made trenchant criticisms of Roman Catholic Marian devotion he wrote about the Virgin relatively frequently and usually respectfully. A sermon preached in 1522 on Mary's birth exemplifies this: while "it is right that she is honoured correctly . . . priests and monks have expanded the honouring of a woman and lifted Mary so high that they have made a goddess (like those of the pagans) out of a modest servant."[15] For Luther—probably drawing on Augustine—Mary had demonstrated that she was a woman of extraordinary faith (an idea also to be found in the writings of Zwingli and other early reformers).[16] Rejecting medieval innovations that celebrated Mary as queen of heaven—Luther instanced the hymns "Salve regina" and "Regina coeli"—he dismissed the Ascension as "completely papist, that is, full of blasphemy and established without any grounding in Scripture."[17] In his German translation of the Bible he followed Erasmus and described Mary as "gracious one" rather than "full of grace," regardless of the fact that "the papists are going wild about me."[18] Despite his insistence on scripture, Luther, in common with most other reformers, believed in the perpetual virginity of Mary. (Milton himself deployed this belief in support of divorce in the *Judgement of Martin Bucer*: "Now the proper and ultimate end of marriage is not copulation, or children, for then there was not true matrimony between Joseph and Mary" [*CPW*, 2:465].)[19]

The requirements of preaching on the Annunciation demanded that Luther enlist his narrative skills along with the Gospels, supplying some of the human psychology that is absent in them: "Such words [of the angel Gabriel] made the pious child blush and took her breath away with shock, for she did not know what they were about."[20] In a similar vein, in his *Commentary on the Magnificat* (1521), Luther described Mary's humility: "She seeks not any glory, but goes about her usual household duties, milking the cows, cooking the meals, washing pots and kettles, sweeping out the rooms, and performing the work of a maidservant or housemother in lowly and despised tasks."[21] Startlingly, the commentary ends with "May Christ grant us this through the intercession and for the sake of His dear Mother Mary! Amen."[22]

On the subject of relics of lactation, Calvin was more scathing than Erasmus: "Had the breasts of the most Holy Virgin yielded a more copious supply than is given by a cow, or had she continued to nurse during her whole lifetime, she scarcely could have furnished the quantity which is exhibited."[23] He objected to Marian epithets, "proud titles" such as "Queene of heaven, the source of salvation, the gate of life."[24] In the *Institutes* he clearly rejected the practice of calling on "the holy virgin to bid her son do what they request."[25] Nevertheless, Calvin held that Mary had things to teach Christians. When faced with the difficulty of explaining Christ's assertion "This is my body," he observed that "following the holy virgin's example [at the Annunciation], we do not regard it as unlawful for ourselves in a difficult matter to inquire how it can take place."[26] Mary was also an authority: "For wee doe willingly receive her as a teacher, and wee obey her doctrine and her preceptes."[27] The latter quotation is from Calvin's *Harmonie upon the Three Evangelistes.* Calvin does not write extensively on Mary, but of necessity she appears in his commentaries on the opening of Matthew and Luke, a fact that has not escaped readers of *Paradise Regained.*[28] For now, however, it is enough to note that Mary's teaching authority derived from her experience, which she kept "layde uppe in her heart, that afterwards she might bring the same from thence with other treasures."[29]

In the English Reformation the churchmen of Edward VI and Elizabeth I condemned what was seen as Mariolatry in terms that are familiar from the magisterial reformers.[30] Nevertheless, "Attacks on the Virgin Mary led to a redefinition of her significance rather than to her disappearance," and she was still highly visible in everyday life.[31] The year still began on March 25, the feast of the Annunciation, and, as Milton's own family testifies, Mary was a common given name, along with that of Anne, her mother. Although statues had been removed from them, cathedrals and churches commemorated Mary. The 1559 and 1662 versions of *The Book of Common Prayer* included the familiar Christocentric texts in the Nicene and Athanasian creeds (with their respective statements that Christ "was incarnate by the Holy Ghost of the Virgin Mary" and was "of the substance of his Mother," elements that were reaffirmed in the Thirty-Nine Articles), and the Magnificat was recited at every Evening Prayer.[32] In the liturgical calendar the Annunciation and the Purification remained major feasts, and there were, in addition, celebrations of the Visitation, the Nativity of the Blessed Virgin Mary, the Conception of the Blessed Virgin Mary, and the feast of St. Anne, mother to the Blessed Virgin Mary.[33] Reformed skepticism about Catholic excesses was not permitted to spill over into defamation: thus in 1629 the churchwardens of Romsey denounced a parishioner "for saying that the Virgin Mary was an harlot," and in the 1630s some members of the clergy were reported for their "irreverent" comments about her.[34]

The most striking Anglican statement of the virtues of Mary appeared in Anthony Stafford's *The Femall Glory* (1635). Stafford was a Laudian and anti-Puritan, but he was certainly not a Roman Catholic. In addition to writing religious works, he produced several books that were concerned with fashioning a gentleman along the lines of his ideal, Sir Philip Sidney. *Femall Glory* had a similarly educative purpose alongside its religious one.[35] The work acknowledged two audiences: female readers ("O make the emulation of this chaste Turtle your only study!") and male ones ("Neither doth she only require your Gratitude, but your Imitation").[36] For Stafford, Mary was "in Dignity next God himself," and he disapproved of her undervaluation by some Protestants, who showed her less respect than the Qur'an did: "Till they are good Marians, they shall never be good Christians; while they derogate from the dignity of the Mother, they cannot truly honour the Sonne."[37] At the same time he was clear that "no lesse is her shame, or rather, indeed, her trembling when pennes prophanely prodigall ascribe that honour to her which is onely proper, and due to that Deity from which she received her grace and being."[38] In support of this, Strafford displayed his scholarship. He was critical of Erasmus and drew on patristic sources and quotations from "an acute Protestant Doctor," as well as Melanchthon and Bullinger.[39] He ended with long lists of authors who wrote in praise of Mary and rulers who were devoted to her.

Thus far, Stafford is, for his circle, relatively uncontroversial. His is the sort of position that can be found, for example, in the writing of Richard Sheldon, a former Catholic priest who took orders in the Church of England and went into royal service under James I, employment that came to an end because of his anti-Catholic views and his distrust of Henrietta Maria.[40] Sheldon too observed that "I little regard those fonde Disciplinarians, who speake coldly of her [Mary], or of her blessed praises," though he was adamant that the Virgin was not "a secondarie Mediatrisse with her sonne" and that those who gave Mary the attributes of a goddess were deplorable.[41]

While insisting that it was following the theological line to be found in writings such as Sheldon's, *The Femall Glory* shows much more of an affinity with Rome. Immediately noticeable are its illustrations; the one of the Assumption in particular would have inflamed anyone opposed to Marian imagery.[42] The book opens with various poetic tributes, including "The Ghyrlond of the Blessed Virgin Marie," by B. I. (possibly Ben Jonson). This declares that Mary is "Alike of kin, to that most blesses Trine" and employs traditional Catholic epithets, some of them derived from the Hours of the Virgin and the Litany of Loreto: "Tree of Life . . . House of gold . . . Gate of heavens power, The Morning star . . . Great Queen of Queens . . . spotless Mirrour . . . Seat of Sapience . . . Throne of glory . . . Daughter, Mother, Spouse of GOD."[43] These are the sorts of "proud titles" that Calvin execrated and that were commonly attacked by subsequent writers who realized how integral they were to papist practices.[44]

In the course of retelling parts of Mary's life from the Bible and exploring their significance, Stafford found himself in the position that Luther had been in, in that the Gospels needed some filling out: "But what the Scripture omitteth, must be supplied by our charitable imagination, which cannot but conceive all those her Actions buried in silence, to have beene of the same pure thred with the rest of her life."[45] Stafford's fleshing out of Gospel passages was somewhat more risqué than Luther's. In *The Femall Glory*, at the Annunciation, Mary initially mistakes Gabriel, "thinking him to be a man subject to abhorred Lust," so that she "therefore feared violence."[46]

Unsurprisingly then, Stafford's book attracted harsh criticism. Henry Burton thundered that it "mightily deifies the Virgin Mary. . . . Loe heere a change of our God into a Goddesse," and Laud found it necessary to dissociate himself from its content in his trial in 1644.[47] The 1640s saw a crackdown on crypto-papistry, and its legislation shows not only that Marian images survived in pre-Reformation stained glass but that windows incorporating images of the Virgin had been installed in the previous two decades.[48] Having been attacked and repaired over a period of sixty years, the well-known London landmark Cheapside Cross was finally dismantled in 1643.[49] One godly author celebrating this fact noted that when this was done it was revealed that its statues could be animated by hidden mechanisms and that a pipe system allowed its image of Mary to lactate.[50] Marian devotion was never far removed from deceit as well as idolatry.

The Virgin continued to have a literary presence as well as a theological one, although this was, of course, much reduced from that of pre-Reformation England. The importance of Mary in early modern literature has recently come in for more emphasis. It is now common to remark that the statue of Queen Hermione in *The Winter's Tale* is reminiscent of the Marian statuary of an earlier era.[51] The critical burden that Shakespeare bears is such that very little that might be said has not been said, so attention to the Virgin's roles in the plays of Marston, Chapman, Dekker, and Elizabeth Cary might be better academic weathervanes.[52]

One of the best-known literary manifestations of the Virgin linked her with Queen Elizabeth, who, particularly after her death, acquired some of her associations.[53] For readers of Milton, Spenser's treatment of Marian imagery is probably the most interesting. It has been suggested that in *The Faerie Queene* Belphoebe is described with vocabulary usually associated with the Virgin, while Britomart encounters her in the statue in the Temple of Isis as well as taking on some of her attributes.[54] Helen Hackett points out how *The Shepherd's Calendar* invokes Mary, although not in the traditional manner. Her explanation of what Spenser does is worth quoting at length, as it may have more general applicability: "On the one hand Spenser might be seen as employing Marian iconography consciously but surreptitiously, dressing it in terms of the classical mythography of Ovidian metamorphosis, Virgilian prophecy, and the figure of Venus Virgo. He is thus able to deploy deep-seated Marian traditions . . . while avoiding the appearance of quasi Catholicism. Alternatively, he can be seen as not adopting Marian iconography, but reappropriating the myth of the holy virgin-bride-mother for Protestantism."[55]

It is unsurprising that the works of poets who were, who had been, or who became Roman Catholics, such as Donne, Jonson, Southwell,

Crashaw, and Henry Constable, included elements of the Marian devotion that was so important to the old faith. However, Protestant authors evinced their regard for Mary as well, and in ways that showed her ties to pre-Reformation piety. Mary's titles had not disappeared: Sylvester's translation of DuBartas's "The Triumph of Faith" celebrated "A Virgin pure in body and in minde, / Christ's Mother, Sister, Spouse, and Daughter deer," while in the second part of *Silex Scintillans* (1655), Vaughan's "The Knot" greeted the "Bright Queen of Heaven! God's Virgin Spouse."[56] Fletcher's biblical epic *Christ's Triumph Over Death* included an account of Mary's suffering at the Crucifixion, a readily understandable extrapolation from the Gospels, but one that threatened to reduce the purely Christocentric process of redemption:

> Ah blessed Virgin, what high Angels art
> Can ever coumpt thy teares, or sing thy smart,
> When every naile, that pierst his hand, did pierce thy heart?[57]

Protestant clergy also contributed to Marian literature: Herbert produced an "Anagram of the Virgin Marie," and in "To all Angels and Saints" he lamented that her role as advocate was unacceptable to James I:

> I would addresse
> My vows to thee most gladly, blessed Maid,
> And Mother of my God, In my distresse.
> . . . .
> But now (alas!) I dare not; for our King,
> Whom we do all joyntly adore and praise,
>   Bids no such thing:[58]

More specifically of interest with regard to *Paradise Regained* is the narrative verse that dealt with the life of Mary. The most obvious example of this is *The Life and Death of the Most Blessed Among Women, the Virgin Mary Mother of Our Lord Jesus* (1620) by "the Water Poet," John Taylor. Both its dedication to Mary, Countess of Buckingham—a reluctant convert from Catholicism and the mother of James I's favorite—and its explanation of having being based on a volume Taylor found in Antwerp from which he took the best and omitted the poison were alarming to part of his audience; nevertheless, Taylor was a committed Protestant, and he was adamant that prayer should be addressed only to the Trinity:

> I will no prayers nor invocations frame,
> For intercession to this heavenly Dame:
> Nor to her name one fruitlesse word shall runne,
> To be my Mediatresse to her Sonne.[59]

It seems that he may have intended the work as an ecumenical bridge that could be acceptable to both "pious Protestants and charitable Catholics," and although the patience of the latter might be tried by its argument that Romanists dishonor the Virgin by their superstition, the narrative allowed him to cover material that was part of a shared heritage.[60]

Aemilia Lanyer's *Salve Deus Rex Iudaeorum* (1611) is a poem most often discussed (both in itself and in relation to Milton) on the basis of its treatment of Eve.[61] Eve's story is only inset in a narrative of the passion of Christ. Like Fletcher—but to a much more sustained degree—Lanyer describes Mary's perspective on Calvary: she is "His woefull Mother wayting on her Sonne, / All comfortlesse in depth of sorow drowned," the beginning of a description that is sustained over sixteen stanzas and that includes an analeptic account of the Annunciation.[62] *Salve Deus* is an interesting blending of reformed and Catholic attitudes to Mary, and were there to be any direct evidence that Milton knew the text, it would be a touchstone of scholarship on *Paradise Regained*, another treatment of part of the life of Christ that includes verses detailing the actions and inner life of the Virgin. As it is, Lanyer's work, along with that of the rest of the poets mentioned here, is included in this chapter not principally because Milton may have known it but because it is an index of the literary milieu in which he wrote and shows the possibilities of the treatment of Mary that were realized in the seventeenth century.

Given all of this, it may seem unnecessary to discuss Milton in the light of Catholicism. After all, it could be argued that the whole business of looking at Milton against a Catholic background is wrongheaded, since it puts him in the position of reacting, an automatically subordinate one. Nevertheless, it should be emphasized that Catholic Marian piety continued to be a threat to the state and, as such, was not a minor theological aberration. In *A Treatise of Civil Power*, Milton justified excluding Catholics from toleration because "Their religion the more considered, the less can be acknowledged a religion; but a Roman principalitie rather" (*CPW*, 7:254). Roman Catholicism's errors were politically as well as theologically pressing, and devotion to the Virgin played a part in this; thus, for example, the Jesuit Henry Garnett and other Roman Catholics of his day had associated the Virgin with military imagery.[63] Garnett's combat was a spiritual one that substituted rosary beads for armor, but as he had been executed for his alleged part in the Gunpowder Plot (he had, in fact done everything he could to prevent it), this was one of the niceties that had been put to one side in the inevitable hysteria that surrounded his trial.[64] Mary also made appearances on real battlefields. She had been named *generalissima* of the Imperial forces during the Thirty Years War, and in Milton's lifetime several Catholic countries dedicated themselves to the Virgin (including France in 1638, Portugal in 1644, and Poland in 1656).[65] One English traveler noted the founding of the military order of the Immaculate Conception by Urban VIII in 1614, quoting a letter that described "the most universall millitary order of Religion, that hath ever beene knowne in the World: It sweareth Feallty and obedience to the holy Apostlicall Sea of Rome" and is "well provided with Ammunition and Arms, and good tall shiping."[66]

Henry Garnett's death had not put an end to the damage that he could do: "Books are not absolutely dead things, but do contain a potencie of life in them to be as active as that soule whose progeny they are" (*Areopagitica, CPW*, 2:492). He had founded Marian sodalities (one for men and one for women) and had published *The Societie of the Rosary* (ca. 1594). The danger posed by recusant books—smuggled into the country or clandestinely produced at home—had been recognized immediately. A report to Robert Cecil in 1600 alerted him to a foreign distributor in possession of "a great number" of copies of *The Primer or Office of the Blessed Virgin Mary*.[67] This was the first English translation of a popular work that went through eighteen editions before 1658.[68] Of course Marian texts appeared in most recusant publications, and the desire to suppress the popish aspects of devotion to the Virgin in part informed James I's Act of 1603 that made it an offense to "bring from beyond Sea, Print, Sell or Buy any Popish primmers, Ladies Psalters, Manuals, Rosaries, Portals, Legends, or Lives of Saints."[69] Famously, Milton excluded Catholic books from his critique of censorship in *Areopagitica* (*CPW*, 2:565). By the time *Of True Religion* was published, the Restoration had ushered in the lamentable situation in which "We suffer the Idolatrous books of Papists . . . to be sold and read as common as our own" (*CPW*, 8.437).

Throughout the seventeenth century the possession of rosaries acted as a litmus test for Catholicism and became the paraphernalia of Protestant satire. A broadsheet of 1641 itemized the contents of a Jesuit's "Popish pack" as "a truss of trinkets, holy crosses, beads, / Religious relics, Ave-Marias, creeds," along with "Our lady's image."[70] Milton played with similar ingredients in *Paradise Lost* when he mocked "Reliques, Beads, / Indulgences, Dispenses, Pardons, Bulls" (3.491–92). This was the humorous side of all too serious procedures regularly used to identify homegrown sedition and to police the ports. In 1637 the Dover authorities arrested one George Moore, suspected as a priest "on account of certain rosaries which he had about him."[71] The importance of beads was such that even their absence was significant enough to be recorded: in 1601 the mayor of Dover noted that a sailor he was questioning "brought no beads nor crucifixes nor letters with him to England" while another, who had for a time been a student at Douay, had "neither letters, pictures, bulls, beads, or any other superstitious thing by him."[72] The Restoration did not alter this, as can be seen in a 1667 account of a Frenchman who was arrested near the coast in Norfolk. In addition to having "a crucifix and beads," he possessed "a pound of brimstone, and directions to make wild fire."[73]

Politics, literature, and Mary intersected in the person of Henrietta Maria, who established the Arch-Confraternity of the Holy Rosary based in her chapel at Somerset House.[74] (This monument to idolatry was tolerated until the 1640s, when its hangings depicting the Virgin were removed and its pictures were whitewashed over.)[75] While William Prynne denounced the queen as a "Mediatrix" in the king's own bed, other writers dedicated books to her in recognition of her temporal powers of intercession.[76] She nominated Francis Lenton (d. 1653) to the honorary position of Queen's Poet, in return for which he produced verse that associated her with Mary.[77] He was not the only author to do so. Ben Jonson's "An Epigram to the Queen, Then Lying In, 1630" was not calculated to recommend itself to all sensibilities:

Hail Mary, full of grace! it once was said,
And by an angel, to the blessed'st maid,
The mother of our Lord: why may not I
Without profaneness, yet, a poet, cry
Hail Mary, full of honours! to my queen,
        The mother of our prince?[78]

Of course, Jonson was also involved in court masques, a genre that associated the temporal and heavenly queens. It was precisely entertainment of this sort that attracted the implicit criticism of Milton in *A Mask Presented at Ludlow Castle* (1634), where the chastity of the Lady is in stark contrast to the morals of Henrietta Maria. Comus "is the court masquer: he wields 'dazzling spells' and marvellous spectacles but they only 'cheat the eye with blear illusion.'"[79] This may have an echo in *Paradise Regained*, where Satan

    . . . to him takes a chosen band
    Of Spirits likest to himself in guile
    To be at hand, and at his beck appear,
    If cause were to be unfold some active Scene
    Of various persons each to know his part.
                            (2.236–40)

Despite all of this, it should be borne in mind that Milton's contemporaries did not see every episode of Marian devotion as the seed of the destruction of the state. This is nicely demonstrated in a report sent to Joseph Williamson in 1667. In addition to holding various regular civil service positions, Williamson was the realm's chief intelligencer "and a victim of the fear of Catholics."[80] Nevertheless, one of his agents felt free to grumble that upon investigating a complaint of the ever-vigilant anti-Catholic William Prynne, all he had found was "not above a dozen simple women, and three or four inconsiderable men, who were at their beads." This squandering of time impeded attention to more urgent tasks. Prynne and his like "can see mountains through millstones, take alarm at the creeping of a snail," and Prynne himself "can find high treason in a bulrush, and innocence in a scorpion."[81]

The young Milton of *A Masque* seems to have thought along the same lines as Williamson's informer when he allowed a hermit his beads (391). This, however, is not representative of Milton's attitude to Catholic Marian piety. Although it would have been extraordinary to have written a poem on the Nativity without Mary, in "On the Morning of Christ's Nativity" Milton did the next best thing: the Virgin is never named, and when she does appear in the text the reader cannot forget that her importance depends on her son who is "Of wedded Maid, and Virgin Mother born" (3).[82] The words "see the Virgin blest" are immediately followed by "Hath laid her Babe to rest" (237); there is no reflection on, for example, the difficulties of giving birth in the miserable surroundings in which Mary found herself. Similarly, Milton's prose works have little to say about the Virgin. He is respectful of her position as the mother of God and is happy to invoke the authority of the Magnificat's "Cutt down Dynasta's or proud Monarchs from the throne" (*Tenure of Kings and Magistrates, CWJM*, 6:164), but he is, of course, aware of the excesses associated with her cult. In *Of Prelatical Episcopacy*, Irenaeus of Lyon is dismissed as an obviously and generally flawed authority on account of his claims "that the obedience of Mary was the cause of salvation to her selfe, and all mankind," and that "the Virgin Mary might be made the Advocate of the Virgin Eve" (*CPW*, 1:642).[83] At the other end of his writing career, the spiritual life of Charles I, as ventriloquized by *Eikon Basilike*, is ridiculed in the monarch's "out-babling Creeds and Ave's" in chapter 23 of *Eikonoklastes*, a work that is also scathing about Henrietta Maria (*CWJM*, 6:394). When, spectacularly, Milton realized that one of the king's prayers had been plagiarized from Sidney's *Arcadia*, trumpery and heathenism were rolled into the dismissal of his enemy's "Idoliz'd Book, and the whole rosarie of his Prayers" (*CWJM*, 6:293). Just as for Beza, a "multitude of beads and rosaries" compares unfavorably with true prayers (*Tetrachordon, CPW*, 2:690), and being measured against a "lay Papist of Loretto" is a low point for any Protestant (*Areopagitica, CPW*, 2:543–44).

With the exception of *Paradise Regained*, the work of Milton's in which Mary most often appears is *Paradise Lost*. In book 5 she is foreseen in the lines:

> . . . On whom the Angel *Haile*
> Bestowd, the holy salutation us'd

> Long after to blest *Marie*, second *Eve*.
>   Haile Mother of Mankind . . .
>   (5.385–88).[84]

Adam too refers to her, when he begins to understand the Incarnation and

> Why our great expectation should be call'd
> The seed of Woman: Virgin Mother, Haile,
> High in the love of Heav'n, yet from my Loynes
> Thou shalt proceed, and from thy Womb the Son
> Of God most High; So God with man unites.
>   (12.378–82)

The "seed of woman" is a reference to Genesis 3:15, where God curses the snake: "I will put enmitie betweene thee and the woman, and betweene thy seed and her seed: it shal bruise thy head, and thou shalt bruise his heele." The Vulgate had rendered this as "ipsa conteret caput tuum" (*she* will crush your head), and this had eventually acquired the Marian explanation outlined in the notes of the Roman Catholic translation of the Bible: "Protestants wil not admitte this reading, *ipsa conteret*, she shal bruise, lest our Blessed Ladie should be said anie way to bruise the serpents head."[85] Unsurprisingly, Milton rejected this: "Between Thee and the Woman I will put / Enmitie, and between thine and her Seed; / Her Seed shall bruse thy head, thou bruise his heel" (10.179–81).[86]

The Virgin's presence in the rest of *Paradise Lost* is less direct. Jesus is "son of *Mary* second *Eve*" (10.183), and, given the poem's basis in Genesis, Marian references explicitly hinge on the Eve/Mary typology.[87] When Satan appears "Squat like a Toad, close at the eare of *Eve*" (4.800), the scene is a twisted foreshadowing of the Annunciation.[88] Anne Barbeau Gardiner has argued that "Milton seems to inscribe into Satan's hymn of praise to Eve several titles of glory usually reserved for the Virgin Mary."[89] As has been seen, these titles were firmly rejected by the majority of Protestant writers. Drawing on hymns in *The Primer or Office of the Blessed Virgin Mary*, Gardiner links, for example, the "Regina angelorum" with Satan's "Goddess among Gods, ador'd and serv'd / By Angels numberless, thy daily Train" (9.547–48), and the "Ave virgo singularis" with Satan's "sole Wonder" (9.533). In a similar manner, Gardiner addresses the phrases "Celestial beautie" (9.540) and "Queen of this Universe" (9.684) among others.[90] It is not clear that her pairing of the "Ave virgo" with "Fairest resemblance of thy Maker faire" (9.538) works as well as her other examples, but Milton's line does recall Dante's description of Mary as "the face that is most like the face of Christ" in *Paradiso* 32.85–86.[91]

If one smuggled "Celestial Patroness" (9.21) into Gardiner's list, astute readers would immediately see the sleight of hand, for this was Milton's description of Urania, whom the poet had earlier called on to "Descend from Heav'n" (*PL* 7.1). Yet "Celestial Patroness" clearly echoes Marian piety. This arises from the degree of interchangeability of imagery for female divinities, something Protestant authors were well aware of, since they used it as an etiology of Mary's titles: "May it not be that you have learned these titles of the Idolaters, who called Juno & Diana Queenes of Heaven?" Cybele, Minerva, Carna, Juno Sophia, and Hecate provide other heathenish models for Catholic Mariolatry.[92] In the Nativity Ode, "Heav'ns Queen and Mother both" (200) is Ashtoreth, not Mary.[93] Gardiner also points out that Satan's false promises regarding Eve's future glory are prefigurations of the Assumption.[94] Once more, there is the difficulty of sorting out generic elements of an apotheosis-like event from the details of a specific one. When in "An Epitaph on the Marchioness of Winchester" Milton writes of his subject, "thou bright Saint high sit'st in glory . . . With thee there clad in radiant sheen, / No Marchioness, but now a Queen" (61, 73–74), for all that the lady was from a prominent Catholic family, he is hardly likely to be either endorsing or parodying Marian epithets.[95] These echoes, then, though suggestive, are not decisive.

The attention that Milton gives to Mary in *Paradise Regained* is unexpected—it is neither predictable from his work nor dictated by literary fashion. As has been seen, there is what Pelikan called the "positive" Marian theology of the reformers, but Milton had not shown much interest in this. Certainly, a poem that deals in part with Jesus's childhood would strain to avoid allocating a role to Mary (although the Nativity Ode nearly managed it), and that she should be a virtuous and holy woman is no surprise. However, *Paradise Regained* goes significantly farther. What is at issue is not merely how often the Virgin is mentioned— the poem retells the Annunciation three times—but that it directly represents Mary's perspective on her situation. When Jesus does not appear home after his baptism, the reader learns that "Motherly cares and fears got head, and raised / Some troubl'd thoughts, which she in sighs thus clad" (2.64–65); then Mary has a monologue of nearly forty lines in length, in which, in addition to providing information about Christ, she reflects on the difficulties of her lot. Although no one doubted the tribulations of the Virgin, representing them through her own eyes was associated with Roman Catholicism.

Mary's virtues, on the other hand, are perfectly in keeping with the reformed tradition. Her response to her vocation shows her to be obedient and faithful, "with patience . . . inur'd" (2.102), and as accepting the suffering that is her lot: "Afflicted I may be, it seems, and blest; / I will not argue that, nor will repine" (2.93–94). Even when Jesus does not return home as expected, her breast is "calm" (2.63). This composure had patristic warrant, since Ambrose of Milan had described her in *De virginibus* in the following terms: "Never an agitated movement, never a hurried step, never a raised voice. The very appearance of her person reflected the holiness of her mind."[96] Shortly afterwards Ambrose continued, "Thus Mary observed everyone, as if she had something to learn from everyone . . . so that she was more like a teacher than a disciple."[97] Her role as teacher is one of her most remarkable features in *Paradise Regained* and one that, in consequence, has attracted significant comment.[98] In book 1, Jesus recounts how Mary instructed him, helping him realize who, as Son of God, he was; this is a good deal more active than Luke's "But Mary kept all these things, and pondered them in her heart" (2:19).

There is an obvious degree of overlap between the qualities of Mary and those of her son, for all that he goes into the desert and defeats Satan and she stays at home.[99] The figure of the Virgin is clearly opposed to that of the fallen angel. Both of them watch Jesus growing up and try to fathom him, and both of them take him to the Temple, but with opposite results.[100] The values of the Magnificat are challenged in Satan's temptations of the Virgin's son.[101] In contrast, just as Mary is "Meekly compos'd" (2.108), Jesus is "meek and with untroubl'd mind" (4.401). The question is how much can be read into this. On the one hand, all good people share certain characteristics, and the distinctions between stereotypically masculine and feminine virtues are eroded in a poem that eschews armed combat for spiritual struggle. On the other hand, Mary and Jesus do appear to have a particularly close affective and psychological bond. Christ says, "These growing thoughts my Mother soon perceiving / By words at times cast forth" (1.227), before repeating what she said. Just as Mary had pondered her son's words, he in turn ponders hers as she mediates God's plan for him (it should be noted that Catholicism's "Mediatrix" is more bound up with advocacy). Humble on her own account ("I look't for some great change; to Honour? no, / But trouble, as old *Simeon* plain fore-told" [2.86–87]), the Virgin treasures a great future for her son: "Thou shouldst be great and sit on *David*'s Throne / And of thy Kingdom there should be no end" (1.240–41). It is appropriate that at the end of the poem, instead of simply returning to his dwelling, he "Home to his Mothers house private return'd" (4.639). Given that the poem earlier included Mary's unease at his absence, her delight at his return is implicit in this line, a phenomenon that has its parallel in contemporary Catholics' confidence that Jesus appeared to his mother after his resurrection.[102]

Adducing such parallels for parts of *Paradise Regained* is not intended to suggest that it is a crypto-Catholic work. It has none of the central elements of a piety that Milton had rejected elsewhere—so, for example, it never comes close to using the vocabulary associated with the Virgin's queenly titles—and in harmony with *Paradise Lost* it clearly rejects the Marian reading of Genesis 3:15: Satan is "With dread attending when that fatal wound / Shall be inflicted by the seed of Eve / Upon my head" (1.53–55). Given that the poem emerged from a milieu when Milton's countrymen had showed that they were not immune from egregious religious and political errors, it exhibits very little concern about how Mary might be read (recall the clarifications that other Protestant writers had felt requisite when the Virgin was being praised).[103] This is all the more notable since *Paradise Regained* is "a poem-long dramatization of the rejection by the hero, Jesus, of any disposition toward any kind of idolatry."[104] At its climax Satan is told, "The first of all Commandments, Thou shalt worship / The Lord thy God, and only him shalt serve" (4.176–77). It is a didactic work (God, Gabriel, Mary, and Jesus are teachers) that acknowledges the power of words. Jesus hopes "to vanquish by wisdom hellish wiles" (1.175). The wiles of the misinterpreters of Mary do not, it seems, require vanquishing, although Milton would have been as quick to see possible Romish echoes as any of his contemporaries.

Various explanations for this unusual feature of the poem spring to mind. As they are unsatisfactory, they will be dealt with briefly. First, it might be suggested that because Jesus's strategy is "By winning words to conquer willing hearts" (1.222), Milton, like Taylor, is using Mary as an ecumenical bridge for pious Protestants and charitable Catholics. This seems to be a logical rather than an actual possibility: there is no evidence for this strategy in any other aspect of the poem, and it would be difficult to reconcile with anything else Milton wrote at the time. On the other hand, perhaps the opposite is the case and "Milton despoils the Catholics"?[105] He may wish to show the robustness of the Protestant regard for Mary. If this is true, he does so without any combativeness, and although the poem eschews martial violence, it does not shy away from theological confrontation. Alternatively, it could be objected that since Catholic piety was based on postbiblical accretions, even to dismiss them would be anachronistic, but as the reader is taken to be familiar with Lyonesse and Lancelot (2.360–61) this is not the case. A slightly less specific version of this, taking its point of departure from the quip that "there is only one thing in the world worse than being talked about, and that is not being talked about," is a stronger one, with the virtue that it might explain how comparatively infrequently Milton uses Mary in his other writing.[106]

To sum up, Milton need not have given the quality or quantity of attention to Mary that he does in *Paradise Regained*. Roman Catholic views of the Virgin were a live feature of theological and literary controversies when Milton was writing, and Mary was enlisted in political opposition to the English state that he cherished, yet he does not spare three words to clarify, for example, that although Mary is not seen to sin, she was not sinless. There is no ready explanation for this. On the one hand, proponents of the "new Milton criticism" can adduce *Paradise Regained* as exemplifying a conflicted Milton, a case where a problem should not be solved that he himself resisted.[107] Anyone wary of such novelties can fall back on the wisdom of an anonymous contemporary: "He is such an enemy to usual practices that I believe when he is condemned to travel to Tyburn in a cart, he will petition for the favour to be the first man that ever was driven thither in a wheel-barrow."[108]

NOTES

1. Michael O'Carroll, *Theotokos: A Theological Encyclopaedia of the Blessed Virgin Mary* (Wilmington, DE: Michael Glazier, 1986), 181.

2. Heinrich Denzinger et al., eds., *Enchiridion Symbolorum Definitiorum et Declarationum de Rebus Fidei et Morum*, 43rd ed. (San Francisco: Ignatius Press, 2012), 458.

3. Ibid., 357.

4. O'Carroll, *Theotokos*, 180–82.

5. John Foxe, *The Unabridged Acts and Monuments Online (1578 edition)* (Sheffield: hriOnline, 2011), 825 www.johnfoxe.org.

6. Diarmaid MacCulloch, "Mary and Sixteenth-Century Protestants," in *The Church and Mary: Papers Read at the 2001 Summer Meeting and the 2002 Winter Meeting of the Ecclesiastical History Society*, ed. R. N. Swanson, Studies in Church History (Woodbridge: Boydell and Brewer, 2004), 192.

7. Desiderius Erasmus, *The Praise of Folly*, ed. and trans. Clarence H. Miller (New Haven, CT: Yale University Press, 1979), 65.

8. Ibid., 75.

9. Desiderius Erasmus, *The Colloquies of Erasmus*, ed. and trans. Craig R. Thompson (Chicago: University of Chicago Press, 1965), 295.

10. Biblical quotations are taken from the Authorized Version of 1611.

11. George Huntston Williams, *The Radical Reformation*, 3rd ed. (Kirksville, MO: Truman State University Press, 2000), 481; *The Geneva Bible: A Facsimile of the 1560 Edition* (Peabody, MA: Hendrikson, 2012).

12. MacCulloch, "Sixteenth-Century Protestants," 193.

13. *Enchiridion Militis Christiani*, in Desiderius Erasmus, *Enchiridion Militis Christiani. De Contemptu Mundi. De Vidua Christiana*, ed. John W. O'Malley, Collected Works of Erasmus 66 (Toronto: University of Toronto Press, 1988), 73. Cf. John Calvin, *A Harmonie upon the Three Evangelistes Matthewe, Marke, and Luke, with the Commentarie of M. John Calvine*, trans. Eusebius Paget (London: Thomas Adams, 1610), 338.

14. Jaroslav Pelikan, *Mary through the Centuries* (New Haven, CT: Yale University Press, 1996), 157.

15. Susan C. Karant-Nunn and Merry E. Weisner-Hanks, eds., *Luther on Women: A Sourcebook* (Cambridge: Cambridge University Press, 2003), 35.

16. Pelikan, *Mary through the Centuries*, 160; Bridget Heal, *The Cult of the Virgin Mary in Early Modern Germany: Protestant and Catholic Piety, 1500–1648*, Past and Present Publications (Cambridge: Cambridge University Press, 2007), 61. Augustine stressed Mary's faith: "By believing, [she] conceived Him whom she, by believing, brought forth." Augustine of Hippo, *Sermons on the*

Liturgical Seasons, sermon 215.4, trans. Mary Sarah Muldowney, The Fathers of the Church 38 (Washington, DC: Catholic University of America Press, 1959), 145.

17. Karant-Nunn and Weisner-Hanks, *Luther on Women*, 36, 46.

18. Martin Luther, "On Translating: An Open Letter," in *Selected Writings of Martin Luther*, ed. Theodore G. Tappert, 4 vols. (Minneapolis: Fortress Press, 2007), 4:183.

19. See Karant-Nunn and Weisner-Hanks, *Luther on Women*, 56; Heal, *Cult*, 57.

20. Karant-Nunn and Weisner-Hanks, *Luther on Women*, 39.

21. Ibid., 46.

22. Cited in Pelikan, *Mary through the Centuries*, 159.

23. John Calvin, *Calvin's Tracts and Treatises*, trans. Henry Beveridge (Grand Rapids, MI: Eerdmans, 1958), 317.

24. Calvin, *Harmonie*, 35.

25. John Calvin, *Institutes of the Christian Religion* 3.20.22, ed. John T. McNeill, 2 vols., The Library of Christian Classics 20 (Louisville, KY: Westminster John Knox Press, 1960), 881.

26. Calvin, *Institutes* 4.17.25, ed. McNeill, 1392.

27. Calvin, *Harmonie*, 36.

28. See, for example, Carolyn H. Smith, "The Virgin Mary in *Paradise Regain'd*," *South Atlantic Quarterly* 71 (1972): 558–59; Theresa M. DiPasquale, *Reconfiguring the Sacred Feminine: The Poems of John Donne, Aemilia Lanyer, and John Milton*, Medieval and Renaissance Literary Studies (Pittsburgh, PA: Duquesne University Press, 2008), 292–301.

29. Calvin, *Harmonie*, 103.

30. An overview of the history of Mary in the later sixteenth century can be found in Christine Peters, *Patterns of Piety: Women, Gender and Religion in Late Medieval and Reformation England*, Cambridge Studies in Early Modern British History (Cambridge: Cambridge University Press, 2003), 207–27; Paul Williams, "The English Reformers and the Blessed Virgin Mary," in *Mary: The Complete Resource*, ed. Sarah Jane Boss (Oxford: Oxford University Press, 2007), 238–55.

31. Peters, *Patterns of Piety*, 243.

32. Quotations are from the 1662 edition. Brian Cummings, ed., *The Book of Common Prayer: The Texts of 1549, 1559, and 1662* (Oxford: Oxford University Press, 2011), 259, 392.

33. Ibid., 222–33.

34. John Bruce and William Douglas Hamilton, eds., *Calendar of State Papers, Domestic Series, of the Reign of Charles I*, 22 vols. (London: Longmans, Green, 1858–93), 3:587, 10:262, 12:539.

35. Arnold Hunt, "Stafford, Anthony," in *ODNB*.

36. Anthony Stafford, *The Femall Glory: Or, the Life, and Death of Our Blessed Lady, the Holy Virgin Mary, Gods Owne Immaculate Mother to Whose Sacred Memory the Author Dedicates These his Humble Endeavours* (London: Thomas Harper for John Waterson, 1635), B5, B6.

37. Ibid., B6v, 223, 225.

38. Ibid., 9.

39. Ibid., 88, 182, 184, 188, 210.

40. Hunt, "Stafford, Anthony."

41. Richard Sheldon, *A Survey of the Miracles of the Church of Rome, Proving Them to be Antichristian. Wherein are Examined Six Fundamentall Reasons of John Flood Ignatian, Published by Him in Defence of Popish Miracles* (London: Edward Griffin, 1616), 125, 155.

42. Stafford, *Femall Glory*, 209.

43. Ibid., C7–C8v. See Robert S. Miola, "Ben Jonson, Catholic Poet," *Renaissance and Reformation* 25, no. 4 (2001): 110–11.

44. See, for example, Henry Ainsworth, *An Arrow Against Idolatrie Taken Out of the Quiver of the Lord of Hosts* ([Amsterdam]: n.p., 1624), 108; François de Cro, *The Three Conformities. Or the Harmony and Agreement of the Romish Church with Gentilisme, Iudaisme and Auncient Heresies*, trans. William Hart (London: Edward Griffin, 1620), 42.

45. Stafford, *Femall Glory*, 147.

46. Ibid., 36–37.

47. Henry Burton, *For God and the King: The Summe of Two Sermons* ([Amsterdam]: [J. F. Stam], 1636), 123; *The Works of the Most Reverend Father in God, William Laud, D.D.*, vol. 4 (Oxford: John Henry Parker, 1854), 288.

48. Julie Spraggon, *Puritan Iconoclasm during the English Civil War*, Studies in Modern British Religious History 6 (Woodbridge: Boydell Press, 2003), 67, 89, 156.

49. For an account of the controversy surrounding the cross, see David Cressy, *Agnes Bowker's Cat: Travesties and Transgressions in Tudor and Stuart England* (Oxford: Oxford University Press, 2001), 234–50.

50. Thomas Ady, *A Perfect Discovery of Witches* (London: R. I., 1661), 43.

51. Ruth Vanita, "Mariological Memory in *The Winter's Tale* and *Henry VIII*," *Studies in English Literature* 40, no. 2 (2000): 321; Ruben Espinosa, *Masculinity and Marian Efficacy in Shakespeare's England*, Women and Gender in the Early Modern World (Aldershot: Ashgate, 2011), 167; Gary Waller, *The Virgin Mary in Late Medieval and Early Modern English Literature and Popular Culture* (Cambridge: Cambridge University Press, 2011), 178. For Mary in other plays by Shakespeare, see *Marian Moments in Early Modern British Drama*, ed. Regina Buccola and Lisa Hopkins, Studies in Performance and Early Modern Drama (Aldershot: Ashgate, 2007), 21–110; Waller, *Virgin Mary*, 157–80.

52. Buccola and Hopkins, *Marian Moments*, chaps. 6–9.

53. See Helen Hackett, *Virgin Mother, Maiden Queen: Elizabeth I and the Cult of the Virgin Mary* (Basingstoke: Macmillan, 1995). Hackett critiques those who suggest that Elizabeth adapted Mary's role for herself (6–12), emphasizing instead how English queens (including, for example, Anne Boleyn and Mary I) were associated with the heavenly one (29–37).

54. Waller, *Virgin Mary*, 122; Jill Delsigne, "Reading Catholic Art in Edmund Spenser's Temple of Isis," *Studies in Philology* 109, no. 3 (2012): 211.

55. Hackett, *Virgin Mother*, 111–12.

56. Guillaume de Salluste Du Bartas, *Du Bartas his Devine Weekes and Workes*, trans. Josuah Sylvester (London: Humfrey Lounes, 1611), 690; Henry Vaughan, *The Complete Poems*, ed. Alan Rudrum, rev. ed., Penguin Classics (Harmondsworth: Penguin, 1995), 272.

57. *The Poetical Works of Giles and Phineas Fletcher*, ed. F. S. Boas, 2 vols. (Cambridge: Cambridge University Press, 1908–9), 1:74.

58. *The English Poems of George Herbert*, ed. Helen Wilcox (Cambridge: Cambridge University Press, 2007), 281. See the overview of the discussions of the poem's "theological tensions" and the commentary in ibid., 280–84, and Waller, *Virgin Mary*, 195–96.

59. John Taylor, *The Life and Death of the Most Blessed Among Women, the Virgin Mary Mother of Our Lord Jesus. With the Murder of the Infants in Bethlehem, Judas his Treason, and the Confession of the Good Theife and the Bad* (London: G. Eld, 1620), A8v. For Taylor's Protestantism, see Bernard Capp, "Taylor, John," in *ODNB*.

60. Taylor, *Life and Death*, A5v, A7.

61. Mary's role in the poem is discussed in DiPasquale, *Reconfiguring the Sacred Feminine*, 132–38, 173–77.

62. Aemilia Lanyer, *The Poems of Aemilia Lanyer: Salve Deus Rex Judæorum*, ed. Suzanne Woods (Oxford: Oxford University Press, 1993), 94.

63. Lisa McClain, *Lest We Be Damned: Practical Innovation and Lived Experience among Catholics in Protestant England, 1559–1642* (New York: Routledge, 2004), 97–98.

64. For the details of Garnett's life, see Thomas M. McCoog, "Garnett, Henry," in *ODNB*.

65. Trevor Johnson, "Mary in Early Modern Europe," in Boss, *Mary*, 365–66.

66. James Wadsworth, *Further Observations of the English Spanish Pilgrime . . .* (London: Felix Kyngston for Nathaniel Butter, 1630), 30–31.

67. R. A. Roberts, ed., *Calendar of the Manuscripts of the Most Hon. the Marquis of Salisbury . . . Preserved at Hatfield House, Hertfordshire*, 13 vols. (London: HMSO, 1883–1915), 10:62.

68. J. M. Blom, *The Post-Tridentine English Primer*, Catholic Record Society Publications (Monograph Series) 3 (n.p.: Catholic Record Society, 1982),
168–71.

69. Cited in ibid., 35.

70. Reprinted in John N. King, *Milton and Religious Controversy: Satire
and Polemic in Paradise Lost* (Cambridge: Cambridge University Press,
2000), 196.

71. Bruce and Hamilton, *Calendar [Charles I]*, 12:75.

72. Roberts, *Calendar*, 11:531, 12:84.

73. Mary Anne Everett Green et al., eds., *Calendar of State Papers, Domestic Series, of the Reign of Charles II*, 28 vols. (London: Longman, Green,
Reader and Dyer and HMSO, 1860–1939), 8:148.

74. Frances E. Dolan, *Whores of Babylon: Catholicism, Gender, and
Seventeenth-Century Print Culture* (Ithaca, NY: Cornell University Press,
1999), 121.

75. Spraggon, *Puritan Iconoclasm*, 95.

76. Dolan, *Whores of Babylon*, 120.

77. Jerome de Groot, "Lenton, Francis," in *ODNB*.

78. *Ben Jonson: A Critical Edition of the Major Works*, ed. Ian Donaldson,
Oxford Authors (Oxford: Oxford University Press, 1985), 391.

79. Barbara K. Lewalski, "Milton's *Comus* and the Politics of Masquing,"
in *The Politics of the Stuart Masque*, ed. David Bevington and Peter Holbrook
(Cambridge: Cambridge University Press, 1998), 309, 311.

80. Alan Marshall, "Williamson, Sir Joseph," in *ODNB*.

81. Green et al., *Calendar [Charles II]*, 7:550.

82. In *The Shorter Poems*, ed. Barbara K. Lewalski and Estelle Hann,
CWJM, vol. 3. Quotations from Milton's shorter poems are taken from this
edition.

83. On the basis of the Magnificat, Milton's nephew, Edward Phillips regarded Mary as "the most Divine and Seraphic of all Poets." Dayton Haskin,
Milton's Burden of Interpretation (Philadelphia: University of Pennsylvania Press,
1994), 128, 263n14.

84. See also *PL* 11.158–61.

85. *Biblia Sacra Iuxta Vulgatam Versionem*, 4th ed. (Stuttgart: Deutsche
Bibelgesellschaft, 1994). See O'Carroll, *Theotokos*, 371; Pelikan, *Mary through
the Centuries*, 91–92. For the notes, see *The Holie Bible Faithfully Translated into
English, Out of the Authentical Latin* (Douay: Laurence Kellham, 1609), 12.

86. See also Adam's address to Eve in 11.155 and his rejoicing in
12.363–65 (along with Michael's correction of him).

87. For the origins of the Eve/Mary type, see John Flood, *Representations
of Eve in Antiquity and the English Middle Ages*, Routledge Studies in Medieval

Religion and Culture 9 (New York: Routledge, 2011), 14–16. The bibliography of studies of *Paradise Lost* that deal with this type is vast. For summaries of the main points, see Herbert H. Petit, "The Second Eve in *Paradise Regained*," *Papers of the Michigan Academy of Science, Arts, and Letters* 44 (1959); Mary Christopher Pecheux, "The Concept of the Second Eve in Paradise Lost," *PMLA* 75, no. 4 (1960): 359–66.

88. Roland Mushat Frye, *Milton's Imagery and the Visual Arts: Iconographic Tradition in the Epic Poems* (Princeton, NJ: Princeton University Press, 1978), 100.

89. Anne Barbeau Gardiner, "Milton's Parody of Catholic Hymns in Eve's Temptation and Fall: Original Sin as a Paradigm of 'Secret Idolatries,'" *Studies in Philology* 91, no. 2 (1994): 220.

90. Ibid., 220–21.

91. For Dante, see Pelikan, *Mary through the Centuries*, 139.

92. Cro, *Three Conformities*, 42–43. For interchangeability, see Hackett, *Virgin Mother*, 13–15.

93. See Barbara K. Lewalski, "Milton and Idolatry," *Studies in English Literature* 43, no. 1 (2003): 215.

94. Gardiner, "Milton's Parody," 227.

95. For the Marchioness's family, see Gordon Campbell and Thomas N. Corns, *John Milton: Life, Work and Thought* (Oxford: Oxford University Press, 2010), 57.

96. Luigi Gambero, *Mary and the Fathers of the Church: The Blessed Virgin Mary in Patristic Thought*, trans. Thomas Buffer (San Francisco: Ignatius Press, 1999), 200.

97. Ibid., 200–201.

98. Petit, "Second Eve," 368; Haskin, *Milton's Burden*, 128; DiPasquale, *Reconfiguring the Sacred Feminine*, 295.

99. See Walter MacKellar, ed., *A Variorum Commentary on the Poems of John Milton: Paradise Regained*, vol. 4 (London: Routledge and Kegan Paul, 1975), 31.

100. David Gay, *The Endless Kingdom: Milton's Scriptural Society* (Newark: University of Delaware Press, 2002), 172.

101. Haskin, *Milton's Burden*, 134.

102. A. G., *The Widdowes Mite, Cast Into the Treasure-house of the Prerogatiues, and Prayses of our B. Lady, the Immaculate, and Most Glorious Virgin Mary, the Mother of God* (Saint-Omer, 1619), 62; John Falconer, *The Mirrour of Created Perfection. Or The Life of the Most Blessed Virgin Mary Mother of God* ([Saint-Omer]: [English College], 1632), 112.

103. One possibility comes to mind. Luke 2:51 says that Jesus went home from the Temple with his parents "and was subject unto them." Although the

Temple episode is told twice in *Paradise Regained*, there is no hint of this verse. It is possible that, like Erasmus, Milton wishes to avoid any suggestion that Jesus is at Mary's command.

104. Lewalski, "Milton and Idolatry," 224.

105. Marjorie O'Rourke Boyle, "Home to Mother: Regaining Milton's Paradise," *Modern Philology* 97, no. 4 (2000): 508. This phrase is not used specifically in this context in the paper and should not be taken as a summary of it.

106. Oscar Wilde, *The Picture of Dorian Gray: The 1890 and 1891 Texts*, ed. Joseph Bristow, *The Complete Works of Oscar Wilde* 3 (Oxford: Oxford University Press, 2005), 170.

107. See Peter C. Herman and Elizabeth Sauer, "Introduction: Paradigms Lost, Paradigms Found: The New Milton Criticism," in *The New Milton Criticism*, ed. Peter C. Herman and Elizabeth Sauer (Cambridge: Cambridge University Press, 2012), 1, 3.

108. Quoted in Campbell and Corns, *Life*, 312.

Contributors

ALASTAIR BELLANY is Associate Professor of History at Rutgers University. He is the author of *The Politics of Court Scandal in Early Modern England* (Cambridge: Cambridge University Press, 2002) and coeditor (with Andrew McRae) of "Early Stuart Libels: An Edition of Poetry from Manuscript Sources" (2005). His most recent book, *The Murder of King James I*, cowritten with Thomas Cogswell, appeared from Yale University Press in the fall of 2015.

THOMAS COGSWELL, Professor of History at the University of California, Riverside, has written *The Blessed Revolution: Politics and the Coming of War, 1621–1624* (Cambridge: Cambridge University Press, 1989); *Home Divisions: Aristocracy, the State and Provincial Conflict* (Stanford, CA: Stanford University Press, 1998); and with Alastair Bellany, *The Murder of King James I* (New Haven, CT: Yale University Press, 2015).

THOMAS N. CORNS is Emeritus Professor of English Literature at Bangor University. His recent publications include *John Milton and the Manuscript of "De Doctrina Christiana"* (Oxford: Oxford University Press, 2007) (with Gordon Campbell, John K. Hale, and Fiona Tweedie); *A History of Seventeenth-Century English Literature* (Oxford: Blackwell, 2007); *John Milton: Life, Work, and Thought* (Oxford: Oxford University Press, 2008) (with Gordon Campbell); and his edited *A New Companion to Milton* (Malden, MA: Wiley Blackwell, 2016). He edited *The Complete*

Works of Gerrard Winstanley (Oxford: Oxford University Press, 2009) (with Ann Hughes and David Loewenstein) and *The Milton Encyclopedia* (New Haven, CT: Yale University Press, 2012). With Gordon Campbell, he is the general editor of *The Complete Works of John Milton* (Oxford: Oxford University Press, 2008–). He is an Honored Scholar of the Milton Society of America, a Fellow of the British Academy and the Royal Historical Society, and a Foundation Fellow of the English Association. His current projects include editing *Paradise Lost* for *The Complete Works* (with David Loewenstein).

RONALD CORTHELL is Professor of English at Purdue University Northwest. He is the author of *Ideology and Desire in Renaissance Poetry: The Subject of Donne* (Detroit, MI: Wayne State University Press, 1997) and coeditor, with Arthur F. Marotti, Frances E. Dolan, and Christopher F. Highley, of *Catholic Culture in Early Modern England* (Notre Dame, IN: University of Notre Dame Press, 2007). From 1989 to 2011, he served as editor of *Prose Studies: History, Theory, Criticism*, including special issues on Milton's prose in 2011 and, coedited with Thomas N. Corns, in 1997.

ANGELICA DURAN is Professor of English and Comparative Literature at Purdue University, where she has also served as Purdue's Director of Religious Studies (2009–13). She is the editor of *A Concise Companion to Milton* (Malden, MA: Wiley Blackwell, 2007, pbk. and rev. 2011) and *The King James Bible across Borders and Centuries* (Pittsburgh, PA: Duquesne University Press, 2014), the lead editor of *Mo Yan in Context* (West Lafayette, IN: Purdue University Press, 2014) and *Milton in Translation* (Oxford: Oxford University Press, 2017), and the author of *The Age of Milton and the Scientific Revolution* (Pittsburgh: Duquesne University Press, 2007). She is the Treasurer (2012–21) of the Milton Society of America and a member of the editorial board of *Milton Quarterly* (2005–).

MARTIN DZELZAINIS is Professor of Renaissance Literature and Thought at the University of Leicester. He is currently editing the Histories for *The Complete Works of John Milton*; Andrew Marvell's verse and prose for the Oxford Twenty-First-Century Authors series; and (with

Edward Holberton) *The Oxford Handbook of Andrew Marvell* (all for Oxford University Press). He is also general editor, with Paul Seaward, of the Oxford University Press edition of *The Works of Edward Hyde, Earl of Clarendon*.

JOHN FLOOD is Senior Lecturer in the Department of English of the University of Groningen. He specializes in medieval and early modern literature. His most recent book is *The Works of Walter Quin, an Irishman at the Stuart Courts* (Dublin: Four Courts Press, 2014), and he is the author of *Representations of Eve in Antiquity and the English Middle Ages* (London: Routledge, 2010). He has coedited collections on *Robert Grosseteste and His Intellectual Milieu* (Toronto: Pontifical Institute of Medieval Studies, 2013) and *Heresy and Early English Literature* (Dublin: Four Courts Press, 2010).

ESTELLE HAAN is Professor of English and Neo-Latin Studies at The Queen's University of Belfast. She has authored/edited thirteen books on Milton and on other neo-Latin poets of the long eighteenth century. These include *From Academia to Amicitia: Milton's Latin Writings and the Italian Academies* (Philadelphia: American Philosophical Society, 1998), *Thomas Gray's Latin Poetry* (Leuven: Leuven University Press, 2000), *Andrew Marvell's Latin Poetry* (Leuven: Leuven University Press, 2003), *Vergilius Redivivus: Studies in Joseph Addison's Latin Poetry* (Philadelphia: American Philosophical Society, 2005), *Classical Romantic: Identity in the Latin Poetry of Vincent Bourne* (Philadelphia: American Philosophical Society, 2007), *Sporting with the Classics: The Latin Poetry of William Dillingham* (Philadelphia: American Philosophical Society, 2010), *Both English and Latin: Bilingualism and Biculturalism in Milton's Neo-Latin Writings* (Philadelphia: American Philosophical Society, 2012), and an edition of Milton's Latin poetry in *The Complete Works of John Milton*, volume 3 (Oxford: Oxford University Press, 2014). She is currently completing an edition of Milton's Latin letters, and is also working on two authored books entitled *"That Puissant City": John Milton's Roman Sojourns 1638–1639*, and *Surprised by Syntax: Reading the Latinity of Paradise Lost*.

ELIZABETH SAUER, Fellow of the Royal Society of Canada, is Professor of English at Brock University, Canada, and a Canada Council Killam Research Laureate. She authored *Milton, Toleration, and Nationhood* (Cambridge: Cambridge University Press, 2014, pbk. 2016), coedited *The New Milton Criticism* (Cambridge: Cambridge University Press, 2012), coedited *Reading the Nation in English Literature* (London: Routledge, 2010), coedited *Milton and Toleration* (Oxford: Oxford University Press, 2007; Milton Society of America book award), edited *Milton and the Climates of Reading* (Toronto: University of Toronto Press, 2006; a *Choice* Outstanding Academic Title); authored *"Paper-Contestations" and Textual Communities in England* (Toronto: University of Toronto Press, 2005), and coedited *Reading Early Modern Women* (New York: Routledge, 2004), winner of the Society for the Study of Early Modern Women Best Collaborative Work. In progress is a book on early modern English nationhood and transatlantic literature, funded by a multiyear Canada Council Insight Grant.

Index

Abbot, George (archbishop), 42
Accademia degli Apatisti, 141
Accademia degli Oziosi, 135, 139
Accademia degli Svogliati, 141,
    159n64
Accademia degli Umoristi, 141, 142,
    143, 159nn63–64, 160n68
Accademia dei Fantastici, 141
Addison, Joseph, 96–97
Albert the Great, 85–86, 170
Alexander VI (Rodrigo Borgia;
    pope), 105
Alexander VII: *Sollicitudo Omnium
    Ecclesiarum*, 170
Allen, William: *A True, Sincere, and
    Modest Defense of English Catho-
    lics*, 9
Alpers, Paul, 108–9
Ambrose of Milan: *De virginibus*,
    185
Anabaptists, 94
Andrewes, Lancelot, 106–7, 125n16
Aquinas, Thomas, 85–86
Arch-Confraternity of the Holy
    Rosary, 180

Arians, 94
Ariosto, Ludovico, 138
    Orlando Furioso, 97
Arminianism, 41, 94, 96, 98
Athanasian creed, 173
Athanasius of Alexandria, 10
Augustine, Saint, 170, 172, 188n16
Augustinian Hermits, 156n29
Austin, R. G., 165n117

baptism, 90–91
Barberini, Antonio (cardinal), 142
Barberini, Francesco (cardinal), 142,
    160n70
Baroni, Adriana, 140
Baroni, Leonora, 159n64, 162n87
    *Applausi Poetici Alle Glorie della
    Signora Leonora Baroni*, 140,
    142, 143, 144, 158n55,
    158n58, 162n79
    Milton on, 131, 132, 133, 141–47
Basing House, 3
Bastwick, John
    on Laudianism, 23, 35n20
    Letany of John Bastwick, 23

Bate, George, 48

Baxter, Margery, 84, 86

Baxter, Richard, 66, 70, 75

Bellarmine, Robert (cardinal), 76, 96

Benigni, Domenico, 144

Bentley, Richard, 96–97

Berthold, Saint, 124n5

Beza, Theodore, 182

Biddle, John, 68

Blake, Admiral Robert, 107

Blasphemy Act, 71, 81n25, 82n27

Blasphemy Ordinance of 1648, 87, 90

Boleyn, Anne, 191n53

Book of Common Prayer, 91, 92, 173

Borrow, George: *The Bible in Spain*, 123n2

Bossy, John, 6–7

Bradner, Leicester, 149

Buchanan, George, 156n29

Buckingham, 1st Duke of (George Villiers),
　and James I's death, 40, 43, 45, 47, 48, 49, 50, 51–53, 54, 55, 56
　and Marquis of Hamilton's death, 43, 44
　relationship with Charles I, 39, 40, 43–44, 46, 47, 50, 51–53, 54, 57–58

Bullinger, Heinrich, 174

Burghley's *Execution of Justice in England*, 9

Burton, Henry, 23
　on popery, 22
　on Stafford, 175

Bush, Douglas, 138

Byard, Margaret, 158n60

Calvin, John
　Harmonie upon the Three Evangelistes, 173
　Institutes of the Christian Religion, 173
　and Milton, 11, 87, 90, 93–94, 95, 98
　on Virgin Mary, 173, 175

Campbell, Gordon, 132, 141–42, 160n70

Campion, Edmund, 7, 88, 96

Cardoini, Camillo, 132

Carew, Thomas, 2

Carey, John, 109–10

Carmelites, 156n29

Cary, Elizabeth, 176

Catechesis Ecclesiarum Quae in Regno Poloniae, 68

Catesby, Robert, 105

Cecil, Robert, 179

Certain Briefe Treatises, 29

Chapman, George, 176

Charge of the Army, The, 50

Charlemagne, 112–13

Charles I, 2, 23, 26, 107, 113
　and death of James I, 39, 44–50, 51–52, 55, 56, 58, 59
　dissolution of 1626 Parliament, 39, 40, 43–44, 45, 46, 51, 52–53, 54, 56, 58, 59
　execution of, 18–19, 39–40, 50–52, 55, 57, 59
　Milton on, 18–19, 20–21, 28, 39–40, 53, 54, 58, 182
　relationship with Buckingham, 39, 40, 43–44, 46, 47, 50, 51–53, 54, 57–58

Charles II
  Restoration, 4, 93, 111, 180
  during Third Civil War, 54–55,
    56–57
Cheapside Cross, 176
Church of England, 18, 23, 91, 92,
    98, 173–74
Cinzio Passeri Aldobrandini
    (cardinal), 139
Clarendon, Earl of (Edward Hyde),
    66, 70
Clarke, Samuel: *Englands Remem-*
    brancer, 105
Clement IX, 142
Cocco, Sean, 135
Coffey, John, 67
Columbus, Christopher, 116
Con, George, 22
Condé, Prince de, 113
conscience
  Cromwell on, 67
  Milton on, 5, 8, 9, 10, 11, 20, 26,
    66, 74, 76, 78, 92, 102
  Vane the Younger on, 75, 76, 78
Constable, Henry, 177
Cook, John: *King Charls his Case*,
    50–52, 53–54
1 Corinthians 3:13, 15, 88, 89
2 Corinthians
  5:1, 88
  5:10, 88
Corns, Thomas N., 26, 132,
    141–42, 160n70
Corona Regia, 43
Correr, Anzolo, 22–23
Cosin, John: *Collection of Private*
    Devotions, 21–22
Counter-Reformation, 21, 116–17

Covenanters, 54
Cowper, William, 162n84
Crashaw, Richard, 177
  "Saint Mary Magdalene, or the
    Weeper," 125n15
Cromwell, Oliver
  death of, 66
  dissolution of Rump Parliament in
    1653, 67
  Irish campaign, 3, 4
  on liberty of conscience, 67
  as Lord Protector, 66, 67, 68–69
  in Third Civil War, 54
Cromwell, Richard, 70
Cueva y Toledo, Bartolomé de la
    (cardinal), 42

Dante's *Paradiso* 32.85–86, 184
Darnley, Henry Stuart, 58
Dati, Carlo
  Esequie della Maestà Christianiss,
    134
  relationship with Milton, 133–34,
    149, 150, 155n16, 158n49,
    160n72
Declaration of 1648, 40, 46–48, 49,
    50, 51, 53–54
Declaration of Indulgence, 8, 9,
    15n19
Dee, John, 163n97
Defenestration of Prague, 2
Dekker, Thomas, 176
De Lellis, Carlo, 136
Delille, Jacques, 115, 127n37
Dell'Antonio, Andrew, 143
Delsigne, Jill, 146
Denbigh, Countess of (Susan
    Fielding), 21

Deodatus (bishop of Nevers and
    abbot of St. Jointures), 150–53
Dethicke, Sir John, 91–92
Digges, Sir Dudley, 44, 46
Diodati, Carlo, 147–48
Diodati, Charles, 147–48, 150, 151
Diodati, Theodore, 149
*Directory for the Publique Worship of
    God*, 91, 92
Dobranski, Stephen, 20
Dominicans, 97, 102, 156n29,
    160n72, 170
Doni, Giovanni Battista, 160n68
Donne, John, 176–77
    on change of religious allegiance, 6
    Pseudo-Martyr, 6
Donnelly, John P., 117
Drake, Sir Francis, 110
Drogheda massacre, 3, 4
Dryden, John: *The Life of St. Francis
    Xavier*, 127n41
Du Bartas, Guillaume de Saluste:
    "The Triumph of Faith," 177
Duffy, Eamon: *Stripping of the
    Altars*, 7
Du Mortier, Nicolas, 150
DuRocher, Richard, 117–18

Ecclesiasticus (Sirach), 171
Edward VI, 173
Edwards, Karen, 125n19
Eglisham's *The Forerunner of Revenge
    upon the Duke of Buckingham*
    Catholicism of Eglisham, 41–42,
        46, 48, 49, 54, 59
    murder of James I in, 40, 45–46,
        53–54
    murder of Marquis of Hamilton
        in, 43–44

origins of, 41, 42–43
popularity of, 40, 41, 45–46,
    47–48, 57
Eikon Alethine, 52–53
Eikon Basilike, 39, 52, 53, 182
Eikon e Piste, 53
Eliot, Sir John, 44, 46, 51, 58
Elizabeth I, 104, 173, 176, 191n53
Ellison, James, 147
English Civil Wars, 54–55, 56–57,
    98
    anti-Catholicism during, 40–41,
        46
English Pope, The, 27
Erasmus, Desiderius: on Virgin
    Mary, 171–72, 174, 193n103
Escóiquiz, Juan de, 115, 127n35
Eucharist, the, 83–86, 87, 90–91,
    135
Evans, J. Martin: *The Imperial Epic*,
    116
Evelyn, John, 141, 159nn63–64,
    161n76
Exclusion Crisis, 96
Ezekiel 44:2, 171

Featley, Daniel, 42
Felton, John, 40
Ficino, Marsilio: *Pimander*, 145
Fixler, Michael, 66–67
Fletcher's *Christ's Triumph Over
    Death*, 177
Florence, 145, 148, 150, 158n49
    Accademia degli Svogliati, 141,
        159n64
    Milton in, 132, 141, 149, 159n64,
        166n128
Florio, John, 150
Fowler, Alastair, 97

Foxe, John, 170
Francini, Antonio, 149
Franciscans, 97, 124n5, 131, 132, 156n29, 160n72, 170
Francis of Assisi, St., 124n5
Francis Xavier, St., 117
Frank, Joseph, 2
Frederick V, 2
freedom of speech, 29–30, 31, 32
Freeman, James A., 141
Fry, John, 68
Fuchs, Barbara, 126n33

Galations 3:28, 122
Galileo Galilei, 142, 160n72
Gardiner, Anne Barbeau, 183–84
Garnett, Henry: *The Societie of the Rosary*, 179
Genesis 3:15, 183, 186
Goldie, Mark, 73
Gondomar, Conde de, 42
Grand Remonstrance of 1641, 19, 46, 73
Greenblatt, Stephen, 118
Gunpowder Plot, 1, 103–5, 154n5, 179
    Guy Fawkes Day, 20, 103
    Milton on, 3, 4, 103–4, 105, 106, 131
    "Remember, Remember the Fifth of November," 105, 106
Guzman, Dominic de, 102, 124n5

Haan, Estelle, 141
Hackett, Helen, 176, 191n53
Hadfield, Andrew, 102
Haigh, Christopher, 7
Hale, John, 134, 149, 155n16
Hall, E. F., 69

Hall, Joseph
    Defence of the Humble Remonstrance, 28
    "Episcopacie by Divine Right Asserted," 28
Hamilton, Marquis of, 41, 42, 43–44
Harris, Neil, 113
    on Milton's similes, 112
Harrison, Thomas, 50
Haskell, Y. A., 163n93
Haviland, Matthew, 1
Hebrides, 108
Heinsius, Nicolaas, 24
Henrietta Maria, Queen, 22, 23, 175, 180–81, 182
Henry VIII, 27
Herbert, George
    "Anagram of the Virgin Marie," 177
    "To all Angels and Saints," 177
Hermes Trismegistus
    Asclepius, 145
    on *mens tertia*, 145–46, 164n101
    Pymander, 145, 146, 163n97, 164n101
hermeticism, 143, 145–47, 163n97
Hermida, Benito, 115, 127n35
Hill, Christopher, 95–96
    The Experience of Defeat, 67
Holste, Lukas, 142–43, 160n70, 161nn74–75, 162n78
Holy Roman Empire, 2, 119
Holy Spirit, 145–46, 164n101, 172, 173
Hooker, Richard, 83
Horace's *Epistles* 1.11.27, 132, 154n7
Howell, James: *An Inquisition after Blood*, 52

Hughes, Merritt, 129n51
Humble Proposals of 1652, 71,
    81n25
Hyde, Sir Edward, 47, 48

idolatry, 72, 73–74, 75, 79
Ignatius Loyola, Saint, 116–17,
    125n19
Immaculate Conception, 170
implicit faith, 10, 11, 12, 74, 76, 93,
    154n9
Irish Catholic revolt, 3, 4
Isaiah 7:14, 171

Jackson, Henry: and *Wickliffes
    Wicket*, 83–84
James, Duke of York, 93, 96
James I, 1, 2, 10, 76, 174–75
    death of, 39–40, 43, 44–59
    and Overbury, 56
    policies regarding Catholicism, 20,
        177, 179
    relationship with Eglisham, 41, 42
    See also Gunpowder Plot
Jesuits, 17, 18, 24, 116–17, 125n19,
    128n43, 179, 180
Jonson, Ben, 176–77
    "An Epigram to the Queen, Then
        Lying In," 180–81
Judges
    5:8, 122
    15:15, 122
    16:3, 122

Kelley, Maurice, 98
Kendall, Willmoore, 73
King, Edward, 108, 109
King, John N., 97
King Iames His Iudgement, 45, 46

Lake, Peter
    The Antichrist's Lewd Hat, 7
    on popery, 18
    on Protestant self-fashioning, 9
Lamb, Charles, 145, 162n79
Lanyer, Aemilia: *Salve Deus Rex
    Iudaeorum*, 178
Lasso de Oropesa, Martin, 124n9
Laud, William, 22, 23–24, 35n20
    attitudes regarding Catholicism
        and Puritanism, 24
    Bastwick on, 23, 35n20
    *Constitutions and Canons Ecclesias-
        ticall*, 24, 26, 28
    execution speech, 32–33
    Milton on, 18–19, 20–21, 26,
        27–28, 30, 33, 97
    trial of, 30, 35n21, 175
Lazarus, 89
Lazzarelli, Lodovico: *Crater Hermetis*,
    146
Leicester's Commonwealth, 43
Lenton, Francis, 180
Leonard, John, 110, 127n37
*Letter from a Gentleman of the Romish
    Religion*, 18
Lewalski, Barbara, 118
Lilburne, John, 23
Lipking, Lawrence, 109, 110
Locke, John, 73, 82n33
Loewenstein, David, 82n27
Lollards, 83–84, 85
Long Parliament, 87, 91
Louis XIII of France, 134
Low, Anthony, 139
Luke
    1:28, 171
    2:19, 185
    2:51, 171, 193n103

Luther, Martin
  Commentary on the Magnificat,
    172
  German Bible translation, 172
  on marriage, 90
  and Milton, 33, 89, 90, 93, 95,
    97, 98
  on mortalism, 89, 90
  Ninety-Five Theses, 88
  on Virgin Mary, 172–73, 175

MacCulloch, Diarmaid, 171
Magdeburg massacre, 2
Magnificat, 174, 182, 185, 192n83
Mans Mortallitie, 90
Manso, Giovanni Battista
  Catholicism of, 133, 134–35,
    148–49
  Erocallia, 156n32
  on Naples and Vesuvius, 135
  relationship with Milton, 133,
    134–35, 136, 148–49, 156n32,
    158n60
  relationship with Tasso, 137–38,
    139, 157n41
  Vita di Torquato Tasso, 138,
    157nn43–44, 158n60
Marescotti, Vincenzo, 144
Marino, Giambattista, 136–37,
  157n43
Marotti, Arthur, 4
  *Religious Ideology and Cultural
    Fantasy*, 7
Marriage Act, 91
Marston, John, 176
Mary, Queen of Scots, 55, 58
Mary I, 191n53
Masson, David, 144, 162n85
Matthew 18:21–35, 122

Mazzocchi, Virgilio, and Marco
  Marazzoli's *Chi soffre, speri*,
    160n69
Mazzolari, Giovanni Maria: *Electrica*,
  163n93
McCoog, Thomas, 7
Melanchthon, Philip, 174
Mercurius Militaris, 49
Mercurius Politicus, 54–55
Mercurius Pragmaticus, 47–48
Milton, Anthony, 7
Milton, John
  attitudes regarding Catholicism
    and conscience, 5, 8, 9, 11, 20,
    26, 74, 76, 102
  attitudes regarding Catholicism in
    Italy, 4, 25, 96, 131–33, 134, 153
  attitudes regarding Catholicism in
    Spain, 101–3, 104, 107, 110,
    111–12, 117, 123n2, 124n5,
    125n19
  attitudes regarding excluding
    Catholicism from toleration,
    6, 8, 11, 67, 72–75, 76, 79,
    82n33, 92–93, 94, 178–80
  on blasphemy, 71, 72, 82n27
  and Calvin, 11, 87, 90, 93–94,
    95, 98
  at Cambridge, 4, 103
  on Charles I's dissolution of 1626
    Parliament, 53, 54, 58
  on Charles I's execution, 18–19,
    39–40
  on Charles I's poisoning of
    James I, 39–40, 53, 58
  on Charles I's spiritual life, 182
  Christology of, 86–88, 96, 98
  on conscience, 5, 8, 9, 10, 11, 20,
    26, 66, 74, 76, 78, 92, 102

Milton, John (*cont.*)
  on Dalila and Tarsus, 121–22,
    129n51
  on divorce, 90, 92, 96, 172
  early life, 2–4
  on epic poems, 157n48
  in Florence, 132, 141, 149,
    159n64, 166n128
  on Fontarabbia, 112–13
  on forcing of religion, 8, 11, 77
  on free commonwealths, 65–66
  on freedom of man, 65–66
  on Galileo, 160n72
  in Geneva, 132, 153
  on Gibraltar, 113, 126n32
  on the good old cause, 65–66
  on guardian angels, 143–44,
    162n85, 163n90
  on Gunpowder Plot, 3, 4, 103–4,
    105, 106, 131
  on idolatry, 73–74, 75
  on implicit faith, 10, 11, 12, 74,
    76, 93, 154n9
  on imprimaturs, 5
  in Italy, 4, 24–25, 131–33, 134,
    136–37, 141–47, 148, 149,
    153, 158n60, 159n64, 160n70,
    161n74, 166n128
  on Laudianism, 18–19, 20–21,
    26, 27–28, 30, 33, 97
  on Leonora Baroni, 131, 132,
    133, 141–47
  on liberty of speech, 30, 31, 32
  and Luther, 33, 89, 90, 93, 95,
    97, 98
  on marriage, 19, 90, 91–92
  on *mens tertia*, 144, 145–46,
    163n96
  on Michael's prophecy (in books
    11 and 12 of *Paradise Lost*),
    114–18, 120, 127n37
  on monarchy and bishops, 24, 26,
    27–28
  on mortalism, 89–90, 96
  on Native Americans, 115–16
  on Paradise of Fools (in book 3 of
    Paradise Lost), 96–98, 102, 111
  on popery, 8–9, 10, 11–12,
    15n19, 18–21, 26–27, 28–32,
    33, 72–75, 76, 93, 102
  Protestant self-fashioning in, 9
  on purgatory, 19, 88–89, 131–32
  relationship with Charles Diodati,
    147, 148, 150, 151
  relationship with Dati, 133–34,
    149, 150, 155n16, 158n49,
    160n72
  relationship with Francesco Bar-
    berini, 142, 160n70
  relationship with Holste, 142–43,
    160n70, 161nn74–75, 162n78
  relationship with Manso, 133,
    134–35, 136, 148–49, 156n32,
    158n60
  relationship with Nedham, 57
  relationship with Vane, 66, 67–68,
    69–71, 77, 80n8, 81n25, 82n38
  on remarriage, 90
  on republicanism, 41, 58
  in Rome, 24, 128n43, 141–47,
    153, 158n60, 160n70, 161n74
  and "Root and Branch" Petition,
    24–25
  on the sacraments, 90–92
  on salvation, 96, 98, 121, 123
  on Scipio Africanus, 119, 128n47

on scripture, 11–12, 19, 32, 74,
  77, 78, 86–87, 88–89, 93–94,
  95–96
on "Spaniolized Bishops," 101–2,
  123n2
on supremacy of the spirit within,
  95–96
on toleration, 8, 67, 72–75, 76,
  79, 82n33, 92–94, 95, 96,
  178–80
on transnationalism, 116, 121, 123
on transubstantiation, 84–85, 86,
  87
on Trinitarianism, 86–87, 98
on Urania as Celestial Patroness,
  184
on Virgin Mary, 169, 170–71,
  172, 182–87
on virtuous human life, 4
on Wycliffe, 26–27, 83
Milton, John, works of
  "Ad Leonoram" epigrams, 131,
    132, 133, 141–47, 158n60,
    162n79, 162nn81–82, 162n84,
    163n93
  "Ad Salsillum," 141, 153n1
  *Animadversions upon the Remon-
    strants Defence*, 24–25, 28–29
  An Apology against Smectymnuus, 97
  Areopagitica, 5, 20, 21, 30–32, 33,
    72–73, 76, 92, 160n72, 180,
    182
  "At a Solemn Musick," 163n94
  "Canzone," 128n49
  De Doctrina Christiana, 84,
    85–89, 90, 91, 92, 94–96, 98
  A Defence of the English People,
    113–14

Defensio Secunda, 133
*The Doctrine and Discipline of
  Divorce*, 19, 69, 90, 92
Eikonoklastes, 39, 53–54, 182
"Elegia Prima," 128n49
"Elegia Quinta," 129n51
Elegiarum Liber, 131, 153n1
"Elegia Tertia," 106–7, 113,
  125n15
Epistolae Familiares (6, 7 and 9),
  150, 160n70
"Epitaphium Damonis," 132,
  133, 147–53, 156n32, 158n49,
  165n117, 166n120,
  166nn127–29
"An Epitaph on the Marchioness
  of Winchester," 184
"For the Liberty of Unlicenc'd
  Printing," 30
The History of Britain, 73, 79,
  104, 120
"In Inventorem Bombardae"/"On
  the Inventor of Gunpowder,"
  103
"In Proditionem
  Bombardicam"/"On the Gun-
  powder Plot," 103
"In Quintum Novembris"/
  "On the Fifth of November,"
  20, 103–4, 105, 106, 132,
  135, 154n5, 156n29,
  161n77
*The Judgement of Martin Bucer
  Concerning Divorce*, 19, 172
"Lycidas," 20, 107, 108–11,
  125n19
"Mansus," 132–33, 134–40,
  153n1, 156n32, 157n43

Milton, John, works of (*cont.*)
  A Mask Presented at Ludlow Castle,
    106, 107–8, 110–11, 132,
    154n7, 163n91, 181, 182
  Observations on Irish articles of
    peace, 4
  Of Prelatical Episcopacy, 28, 182
  Of Reformation, 26–28, 97, 98,
    101–2
  Of True Religion, 3, 8–9, 11–12,
    15n19, 20, 82n28, 89, 93–94,
    96, 180
  "On the Morning of Christ's
    Nativity," 182, 184
  Paradise Lost, 4, 84–85, 96–98,
    102, 106, 107, 109, 111,
    112–13, 114–18, 120, 126n32,
    127n37, 169, 180, 182–84, 186
  Paradise Regained, 106, 111,
    118–21, 122–23, 128n47,
    169–70, 173, 177, 181, 182,
    184–87, 193n103
  Poemata, 131–34, 153n1
  Poems, &c. upon Several Occasions,
    104, 107
  *Poems of Mr John Milton Both
    English and Latin*, 104, 131,
    153n1
  Postscript to *An Answer to a Booke*,
    26
  preface to translation of Bucer's
    *The Judgement of Martin Bucer,
    Concerning Divorce*, 69
  Pro Populo Anglicano Defensio,
    39–40, 57–58
  *The Readie & Easie Way to Estab-
    lish a Free Commonwealth*, 65,
    102
  *The Reason of Church-government
    Urg'd Against Prelaty*, 29, 92,
    102, 154n9, 157n48
  Samson Agonistes, 106, 111,
    121–22, 129n51
  sonnet to Vane, 67–68, 69–70
  Sylvarum Liber, 132, 153n1
  Tenure of Kings and Magistrates, 182
  Tetrachordon, 182
  *A Treatise of Civil Power in Ecclesi-
    astical Causes*, 8, 11, 20, 70, 71,
    73, 77, 179
  Trinity Manuscript, 68–69
Moderate, 49
Morley, Thomas: *A Remonstrance
    of the Barbarous Cruelties and
    Bloudy Murders Committed By
    the Irish Rebels Against the
    Protestants in Ireland...*, 3

Naseby, battle of: camp follower
    massacre at, 3
Nedham, Marchamont
  relationship with Milton, 57
  on Stuart family, 54–55, 58
New Model Army, 3
Newport, Lady (Anne Blount):
    conversion of, 22
Nicene creed, 173
Nicholas, Sir Edward: *Royall
    Apologie*, 48
"Novembris Monstrum," 105

Oath of Allegiance Controversy, 6,
    9–10, 76
Overbury, Sir Thomas, 56
Overton, Richard: *Mans Mortallitie*,
    90

Ovid's *Metamorphoses*: river Tagus
   in, 106
Owen, John, 67, 68, 69, 149

Parker, Henry: *The True Portraiture
   of the Kings of England*, 55–56
Pecke, Samuel
   on Laud, 32–33
   Perfect Diurnall, 32–33
Pelikan, Jaroslav, 172, 184
Persons, Robert, 7
   *A Brief Discourse containing
     certayne Reasons why Catholiques
     refuse to go to Church*, 9
   on explicit vs. implicit faith, 11
   on salvation and faith, 10–11
   *The Warn-word to Sir Francis
     Hastinges Wast-word*, 10–11
1 Peter 4:12, 88, 89
Peter de La Palu, 86
Peter Lombard, 170
Philip II, 110, 127n39
Philip IV, 170
Phillips, Edward, 192n83
political loyalty and religious belief,
   9–10, 17, 18, 19–21, 22
popery
   Burton on, 22
   Lake on, 18
   and Laudianism, 24
   Milton on, 8–9, 10, 11–12,
     15n19, 18–21, 26–27, 28–32,
     33, 72–75, 76, 93, 102
   Prynne on, 22
   Smart on, 21–22
   Vane the Younger on, 75, 76–77,
     78
Popish Plot (1678–81), 9, 96

Presbyterians, 26, 73, 92
Preston, Roland, 75–76
Pride's Purge, 50
*Primer or Office of the Blessed Virgin
   Mary, The*, 179, 183
Prynne, William, 23, 46, 180, 181
   on Laud, 33
   on popery, 22
Puritans, 17, 18, 19, 23, 24, 59, 67,
   95, 96
Pym, John, 19, 29–30, 40
Pynchon, William, 68

Questier, Michael
   The Antichrist's Lewd Hat, 7
   on Oath of Allegiance, 10
Quint, David, 128n47

Racovian Catechism, 68
Raleigh, Sir Walter, 115
Raymond, Joad, 144, 163n90
recusants, 23, 41, 179
"Remember, Remember the Fifth of
   November," 105, 106
Restoration, 4, 93, 111, 180
Revelation 13:1, 153n2
Riccio, David, 58
Roman Empire, 119, 126n33
Roman Inquisition, 170
Rome
   Accademia degli Umoristi, 141,
     142, 143, 159nn63–64, 160n68
   Milton in, 24, 128n43, 141–47,
     153, 158n60, 160n70, 161n74
Ronconi, Francesco, 158n55,
   158n58
"Root and Branch" Petition, 24–25
rosaries, 180, 181, 182

Rosell, Cayetano, 128n47
Rospigliosi, Giulio (cardinal), 142
Rosselli, Hannibal, 163n97
  on *mens tertia*, 145–46
Rouse, John, 161n75
*Royall Legacies of Charles the First,
  The*, 52
Rupert of the Rhine, Prince, 107
Rutland's *Humble Petition*, 49–50

Salmasius, Claudius, 58
  on regicide, 39–40, 57
salvation, 10–11, 96, 98, 121, 123
Salzilli, Giovanni, 141
Satyrical Catechisme, A, 49
Scipio Africanus, Publius Cornelius,
  119, 128n47
Scotland, 54–55, 56–57
Scott, Thomas, 44–45, 46
Servetus, Michael, 87
Shakespeare, William
  Macbeth, 108
  statue of Queen Hermione in
    Winter's Tale, 176
Shawcross, John, 101
Sheldon, Richard, 174–75
Shell, Alison
  *Catholicism, Controversy, and the
    English Literary Imagination*, 7
  *Oral Culture and Catholicism in
    Early Modern England*, 7
Sidney, Sir Philip, 174
  Arcadia, 182
Simmons, Matthew, 47
Sixtus IV: *Grave Nimis*, 170
Smart, Peter: on popery, 21–22
Smectymnuus, 28
  An Answer to a Booke, 26
Smith, Nigel: on toleration, 6

Socinians, 68, 94
Solemn League and Covenant
  (1643), 73
Sommerville, Johann P., 15n24
Song of Roland, 112
Song of Songs, 171
Southwell, Robert, 7, 176–77
  *Humble Supplication to her
    Majestie*, 9
Spanish Armada, 1, 104, 105
Spanish Empire
  Black Legend of, 104–5, 111
  Catholicism in, 101–4, 110,
    115–17, 123n2, 125n19
  Charles V, 115
  Philip II, 110, 127n39
  Philip IV, 170
Spanish Match, 42
Spenser, Edmund
  The Faerie Queene, 176
  The Shepherd's Calendar, 176
Stafford, Anthony
  The Femall Glory, 174–75
  on Virgin Mary, 174–75
Stavely, Keith, 15n19
St. Michael Mount, 108
Stradling, R. A., 111
Stubbe, Henry, 67
  *An Essay in Defence of the Good
    Old Cause*, 75–76
  on Preston, 75–76
  on toleration, 76
  on Vane, 75
Sylvester, Josuah, 177

Tasso, Torquato
  Gerusalemme Conquistata, 138,
    139
  Il Manso, 137, 138

insanity of, 158n60
relationship with Manso, 137–38,
   139, 157n41
Taylor, John: *The Life and Death of*
   the Most Blessed Among Women,
   the Virgin Mary Mother of Our
   Lord Jesus, 177–78, 187
Testi, Fulvio, 143, 144, 162n87
Thirty-Nine Articles, 173
Thirty Years' War, 2, 41, 179
Thomason, George, 70–71
Tillyard, E. M. W., 127n37
2 Timothy 4:8, 88
toleration, 6, 15n19, 32, 68, 132
   Locke on, 82n33
   Milton on, 8, 67, 72–75, 76, 79,
      82n33, 92–94, 95, 96, 178–80
   Vane the Younger on, 67, 72, 74,
      75, 76, 79, 82n33
transubstantiation, 83–86, 87
Treasons Anatomie, 48
Treaty of the Pyrenees, 111, 113
Trumbull, William, 42
Tumbleson, Raymond: *Catholicism*
   in the English Protestant Imagi-
   nation, 7
Tutino, Stefania: *Law and Con-*
   science, 10, 15n25

United Provinces, 96
Unmasking of Murther, The, 105
Urban VIII, 179

Valla, Lorenzo, 171
Vane the Younger, Sir Henry
   on blasphemy, 71–72
   on conscience, 75, 76, 78
   The Healing Question propounded
      and resolved, 66

on idolatry, 72, 75, 79
on implicit faith, 76–78
on popery, 75, 76–77, 78
relationship with Milton, 66,
   67–68, 69–71, 77, 80n8,
   81n25, 82n38
on religious hypocrisy, 78–79
The Retired Mans Meditations,
   66–67
on Spaniards and native Ameri-
   cans, 79
on toleration, 67, 72, 74, 75, 76,
   79, 82n33
withdrawal from politics, 67
Zeal Examined, 68, 70–72, 75, 76,
   77–78
Van Male, Jean Baptiste, 42
Van Meerbeeck, Jan, 42–43
Vatican Library, 142–43, 161n76
Vaughan, Henry: *Silex Scintillans,*
   177
Vere, Sir Horace, 2
Vicar, John: *Mischeefes Mysterie or*
   Treasons Master-peece, 105, 106
Vindicae contra Tyrannos, 45, 47
Virgil
   Aeneid 2.363, 147
   Aeneid 6.679–80, 143
   Aeneid 6.697, 162n78
   Aeneid 6.700–702, 162n78
   Aeneid 6.878, 165n117
   Eclogue 10.33, 157n36
   on the underworld, 161n77,
      162n78
Virgin Mary
   Annunciation, 172, 173, 174,
      175, 178, 184
   Ascension, 172
   Assumption, 184

Virgin Mary (*cont.*)
  Calvin on, 173, 175
  Erasmus on, 171–72, 174,
    193n103
  Eve/Mary typology, 183, 184
  imagery of, 175–76, 179, 180, 184
  and Immaculate Conception, 170
  Luther on, 172–73, 175
  Magnificat, 174, 182, 185,
    192n83
  as Mediatrix, 180, 186
  Milton on, 169, 170–71, 172,
    182–87
  national dedications to, 179
  Protestant views regarding, 169,
    170–80, 185, 186, 187
  Purification, 174
  relationship with Jesus, 169, 171,
    184, 185–86, 193n103
  relics of, 171, 173
  Stafford on, 174–75
  as teacher, 185, 186
Viscontini, Bartolomeo, 136
Vortsius, Conrad, 41
Vote of No Addresses, 40, 46, 49, 52

Walsham, Alexandra, 7
  Charitable Hatred, 6
  on toleration, 6

Weldon, Sir Anthony: *Court and
    Character of King James*, 56
West, Robert, 144
Wexford massacre, 3, 4
Whitaker, William, 96
  *An Answere to the Ten Reasons of
    Edmund Campion the Jesuit*,
    89, 90
  on the sacraments, 90–91
Widdrington, Roger, 75–76
Wilding, Michael, 31
Williams, Roger, 67, 68
Williamson, Joseph, 181
Winter, Thomas, 105
Wood, Anthony, 57
Woodhouse, A. S. P., 109
Woods, Susanne, 133
Woolrych, Austin, 66
Worden, Blair, 67
Wycliffe, John, 26–27
  Wickliffes Wicket, 83–84

Yates, Frances, 147

Zwingli, Ulrich, 172